Fundamentals of
European Civil Law

and

Impact of the European
Community

Martin Vranken

Lic in Law (Leuven), LLM (Yale), PhD(Leuven)
Associate Professor of Law, University of Melbourne

**BLACKSTONE
PRESS LIMITED**

First published in Great Britain 1997 by Blackstone Press Limited,
9-15 Aldine Street, London W12 8AW   Telephone 0181-740 2277

© Federation Press Pty Ltd

ISBN: 1 85431 691 5

British Library Cataloguing in Publication Data
A CIP catalogue record for this book is available from the British Library.

Typeset by: The Federation Press, Leichhardt, NSW.
Printed by: Australian Print Group, Maryborough, Vic, Australia.

Preface

As suggested by its title, this book presents an outline of the fundamentals of the European civil law. The classic texts on comparative law, especially *An Introduction to Comparative Law* by Zweigert and Kötz and *Major Legal Systems in the World Today* by David and Brierley, form the basis for a discussion of various conceptual issues, such as the notion of comparativism and the concept of legal families, in the introductory chapters of the book. Another classic, *The Civil Law Tradition* by Merryman, has served as a more general but not less important guide and source of reflection throughout the writing of the book. But *Fundamentals of European Civil Law* is different from all three texts in a number of respects. First, this is not a book on comparative law proper as no attempt has been made to systematically compare the civil law with other legal families. Internal comparisons within the civil law do regularly occur though, in particular by way of contrast between the French and German legal systems, so as to stress that the homogeneity of the civil law is not to be taken at face value. Secondly, the book has been written with a common law readership in mind. Specifically, both in the selection of topics and in the manner of their discussion, the common law has been used consciously as a reference point. Thirdly, it seems crucial nowadays to stress that a proper appreciation of the contemporary legal scene in Europe requires consideration of not only national developments but also developments at a supra-national level of the European Community. The book seeks to take account of the ever-increasing penetration of national law by the legal order of the European Community by incorporating the relevant materials on European Community law within each chapter in preference to having a separate chapter at the end of the book. This desire to demonstrate the impact of the European Community on the national law of a growing number of member states has affected the selection of the substantive topics for discussion. Thus, there is no discussion of family law or criminal law, for example, as these areas of the law largely remain untouched (so far) by European Community law.

English commentators tend to adopt, quite understandably, an English "reflex" to their treatment of the civil law. This book has been written from a civil law perspective, although I hope my contact with Australian and New Zealand students over the years allows for sufficient sensitivity to be displayed to the needs of a common law readership. In a typical civil-law fashion, also, *Fundamentals of European Civil Law* moves from the more general to an exploration of the more specific. Chapters 1 to 4 thus sketch the framework within which to assess the practical data provided in the subsequent Chapters 5 to 9. A distinct feature of the book is also its European (civil law) writing style. Specifically, scholarship is recognised throughout the book for its formidable contribution to the shaping of the European civil law that goes beyond what the (common law) label of "secondary" source might suggest.

Because of the civil law perspective adopted in this book, it seemed logical to, by and large, adhere to the distinction between private and public law. The primary focus is on private law and, notwithstanding its growing importance on the Continent, administrative law is beyond the scope of the book. Unnecessary rigidity has been avoided, though. Just as the essence of the civil law, traditionally at least, lies in its private law, so has European Community law been regarded, until fairly recently, as pertaining to the domain of public law only. But, as it is demonstrated in the book, the law of the European Community has clearly started to make inroads into the private domain and this trend is expected to continue in the future. Even aspects of European Community law which might strictly be regarded as public law, such as the four freedoms and European monetary policy, have had their influence on (private) commercial law and practice in the Member States and are discussed in Chapter 8. Also, the precise dividing line between private and public law does not even in the civil law go without debate. Labour law is a case in point: it contains elements of both private and public law and, therefore, it does not fit comfortably into either category. Labour law is dealt with in Chapter 7.

As a practical matter, the main focus of the book is on developments in the French and the German legal systems. Occasional reference only is made to the legal orders of other countries such as, in particular, Belgium, Italy, the Netherlands and Switzerland. In a way this approach reflects a compromise between the search for substance and the desire to avoid clogging the book with too much detail. Also, the French and German legal systems constitute sub-families within the family of the civil law, and each has its "cluster" of derivative legal systems for which it serves as a model (the Belgian and Italian legal systems, for instance, based on the French model, and the Swiss and to some extent now the Dutch systems displaying features of the German model). The Scandinavian legal systems represent a special case altogether. Because of their hybrid nature, they do not form part of the core of the civil law and they are out of place in a book that limits itself to dealing with the fundamentals of the European civil law.

PREFACE

The main reason for writing this book was to encourage and facilitate a deeper understanding of the civil law by those trained in the common law. The challenge was then to maintain a proper balance between the generality and the specificity of the information to be conveyed. Only the reader will be able to tell whether this balance has been achieved.

Martin Vranken
Leuven
September 1996

For Megan and Thomas

Contents

CONTENTS

CONTENTS

CONTENTS

CONTENTS

Abbreviations

AG:	Aktiengesellschaft
BGB:	Bürgerliches Gesetzbuch
BGH:	Bundesgerichtshof
BGHZ:	Entscheidungen des Bundesgerichtshofes in Zivilsachen
BS:	Belgisch staatsblad
Bull civ:	Bulletin des Arrêts de la Cour de Cassation – chambres civiles
B Verf G :	Bundesverfassungsgericht
BW:	Burgerlijk Wetboek
Cass civ:	Cour de Cassation – chambres civiles
Cass com:	Cour de Cassation – chambres commerciales
CFI:	(European) Court of First Instance
CMLR:	Common Market Law Reports
D:	Recueil Dalloz Sirey
DM:	Deutschmark
DP:	Recueil Dalloz Périodique
DS:	Recueil Dalloz Sirey
EC:	European Community
ECB:	European Central Bank
ECJ:	European Court of Justice
ECR:	European Court Reports
ECU:	European Currency Unit
EEA:	European Economic Area
EEC:	European Economic Community
EEIG:	European Economic Interest Grouping
EMCF:	European Monetary Cooperation Fund
EMI:	European Monetary Institute·
EMS:	European Monetary System
EMU:	Economic and Monetary Union
ESCB:	European System of Central Banks
EU:	European Union
Gaz Pal:	Gazette du Palais
GG:	Grundgesetz
GIE:	Groupement d'intérêt économique

ABBREVIATIONS

GmbH:	Gemeinschaft mit beschränkter Haftung
Inf rap:	Informations rapides
HGB:	Handelsgesetzbuch
JCP:	Jurisclasseur périodique
JO:	Journal officiel
JZ:	Juristenzeitung
n:	numéro
NBW:	Nieuw Burgerlijk Wetboek
NJW:	Neue Juristische Wochenschrift
Obs:	Observation
OLG:	Oberlandesgericht
Rev tr dr civ:	Revue trimestrielle de droit civil
RGZ:	Entscheidungen des Reichsgerichts in Zivilsachen
RM:	Reichsmark
RW:	Rechtskundig Weekblad
SA:	Société anonyme
SARL:	Société anonyme à responsabilité limitée
SE:	Societas europaea
SEA:	Single European Act
SNB:	Special Negotiating Body
Somm:	sommaire
StGB:	Strafgesetzbuch
StPO:	Strafprozessordnung
TEU:	Treaty on European Union
TGI:	Tribunal de Grande Instance
UCC:	Uniform Commercial Code
ZGB:	Zivilgesetzbuch
ZPO:	Zivilprozessordnung

Part A

Historical Overview and Conceptual Framework

Chapter 1

Introduction

Even those who look upon the study of law exclusively as a help to professional success have begun to see that the grasp of legal principles is of greater value than mere knowledge of cases and of isolated rules. Such a grasp of principles is, however, unobtainable, unless law is looked upon as an organic whole of which every part is correlated to the other, and unless the origin and growth of each individual institution is examined with the same care as the evolution of a particular species of the fauna or flora of a country is examined by the biologist. Both as regards the examination of the manner in which the various parts of the system are correlated, and as regards the study of the evolution of the particular species, the comparative method is as indispensable to the scientific lawyer as it is to the biologist.

(Schuster 1907: III-IV)

1.1 The Concept of Comparative Law

[101] The development of comparative law as a legal discipline in its own right is of a relatively recent origin. Admittedly, early precedents as regards the study of foreign laws and the use of comparison can be found in the writings of Plato and Aristotle. It has also been suggested that comparative research preceded the drafting of the XII Tables for Rome (David and Brierley 1985:1-2).[1] Montesquieu's *L'Esprit des Lois* was similarly based on comparison. But it is only from the 19th century onwards that the term "comparative law" became established, including a systematic study of its methods and aims. In Europe the first meeting of the *International Congress for Comparative Law* was held at the instigation of Lambert and Saleilles in Paris in 1900. Neither the venue nor the timing proved entirely accidental, as 1900 was the year during which the World Exhibition took place in Paris and there existed a quasi absolute faith in

---

1   A more elaborate history of comparative law can be found in Zweigert and Kötz 1987 I:47-62. See also Hanza 1991 and Kamba 1974:485.

progress generally. This spirit did not leave the legal community untouched, hence the dream of a new world law, a common law of mankind (*droit commun de l'humanité*). The task of comparative law was then to help create this new legal order (Zweigert and Kötz 1987 I:2-3). The tempering effect of two world wars notwithstanding, the foundation of the Rome Institute for the Unification of Private Law *(UNIDROIT)* in 1926 was followed by a decision of the United Nations in 1966 to set up a Commission for the Harmonisation and Unification of International and Commercial Law *(UNCITRAL)*. Other, specialised, agencies include the World Intellectual Property Organisation (WIPO) and the International Labour Organisation (ILO), both based in Geneva.

[102] At a regional level the activities of the European Community (EC) warrant a special mention. The EC has been influential, not only in promoting the harmonisation and the coordination of the national legal orders of its member states, but also in developing its own area of supranational law that cuts across the traditional dichotomy of civil law and common law. In this book the emphasis is largely on the impact of the EC on the substantive law of its constituent countries. But it does not follow that domestic procedural law has been left untouched. According to Art 220 of the Treaty of Rome establishing the European Economic Community the member states shall enter into negotiations with each other with a view to, inter alia, the simplification of formalities governing the reciprocal recognition and enforcement of judgments and arbitration awards. The 1968 Convention on Jurisdiction and the Enforcement of Judgments in Civil and Commercial Matters is said to represent the most substantial achievement to date of the member states in carrying through the program of legal reform that Art 220 of the Treaty enjoins upon them (Dashwood, Hacon, and White, 1987:3-7).

[103] One of the first problems to be tackled by scholars studying this new legal discipline of comparative law concerned its apparent lack of substance. Unlike other fields of law (for instance, contracts or torts), comparative law has no clearly defined and readily identifiable contents or subject matter. Rather, comparative law is in the nature of a black hole in the universe, in that it can accommodate just about anything. It is therefore suggested sometimes that it may be preferable to view comparative law as a particular approach to the study of law: a "method" instead of a "social science".[2] This focus on process rather than substance is captured rather

---

2 A juxtaposition of both labels can be found in Sussman 1970:108 as quoted by Winterton 1975:70.

well in the German (*Rechtsvergleichung* or the comparison of law) and the French (*droit comparé* or law compared) translations of the English term "comparative law". The significance of the debate about substance and procedure must not be exaggerated, though. Even when comparative law is treated as a method of comparing legal systems any such comparison inevitably yields information on the legal systems compared. The term comparative law is then sufficiently broad to cover both the method used in obtaining data and the resulting data themselves (Winterton 1975:70-71).

1.2 Benefits and Pitfalls of Comparative Study

[104] Historically, a primary incentive for comparing different legal systems has been the highly pragmatic objective of domestic law reform. Zweigert and Kötz (1987 I:50) refer to "legislative comparative law" – when foreign laws are examined for purposes of drafting new national laws – as one of two distinct "roots" of comparative law.[3] The wider goal of international unification of the law worldwide – much in vogue at the end of the last century – is not a realistic option at present. Regional harmonisation, on the other hand, may constitute a less futile objective.[4] But even when comparative study for purposes of law reform is undertaken on this more modest scale, it remains a hazardous enterprise. Kahn-Freund (1974:1) has identified and analysed the so-called problem of transplantability. At a general level, the issue is that law – whether it be at home or abroad – never operates in a vacuum and legal systems are understood best when viewed against the backdrop of the historical, political, cultural, social and economic context in which they function. At a more specific level, the problem of transplantability forces a careful consideration as to which particular aspects of foreign law are most suitable for importation into the domestic legal scene. To paraphrase Kahn-Freund (1974:5), it is easier successfully to transfer a mechanical part (say the carburettor or a wheel of a car) than to transfer part of a living organism (the cornea of an eye or a kidney, for instance). An example from

---

3   The second "root" is the "scientific or theoretical "approach to comparative law as discussed in [106] and [107] below. To find the best solutions to legal problems and then to recommend their incorporation into domestic law, has also been called the positivist and utilitarian approach to comparative law. Interestingly, it is said to be more popular in England than elsewhere: Collins:1991:397.

4   See the discussion of comparativism and the European Community in 1.5.

labour law may serve as an illustration of the need to be aware of any differences in the degree of transplantability between legal systems. Thus it may be a relatively straightforward exercise to copy the (rather generous) annual leave entitlements of German workers. Much more risky is a transplantation of the German model of worker representation at the level of the supervisory board of companies. Institutionalised forms of employee participation in Europe are indeed premised upon a fundamental assumption that some commonality of interests exists between workers and management. The labour laws of common-law based legal systems often appear to assume the opposite.[5]

[105] Not surprisingly perhaps, the distinction between "organ" transplants and transplants of "mechanical parts" is easier to state than to apply. By and large, the degree of transferability depends on the distribution of power in society (Blanpain 1993:18). It would seem that this observation has particular significance for, but it is not limited to, labour law. An area of law besides labour law that may prove "resilient" to foreign importation for this very reason is family law (including the law of inheritance). In particular, a feature of the 19th century codification movement in Europe was the importance attached to the protection of property rights as between persons that are related to one another by means of blood ties. The position of the surviving spouse vis-à-vis the descendants or ascendants (or even the brothers or sisters!) of the deceased has been improved in recent years only. In France the so-called reserved part of the deceased's estate (*la réserve*) continues to benefit descendants and ascendants by conferring certain inalienable rights to the property that cannot be disposed of in a will. Depending upon the number of children, the *réserve* comprises minimum one-half and maximum three-quarters of the deceased's estate. If there are no children one-quarter of the estate is reserved for each of the (surviving) parents of the deceased.[6]

[106] It is too narrow to view comparativism as a legitimate enterprise only if it results in proposals for domestic law reform (Sacco 1991:1). Comparative study can in addition be approached as an intellectual

---

5   In Australia and New Zealand, in particular, a system of compulsory arbitration of labour disputes applied for most of this century. The provision for compulsory arbitration was premised on the assumption that the interests of workers and employees are necessarily in conflict with one another, hence the need for third-party intervention in the public interest. In recent years there has been a move away from the centralist model in both countries: Vranken 1994:1.

6   See Frohn 1994:37 for a comparative discussion of the position of the surviving spouse in the contemporary law of succession.

exercise, because it results in a broadening of knowledge that is valuable for its own sake. André Tunc (1988:703), a celebrated French comparative scholar, describes this benefit of comparativism in terms of an enrichment and an opening-up of the mind (*la culture et l'ouverture d'esprit*). Zweigert and Kötz (1987 I:14-15) go one step further. They argue that comparativism is the raison d'être of law as a science, and that the primary aim of all sciences, including law, is knowledge. The knowledge acquired through comparative study then is two-dimensional: comparativism inevitably leads to a better understanding of foreign legal systems; but it also induces a deeper understanding of the law domestically. The former provides knowledge to enlighten the conflicts-of-law student (Baade 1983:500-501). The latter benefit of comparative study is worthwhile on a much wider scale. In particular, comparativism forces a re-consideration of one's own national system of law by encouraging an approach of the domestic legal scene through the eyes of an outsider. By taking distance, the opportunity exists to experience one's own national law from a new and fresh angle. Kahn-Freund (1966:40) summed it up as follows:

> One of the virtues of legal comparison is that it allows a scholar to place himself (or herself) outside the labyrinth of minutiae in which legal thinking so easily looses its way and to see the great contours of the law and its dominant characteristics.

[107] When the above (intellectual) approach to the study of law is adopted, comparativism can become a most sobering exercise. Things that once may have seemed self-evident no longer are. Comparative study leads to a querying of especially those aspects of domestic law that otherwise would be taken for granted. A classic example is the concept of consideration in contract law. In the common law, for an agreement to be enforceable it generally must be supported by consideration. In the civil law, however, a not less sophisticated system of contract law operates notwithstanding the absence of consideration as a prerequisite for the valid formation of the contract. This issue is discussed further in Chapter 5. For now it may suffice to suggest that a student of the common law may wish to reconsider the role of consideration in light of the civil law experience.[7]

[108] The comparative study of law is meritorious not only because it induces a questioning of the seemingly obvious. It also assists in confirming whether and how a particular development in the domestic

---

7   The reverse is probably true as well. The common law notion of consideration may trigger a re-consideration of the stringent criticism by German scholars, in particular, directed at its functional equivalent (*causa*) in legal systems that adhere to the French tradition. See, generally, the discussion in Chapter 5.

legal scene fits in with legal change internationally. The relatively recent doctrine of unconscionability in the common law, for instance, can be compared usefully to functionally similar attempts at curbing the excesses of contractual freedom in the civil law.[8] Similarly, parallels can be drawn between the moves away from fault as the exclusive basis for tort liability in civil law and common law alike.[9] Where it is found that one's own national system of law is not "synchronised" with trends internationally, comparativism raises questions as to the justification of the domestic state of affairs. Because of the growing internationalisation of the world comparativism may even assist in forecasting future domestic developments as ideas and concepts, more than ever before, tend to cross national and regional boundaries (Blanpain 1993:6). Institutionalised worker participation at the place of work serves as a case study in Chapter 7. Of course, the process of cross-fertilisation as triggered by comparative study does often not produce clear "winners" and "losers". Thus a world-wide interest in the German model of institutionalised worker participation need not result in a demise of collective bargaining or a diminished role for unions in those legal systems that contemplate its importation. Rather, the result of any cross-fertilisation may very well be, more modestly, a mitigation of the extremes in the differences between the relevant legal systems. Contemporary developments in blurring the traditional distinction between adversarial and inquisitorial court proceedings in the common law and the civil law, respectively, also illustrate this proposition. The issue of court proceedings is discussed further in Chapter 9.

[109] Maximum benefit is obtained from comparative study when the information about foreign law is put in a national, ie domestic perspective. Only then can comparativism lead to a better understanding of one's own legal system. This is no easy task, though. Kahn-Freund (1974:1) lists several problems that need to be overcome if comparative study is to be successful. First and foremost, there is a need to know about the foreign law to be studied. Specifically, the deeper one's understanding of foreign law (including its surrounding context) from the outset, the richer the results comparative study will yield. Comparative scholars often face the additional challenge of having to come to terms with materials presented in a foreign language. Linguistic idiosyncrasies can never be ruled out entirely, not even – and perhaps especially – when statutes, cases and legal

---

8   See Chapter 5.
9   See Chapter 6. For a recent synthesis of the critique of the fault system in the common law, see Luntz and Hambly 1995:22.

commentaries are available in – often well-intended – English translations. Even academic scholars of the highest international standing get it wrong at times. Blanpain (1993:16) recalls how he inadvertently used the word "eventually" as a translation of the French *éventuellement* for over a decade until it became clear to him that the term "possibly" would have been more accurate. Legal terminology poses problems of its own. A classic example is the French *notaire*, the German *Notar* and the English "notary": the words sound similar but they cover a different reality. The advent of the European Community, especially the membership of the United Kingdom since 1973, proved to be a blessing in this regard as one of the characteristics of the Community is that it is multilingual, and the principle of equality applies to the official languages of all member states.[10] A related problem of comparative study concerns the need to be aware of the so-called box approach to law and the classification of legal issues. Contract, tort and real property are branches of the law that can be found both in the civil law and the common law. Yet, these law subjects do not necessarily have the same contents everywhere. The continental legal systems have never really favoured a rigid distinction between contract and tort. Rather both contract and tort traditionally belong under the more general umbrella of the law of obligations.[11]

1.3 The Comparative Method

[110] A link exists between the contents and the objectives of all law study. This observation is especially pertinent in the case of comparative law as it has been observed already that there is no body of legal rules that can be called "comparative law".[12] A further link exists between the objectives and the methods of law study. Even a pursuit of the most narrow objective of comparative study – specifically, a search for a better understanding of one's own domestic legal system – poses considerable problems of method and technique (Collins 1991:398-399). And the issue

---

10 All the official languages except Irish are working languages of the European institutions. European legislation and case law is therefore available in English, and it is of the highest standard. The official venue for the publication of EC legislation is the *Official Journal*. The official reporting system of the decisions of the European Court of Justice are the *European Court Reports*. It follows that, as the subject matter of the European Community widens to cover aspects of private as well as public law, any translation problems of the comparative researcher are alleviated considerably.

11 See Chapter 2 for a discussion of the Roman-law origin of this phenomenon.

12 See [103] above.

here goes beyond the question as to whether more use ought to be made of the case method when studying and teaching comparative law.[13]

[111] Comparative law is a relatively young discipline and its methodology continues to evolve. Two principal approaches to comparative study have attained some prominence to date. They are the so-called institutional and functional approaches to comparative study (Blanpain 1993:12). The former is relatively formalistic, in that it generally does not look beyond the particular institution, concept or rule that is the subject of comparative study. In contrast, the functional approach takes account of the substantive reasons for the existence (or absence) of any such institution, concept or rule in the legal systems to be compared.[14]

[112] By and large, the functional approach to comparativism is to be preferred because it yields richer results (Blanpain 1993:12; Schregle 1981:22-23) It need not follow, though, that the institutional (or formal) approach lacks merit. Each method reflects a different level of comparative inquiry. An example may clarify this otherwise abstract observation. Labour courts are judicial bodies that are generally found in labour law systems throughout Western Europe with the notable exceptions of Italy and The Netherlands. They owe their origin to the probiviral court or *conseil de prud'hommes* (literally: court of wise men), set up at Lyon pursuant to a Napoleonic law passed in 1806. Historically, the idea behind the probiviral court simply was to have certain labour disputes settled promptly and without expense by a council composed of representatives of employers and employees (Kassalow 1969:169). In a more contemporary context, the very existence of labour courts reflects a political choice to award special treatment to the resolution of (justiciable) labour disputes as opposed to legal disputes in general, whereby the latter continue to be within the jurisdiction of the ordinary courts of law. This observation raises two issues for comparative scholars. First, it may be asked whether different degrees of specialisation exist among labour courts internationally. An institutional approach to comparativism allows that question to be addressed most adequately. Application of this comparative methodology logically entails an internal comparison of the various labour

---

13   Markesinis (1990:1) argues that a major reason for the relative lack of interest in comparative law among (common law) students and practitioners alike is insufficient attention paid to case law by comparativists. On the other hand, however, Sacco (1991:26) observes that in civil law countries, especially in Italy, the comparative study of law has gone hand in hand with greater attention for case law.

14   Compare the distinction between form and substance in Anglo-American law as discussed in Atiyah and Summers (1987).

courts by reference to, inter alia, their personnel, jurisdiction, appellate structure and representation of parties (Vranken 1988:497). Secondly, the comparative research can be widened by adopting a functional (or substantive) approach. The search is then for functional equivalents of the European model of labour courts and it may extend, for example, to a discussion of the American system of personal grievance administration involving private arbitrators. The point is that neither method of comparative research is necessarily superior. To be clear, the functional approach invariably is more difficult: it presupposes that one is able to formulate the correct questions from the very start of the inquiry. In the above example, the question is not simply in which legal systems do labour courts exist. Instead, when a functional approach is adopted the question becomes one as to which means are available for the peaceful resolution of labour disputes.

1.4 Legal Families

(a) The concept of a family of law

[113] The total number of national legal systems in the world today is close to 200, and comparative scholars seeking to study all of them face an impossible task. However, the number of variables can be reduced considerably by bringing together under one heading legal systems that show certain similarities to one another. The concept of legal families allows precisely this. Thus it is a device that facilitates comparative study.

[114] Prima facie it appears difficult to reconcile the concept of legal families with the perception that law is the emanation of the political will of a particular nation at any particular moment in time. Law cannot only be a highly "volatile" product, it also tends to be associated with (at times very patriotic) feelings of belonging and national pride. The 19th century codification movement in Europe is best appreciated against this backdrop. In fact, comparative study is made possible precisely because of this emphasis on differentiation between national legal systems. On the other hand, however, the notion of a family of law assumes that one is able to look beyond the concept of legal system in its narrow sense of the legal rules and institutions pertaining to a particular country. And, of course, only purists would argue that comparative study necessarily involves two or more countries. It is perfectly possible – and legitimate – to engage in comparative work that is limited to one country, eg a country with a federal political structure.

(b) Criteria for classifying legal systems into families

[115] There is no single answer to the question as to which criteria ought to be used to group legal systems along family lines. Much depends upon the nature and the purpose of the comparative study that is being contemplated. If one seeks to analyse the impact of religion on society, for instance, it is imperative to distinguish between the law of the Hindu community, Muslim law, Jewish law and the law of the secular societies in the West. If, on the other hand, one's research domain were to involve indigenous or native legal systems, it can be useful to contrast legal systems with customary or unwritten law and legal systems that rely upon written law. In short, the type of classification devices is influenced by the type and the nature of the comparative inquiry. The geographical scope of study is a relevant consideration as well. The focus of the book is narrowly on the civil law of Western Europe and its distinguishing features vis-à-vis the common law. The observations below are made with this European focus in mind.[15]

[116] It is exceedingly difficult to list the distinguishing features of the European civil law without resorting to generalisations that need lengthy qualifications in order for them to be meaningful. In part, the problem is triggered by the fairly high level of abstraction that the concept of legal family evokes. There is also the consideration that the members of any such family are themselves subject to constant evolution, whereas the use of legal family as a classification device seemingly fails to acknowledge this ongoing change from within. There is, furthermore, the temptation to treat the various fields of law comprising a particular legal system as a homogeneous entity which they may very well not be.[16] Zweigert and Kötz (1987 I:68) argue that the ultimate distinguishing feature of legal systems is their style. Style is a rather vague notion which they clarify by reference to five factors: (1) history, (2) mode of legal thinking; (3) institutions; (4) sources of law; (5) ideology. All are relevant, albeit to varying degrees, in identifying what it is that sets the civil law apart from the common law. Each of these five factors is addressed individually below.

[117] The historical development of a particular legal system is the first factor that influences its overall style. It is a factor that unmistakably sets

---

15 Authoritative overviews of the various legal families throughout the world are by David and Brierley (1985:22) and by Zweigert and Kötz (1987 I:63).

16 The civil code of Belgium, for instance, is a direct copy of its French counterpart. Yet, the development of Belgian labour law has been influenced by German as well as French legal thinking, especially in the area of collective bargaining.

the civil law apart from the common law. Upon closer examination, it is also a factor for internal differentiation within the civil law. History provides then a first indication that the various members of the civil law may be less homogeneous than their common law counterparts. David and Brierley (1985:34) identify several sub-categories of legal systems within the civil law with Latin, Germanic and Scandinavian laws forming three secondary groupings in Europe. Zweigert and Kötz (1987 I:69-70) go one step further and argue that it is misleading to put all three sub-categories into one legal family. In the final analysis, though, even Zweigert and Kötz accept that the Romanistic (France, Italy, Spain, Portugal and the Benelux countries), the Germanic (Germany, Austria, Switzerland), and the Nordic systems have a closer relationship with each other than with the common law. In this book most attention is paid to the French and the German exponents of the civil law.

[118] A second factor that sets civil law and common law apart from each other entails the distinctive mode of legal thinking that each displays. As for the civil law a tendency exists to use abstract terms and, more generally, to adopt a conceptual approach to legal reasoning. The deductive/inductive dichotomy is useful in describing what is meant by this. Under the deductive approach of the civil law, the value of case law is inherently limited in that court decisions are viewed as individual illustrations of, or specific exceptions to, the law as embodied in a general rule, principle, or concept. Legal reasoning in the European civil law occurs then from the top down, moving from the general to the more specific. The distinction by David and Brierley (1985:360-361) between "open" and "closed" systems of legal reasoning makes the same point. The civil law is said to be a closed system in that any legal question that arises can – and, in principle, must – be answered through the interpretation of an existing rule of law. Of course, this approach to the technique of legislative interpretation at times necessitates a high degree of judicial creativity. Applications in the areas of contract and tort law are studied later on in this book. At a more principled level, though, it would appear that the perception of law itself differs in civil law and common law. Law in the civil law is treated as "found" rather than "made" in each individual case through the forces of logical deduction and a preparedness to reason *par analogiam* or *a contrario*. The common law, when viewed through the eyes of the civil law, does not approach law as a science but merely as a method: a method for making distinctions. It is by distinguishing cases that have been decided in the past that the legal rule to be applied to the case at hand is "discovered" by the common law lawyer. Interestingly, from a civil law perspective, this inductive process of discovery in the common law may lead to the formulation of a new rule. In summary, the distinctive mode of legal thinking in the civil law evolves around the technique of interpretation as opposed to differentiation which typifies the common law.

[119] The civil law has its own distinctive institutions. There is an opportunity to discuss several of these in the second part of the book where aspects of substantive law are dealt with. It suffices to merely list some examples at this stage: *cause* in French law,[17] *Geschäftsgrundlage* in German law,[18] and the absence of such concepts as consideration or estoppel throughout the civil law of contract. The significance of this third distinguishing feature in explaining the difference between the legal families of civil law and common law is somewhat overstated, though. There is ample anecdotal evidence to suggest that no inferences can be drawn from the opposite situation as the presence in both legal families of identical legal concepts in name may nevertheless conceal major differences in approach. The French concept of mistake (*erreur*) is a case in point: it has little in common with its common-law counterpart.[19]

[120] Sources of law constitute a traditional criterion for distinguishing between legal families. When applied to the civil/common law dichotomy, statutes as opposed to cases feature as the primary source of law in the civil law and, technically, case law is not a binding source of law at all. Throughout the 20th century, however, there has been some sort of *rapprochement* between civil law and common law, triggered by the penetration of statute in virtually all areas of the common law and the de facto existence of precedent in the civil law. In the chapters on contract, tort, labour law and commercial law there is an opportunity to observe judicial law making in the civil law. However, it must be appreciated that, all in all, the respective approaches of civil law and common law to statutes and cases remain fundamentally different. This is so because the civil law has never had to "accommodate" legislation as a relative newcomer in the otherwise unfettered realm of the common law. Thus it has always been easier for the civil law judiciary to adopt a liberal, purposive approach to statutory interpretation.[20]

---

17   See [523] ff below.

18   See [544] ff below.

19   See Chapter 5.

20   It may also explain why the problem of ageing statutes is perceived differently in civil law and common law. For a discussion, see the bold proposals as regards the American legal scene by Calabresi (1982).

[121] The significance of this last point must not be underestimated. A correlation exists between statutory drafting style and the judicial approach to statutory interpretation. Admittedly, the civil law codes are no longer the sole and, in some areas of law, not even the primary source of regulation, and vast numbers of supplementary statutes have been adopted outside of the codes. But the drafting style of the 19th century codes serves as a reference point that continues to influence the manner of rule formulation to date. In addition, the civil law lawyer tends to read cases through different eyes from the common law lawyer. Distinguishing cases on their facts is an art that is mastered truly only in the common law. In the civil law, by contrast, the search is more readily for the legal principles that underpin the court decisions. The traditional primacy of case law in the common law may have influenced the manner in which statutes are drafted and interpreted. The reverse is true for the civil law: the traditional primacy of statute in the civil law has influenced the manner in which cases are drafted and interpreted.[21]

[122] Ideology is the least useful criterion when distinguishing between civil law and common law. The essence of the political, economic or even cultural foundations of the law in both legal families is too similar for it to be otherwise.

1.5 Comparativism and the European Community

(a) The European legislature

[123] The legal order of the European Community acts as a real-life laboratory for the study of the comparative method, and comparativism plays a crucial role in the "nurturing" of this (relatively) new supranational system of law (Jacobs 1990:99; Hilf 1986:550). Pipkorn (1977: 265-267), a European Community civil servant, gives a clear description of the process that leads to the drafting of proposals for Community legislation. The starting point usually is a call for national reports by qualified experts in the member states. These experts typically are leading academics. When the issues to be addressed by the proposed Community law are of a less complex nature the comparative research is entrusted to just one or two experts. To ensure a common structure and a coherent approach to the relevant problems in the various reports, a questionnaire is prepared which is discussed with the national rapporteurs in advance. The Community has a centralised legal service. However, the leading role in

---

21   See the discussion of the law making process in Chapter 4.

the ultimate drafting of legislative proposals is taken by officials of the Directorate General responsible for the subject matter in question.[22]

[124] The above comments by Pipkorn are made with direct reference to the harmonisation of labour and social laws, but their application is not limited to these fields of law. A core area of private law that has been the subject of ongoing research since 1980 is contract law. The Lando Commission – named after its chair, Professor Ole Lando of Denmark – is a non-governmental body of (mainly academic) lawyers from the EC member states. Drawing selectively upon the national law of the member states, the Commission completed its so-called Principles of European Contract Law in the early 1990s. Officially, the Principles are not legally binding. But they are an essential stepping stone towards the adoption of a truly European Code of Obligations in the future.[23] In 1989 and again in 1994 the European Parliament called for the creation of a European Civil Code. These Principles may form its basis.[24]

(b) The European judiciary

[125] Jacobs (1990:110) has observed that, in contrast with an English court, an essential part of the judicial function of the European Court of Justice consists in legal research. The staff of the Court includes a research and documentation division, comprising lawyers familiar with all the legal systems of the Community. A special role is reserved for the Advocates General (Hartley 1994:60-62). Advocates General have the same status a judges, but they do not participate in the Court's deliberations. According to Art 66 of the Treaty of Rome, the duty of the Advocate General is to make, in open court, a reasoned submission in order to assist the Court. The opinion of the Advocate General is not binding on the Court, but it is invariably considered with great care by the bench. It is reproduced, together with the judgment itself, in the *European Court Reports*.[25] The

---

22 Gordon-Smith 1989:58; Bates 1983:32. The Commission is both the main initiator and executor of Community legislation. The Commission is divided into (ministerial) departments known as Directorate Generals. Two important "departments" are, for example, DG I on External Relations and DG IV on Competition. See also [429] below.

23 Lando 1992:573. The first part of these Principles have now been published. See Lando and Beale 1995.

24 The role of the European Parliament in the law making process of the EC is discussed in [430]-[431] below.

25 *The European Court Reports* are the official reporting system of the European Court of Justice. Because of the need to translate the Court decisions in nearly a dozen Community languages, delays in the reporting of cases are a common occurrence. Case law is reproduced more quickly in the unofficial reporting system of the *Common Market Law Reports*.

opinion of the Advocate General is a rich source of information, comprising a discussion of the facts, reference to the relevant legislative provisions, and a consideration of previous Court decisions. When appropriate, the Advocate General makes express reference to the laws of the member states in an attempt to determine not the lowest common denominator but rather the most appropriate solution to the case at hand.[26]

[126] In principle, the relevance of comparativism applies to all areas of Community law (Hilf 1986:556). In practice, one of the most fertile areas of comparative study by the European Court of Justice to date has been the development of principles governing judicial review (Jacobs 1990:104). An early example as to how comparative law can be used to determine the limits of the powers of the EC Commission is the case of *ASSIDER v High Authority* (case 3/54, [1954-1956] ECR 63) where Advocate General Lagrange sought to explain the notion of "misuse of powers" in Art 33 of the European Coal and Steel Community Treaty (ECSC Treaty) by reference to the administrative laws of the member states. Other principles of Community law that have been identified and/or interpreted by reference to national law include the protection of legitimate interests (*Vertrauensschutz*),[27] the right to be heard (audi alteram partem: *Transocean Marine Paint Association v Commission*, case 17/74 [1974] ECR 1063), the principle of proportionality *(Verhältnismässigkeit: the Internationale Handelsgesellschaft* case, case 11/70 [1970] ECR 1125), and legal professional privilege (*AM and S Europe Ltd v Commission*, case 155/79 [1982] ECR 1575). Even though the comparative reflex of the European Court is often inspired by the opinion of the Advocate General, an open acknowledgment of this "dialogue" between Court and Advocate General has traditionally been absent from the Court decision.[28]

[127] Koopmans, a former judge of the European Court of Justice, sees a bright future for comparative law – both as an academic subject and as a practical tool for analysing and solving legal problems. Possibly, the apparent change in the "legal climate" over the past 10 or 15 years is only partially influenced by the process of European integration. But, in any event, it is his prediction that comparativism will gain further momentum

---

26   The Advocate General is discussed further in [435] below.
27   Westzucker, Case 1/73 [1973] ECR 723. Protection of legitimate expectations is generally preferred to a more literal, but potentially misleading, translation as protection of (legitimate) confidence. See Usher 1974:363; Hartley 1994:152.
28   This same point is made elsewhere in the book. See [435] below.

to the effect that "the twenty-first century may become the era of comparative methods" (Koopmans 1996: 545 and 556).

References

Atiyah, PS, and Summers, RS, 1987, *Form and Substance in Anglo-American Law: A Comparative Study in Legal Reasoning, Legal Theory and Legal Institutions*, Clarendon Press, Oxford.

Baade, H, "Comparative Law and the Practitioner", (1983) 31 *American Journal of Comparative Law* 499.

Bates, TStJN, "The Drafting of European Community Legislation", (1983) *Statute Law Review* 24.

Blanpain, R, 1993, "Comparativism in Labour Law and Industrial Relations", in Blanpain, R, and Engels, C, (eds), *Comparative Labour Law and Industrial Relations in Industrialized Market Economies*, 5th ed, Kluwer, Deventer.

Calabresi, G, 1982, *A Common Law for the Age of Statutes*, Harvard University Press, Cambridge.

Collins, H, "Methods and Aims of Comparative Contract Law", (1991) 11 *Oxford Journal of Legal Studies* 396.

Dashwood, A, Hacon, RJ, and White, RCA, 1987, *A Guide to the Civil Jurisdiction and Judgments Convention*, Kluwer, Deventer.

David, R, and Brierley, JEC, 1985, *Major Legal Systems in the World Today*, 3rd ed, Stevens & Sons, London.

Frohn, EN, 1994, "The Position of the Surviving Spouse in the Law of Succession: Some Comparative Remarks", in Boele-Woelki, K, Grosheide, FW, Hondius, EH, and Steenhoff, GJW, (eds), *Comparability and Evaluation. Essays on Comparative Law, Private International Law and International Commercial Arbitration, in honour of Dimitra Kokkini – Iatridou*, M. Nijhoff, Dordrecht.

Gordon-Smith, D, "The Drafting Process in the European Community", (1989) 10 *Statute Law Review* 56.

Hanza, G, 1991, *Comparative Law and Antiquity*, Akadémiai Kiadó, Budapest.

Hartley, TC, 1994, *The Foundations of European Community Law*, 3rd ed, Clarendon Press, Oxford.

Hilf, M, 1986, "The Role of Comparative Law in the Jurisprudence of the Court of Justice of the European Communities", in De Mestral, A, et al, (eds), *The Limitations of Human Rights in Comparative Constitutional Law*, Y Blais, Cowansville.

Jacobs, F, 1990, "The Uses of Comparative Law in the Law of the European Communities", in Plender, R, (ed), *Legal History and Comparative Law: Essays in Honour of Albert Kiralfy, 1990*, F Cass, London.

Kahn-Freund, O, "On Uses and Misuses of Comparative Law", (1974) 37 *Modern Law Review 1*.

Kahn–Freund, O, "Comparative Law as an Academic Subject", (1966) 82 *Law Quarterly Review* 40.

Kamba, WJ, "Comparative Law: A Theoretical Framework", (1974) 23 *International and Comparative Law Quarterly* 485.

Kassalow, EM, 1969, *Trade Unions and Industrial Relations: An International Comparison*, Random House, New York.

Koopmans, T, "Comparative Law and the Courts", (1996) 45 *International and Comparative Law Quarterly* 545.

Lando, O, and Beale, H, (eds), 1995, *The Principles of European Contract Law. Part I: Performance and Remedies*, Martinus Nijhoff, Dordrecht.

Lando, O, "Principles of European Contract Law: An Alternative to or a Precursor of European Legislation?", (1992) 40 *American Journal of Comparative Law* 573.

Luntz, H, and Hambly, D, 1995, *Torts. Cases and Commentary*, 4th ed, Butterworths, Sydney.

Markesinis, B, "Comparative Law – A Subject in Search of an Audience, (1990) 53 *Modern Law Review* 1.

Pipkorn, J, "Comparative Labour Law in the Harmonisation of Social Standards in the European Community", (1977) 2 *Comparative Labor Law* 260.

Sacco, R, "Legal Formants: A Dynamic Approach to Comparative Law", (1991) 34 *American Journal of Comparative Law* 1.

Schregle, J, "Comparative Industrial Relations: Pitfalls and Potential", (1981) 120 *International Labour Review* 15.

Schuster, EJ, 1907, *The Principles of German Civil Law*, Clarendon Press, Oxford.

Sussman, 1970, "Discussion: The Nature and Teaching of Comparative Law in the Context of Modern Society", in *Proceedings of the Seventh International Symposium on Comparative Law*, 105.

Tunc, A, "L'Enseignement du droit comparé: Présentation", (1988) *Revue internationale de droit comparé* 703.

Usher, JA, "The Influence of National Concepts on Decisions of the European Court", (1976) 1 *European Law Review* 359.

Valticos, N, and von Potobsky G, 1994, "International Labour Law", in Blanpain, R, (ed), *International Encyclopaedia for Labour Law and Industrial Relations*, looseleaf, Kluwer, Deventer.

Vranken, M, "Demise of the Australasian Model of Labour Law in the 1990s", (1994) 16 *Comparative Labor Law Journal* 1.

Vranken, M, "Specialisation and Labour Courts: A Comparative Analysis", (1988) 9 *Comparative Labor Law Journal* 497.

Winterton, G, "Comparative Law Teaching", (1975) 23 *American Journal of Comparative Law* 69.

Zweigert, K, and Kötz H, 1987, *An Introduction to Comparative Law*, 2 Volumes, 2nd ed, Clarendon Press, Oxford.

Chapter 2

History

2.1 Historical Foundations of the European Civil Law

(a) Ius Commune

[201] A study of the history of the civil law offers valuable insights into the factors that helped shape this particular legal family. It also is the first opportunity to demonstrate the relative diversity among members of the civil law as compared to the relatively more homogeneous composition of the common law legal family. In this regard the alternative label of Romano-Germanic family is used occasionally so as to emphasise two major building stones of the civil law, ie Roman law and Germanic customary law (David and Brierley (1985:22)

[202] The year 476 stands for the formal end of the (Western) Roman empire notwithstanding repeated barbarian invasions before 476 (Lambiris 1994:85; Jolowicz 1952:XX). Up until the fifth century, much of Western Europe (including parts of Britain) had been romanised for several centuries. In hindsight this process of romanisation proved to be a relatively civilised affair. Following a period of military conquest the Romans developed a sophisticated civilisation. The backbone of their society was trade and the Mediterranean served as the main commercial artery. The Roman legal system reflected the society it was meant to serve. In practical terms, this meant that Roman law was successful in combining an ability to think in abstract terms with practical common sense (Von Mehren 1957:3-5).

[203] 476 did not signify the end of Roman law. In the West, the invaders did not impose their own, customary law upon the indigenous population. Rather the locals continued to be governed by Roman law. Only, this Roman law degenerated rapidly and it was in essence a "vulgarised"[1] version that survived. The period of the fifth until the 10th century was a period of intellectual decline, characterised by the rise of Islam and by

---

1   The original meaning of "vulgar" is popular. Vulgarised law stands for the proposition that the old Roman law was moulded to suit the needs of a changing society. See Van Caenegem 1992:17.

Muslim control over the Mediterranean. Having first lost its political (Rome) base in the fifth century, Europe next lost its economic centre in the seventh century. Western Europe effectively had its main trade routes cut and, in the result, it turned into a largely rural society. It was a society in which the old Roman law came to be viewed increasingly as remote and unreal. For instance, in the absence of any significant commercial exchange, there was not much call for the Roman law of contracts of sale. In summary, Roman law did survive but in a modified format that reflected the changed environment (Schlesinger 1988:255-256).

[204] In the East the Roman empire was to survive for another thousand years. The seat of the empire was no longer Rome but Byzantium (later called Constantinople and currently known as Istanbul, capital of Turkey). Its most prominent emperor was Justinian. It was Justinian who took the initiative in the sixth century to bring together all Roman laws in one big collection: the *Corpus Iuris Civilis*, also known as the *Corpus Iuris Justinianis*. In doing so, Emperor Justinian changed the outlook of continental Europe forever.

[205] The *Corpus Iuris Civilis* represents the main source of our knowledge of Roman law today. The *Corpus* comprises several books. They are the *Institutes*, which served as a textbook or systematic treatise for students of Roman law; the *Code* and the *Novels*, both containing collections of imperial enactments; and the *Digest* or *Pandects*, which constitutes the most important part of the *Corpus* by far. The *Digest* contains a compilation of the writings of the great Roman jurists, in particular those from the so-called classical period.[2] The *Digest* contains case commentaries – both actual and hypothetical – plus discussions of statutory interpretation. Interestingly, its style is relatively casuistic, and the various topics are not always neatly arranged either. It makes the idea of Roman law as a principled and coherent system of law an over-statement.

[206] The *Corpus Iuris* formed the legal basis of the Byzantine empire for many centuries. The year 1453 marks the definitive end of the (East) Roman empire. At this point in time, Western Europe was experiencing an intellectual renaissance, a process which had started towards the end of the 11th century. Not surprisingly, perhaps, the revival of the West had a solid economic base to it. Following the Crusades and the "liberation" of the Holy Land, the Mediterranean had been reopened as a major West

---

2   The "classical" period officially ended in 235, well before the split of the empire into East and West: Jolowicz 1952:xx.

European trading route. From the 12th century onwards, there occurred a large-scale expansion of commerce the effects of which were not limited to the Mediterranean but with implications further inland as well. Characteristic for this time period was the rapid increase in popularity of fairs, ie organised occasions for commercial exchange (Von Mehren 1957:7). It meant that what were once small towns now had the opportunity to develop into major commercial centres. Vulgarised Roman law was no longer adequate to service this society in change. Instead, the *Corpus Iuris*, a copy of which had been found – quite accidentally – in a library in Pisa, offered a readily available alternative. The *Corpus* was a body of law that at least had the potential of solving satisfactorily many a problem a more active economy and a more cultivated society had to face (Von Mehren 1957:8).

[207] It is important to bear in mind that the "rediscovery" of Roman law as embodied in the *Corpus Iuris* was old law. Not only was the *Corpus* itself several centuries old, the law it contained was even older. To appreciate this fascination with the law of a by-gone era, the intellectual revival in the West is perhaps best understood in terms of a nostalgic reflex: a longing for the good old days; a desire to leave behind the Dark Ages with its superstition and its belief in the super-natural at the expense of logic and reason; a longing for a civilisation (Greek and Roman Antiquity) that was no more (Coing 1973:507-508). And this nostalgic reflex was not confined to law. Other disciplines such as philosophy (Plato), theology and medicine (Aristotle) became caught up in it too. This broad reach need not surprise. It is only in more recent times that law came to be viewed as part of the social sciences along with economics, political science etc. At an earlier stage, law used to be much more closely aligned with philosophy and theology. In turn this explains why once the emphasis was not so much on contemporary (or local) law, but rather the focus was on the more eternal concepts of morality and justice. Its continued impact arguably can be felt more in the modern civil law than in the common law.

[208] Who was to administer this newly "found" law? The people traditionally entrusted with the task of speaking law (the "noblemen") generally lacked the intellect and the knowledge of a legal system that was well over 500 years old. Increasingly, local courts, royal councils, and the church – the main users of the *Corpus* – had to fall back on university-trained lawyers. In time, this led to the birth of a new profession: the *Juristae* (Coing 1973:510-512).

[209] The first university to study the *Corpus Iuris* was located at Bologna. In France large-scale instruction in law started from the 13th century onwards. Germany and Belgium followed suit in the 15th century, and by the 16th and 17th century Scandinavia had been reached as well. Significantly, the various law schools all followed the Bologna model. In practical terms, this meant that throughout Europe law students received the same training in a common law (*ius commune*) comprising Roman law and canon law (*ius utrumque*).

[210] The appearance of canon law in addition to Roman law on the curriculum of the medieval universities was no coincidence. After 476, the Catholic church assumed responsibility for the preservation of the Roman civilisation in the West, both in terms of its laws and its culture. This tended to blur the Roman/canon law distinction somewhat. At about the time of the "discovery" of the *Corpus Iuris*, the Church administration was ready for a major overhaul. The reorganisation of its judicial system started in the second half of the 12th century. The Church needed university-trained people to think through and carry out the required reforms. The Church thus became the primary employer of the *Juristae* and this development also influenced the curriculum (Coing 1973:511). Furthermore, there was the influence of Gratian, a Bolognese monk who is generally credited with having transformed canon law into an independent "system" by producing a collection of canon law materials known as the *Decretum*. Both the *Corpus* and the *Decretum* were taught in tandem.[3]

(b) Factors of differentiation

[211] The *ius commune* of the civil law was brought to a formal end by the national codification movement of the 19th century. But it does not follow that no regional differentiation occurred before that. Not only did the various parts of the Continent differ as regards the timing of their "reception" of Roman law – as discussed above, the actual degree of Roman law penetration was different too. Here is then the first indication as to the diversity among the various members of the civil law family. More specifically, in France Roman law clearly was received more in the South than in the North.[4] The latter part of France became known as the land of customary law (*pays du droit coutumier)* as compared to the land of written law (*pays du droit écrit)* in the South. Written law is a direct

---

3   Gratian has been referred to as "the father of the science of canon law": Kuttner 1983.

4   Precise geographical boundaries are hard to draw. However, the "South" clearly refers to an area that did not include Paris.

reference to the *Corpus Iuris*. Of course, customary law, an unwritten source of law by tradition, was not wholly absent in the South: in fact, customary law in the South was itself (vulgarised) Roman law. On the other hand, customary law in the North did not remain unwritten forever either. Charles VII ordered the official compilation of all customs in the middle of the 15th century. This attempt to stop confusion and legal uncertainty proved to be a mammoth task that took in excess of a century to complete. Little wonder then that the legal system of medieval France has been referred to as a "kaleidoscope" with some 300 local customs, whose influence was often limited to a particular village or city, supplemented by 60 general customs (including the *coutume de Paris* with its influence extending beyond Paris) (Deak and Rheinstein 1936:551). In these circumstances Roman law in the North was used to fill any gaps which inevitably were left by the customary law.

[212] Germany is a different story altogether. Political power was not centralised as in medieval France. On the contrary, the political situation following the reign of the *Hohenstaufen* rulers is typified by a weakening of imperial power. An initiative such as that of French king Charles VII in ordering an official compilation of customary law was therefore unthinkable. In the result there was nothing in place that could provide a buffer against the wholesale adoption of Roman law in 1495. The *Reichskammergerichtsordnung* of 1495 is a legislative act by which Emperor Maximilian tried to bring order in the German system of judicial administration through the centralisation of judicial control. It was part of a larger scheme to restore the power of the monarch. However, the German central court – both the *Reichsgericht* and its successor, the *Reichskammergericht* – lacked the prestige to make its impact felt. The significance of the 1495 legislation then is that it formally acknowledges Roman law as positive law in Germany.[5] This reception of Roman law was triggered by a combination of necessity and choice. On the one hand, the court personnel often had no actual knowledge of local law because of the lack of a central compilation thereof. On the other hand, the German emperors *(Kaiser)* regarded themselves as successors of the Roman emperors *(Caesar)*. Roman law was then no foreign law at all, so ran the argument, which

---

5   It is not entirely clear whether the application of Roman law was imposed or rather whether its application was merely permitted. Schlesinger (1988:267) reproduces an extract from Deak and Rheinstein (1936) to the effect that the judges of the newly established *Reichskammergericht* were "ordered" to decide the cases coming before them according to Roman law. Dawson (1968:189) on the other hand, suggests that the ordinance of 1495 only "authorised" the Court to turn to Roman law.

made its less than selective adoption perfectly acceptable![6] The contrasting approach of France to the adoption of Roman law is captured in the following Latin adage: *non ratione imperii sed imperio rationis* (not by reason of the emperor but because of the superior reason).

[213] The Roman law that was "received" in Germany was not the *Corpus Iuris simpliter* but rather an annotated version. The annotators were individuals teaching law at the medieval European universities. The early annotators are generally known as glossators. Because of the casuistic nature of the *Corpus*, the glossators added short notes ("glosses") to particular passages of the *Corpus*. These glosses typically consisted of comparisons between different texts in an attempt to logically reconcile the various parts of the *Corpus*. From the 13th century onwards, but especially in the 14th and 15th centuries, the glossators were succeeded by the school of post-glossators or commentators (Von Mehren (1957:9). These commentators did not restrict themselves to merely adding short glosses to the *Corpus*. Instead, they engaged in a practice that can only be described as the rewriting of the *Corpus*. In particular, systematic commentaries were produced that focused on specific legal problems. The best known representative of this school of legal commentators is Bartolus. Bartolus refused to take the *Corpus* at face value. Instead, the *Corpus* to him formed the (authoritative) basis for turning law into a science. Significantly, the emphasis by Bartolus was not merely on bringing order into a state of disorder, but rather he was actively interested in system building, even if that meant going beyond the Roman law as laid down in the *Corpus* (Schlesinger 1988:270).

[214] Bartolus' fascination with system building is significant. The lasting effect of the reception of Roman law in Germany concerns the legal method rather than substance of German law. Put differently German law became *verwissenschaftlicht*.[7] There is no equivalent English word to capture the meaning of this expression. In essence, German scholars developed an "addiction" for system building. To them the systematic ordering of legal ideas and concepts became a second nature. Also,

---

6   The main authority for this proposition is Krause, H, 1952 *Kaiserrecht und Rezeption*, Heidelberg, as quoted in Dawson (1968:183). Note that Dawson (1968:183) points out that the actual influence of this idea in promoting the reception of Roman law may have been limited.

7   Wieacker, PRG, 1952 *Privatrechtsgeschichte der Neuzeit*, Gottingen , as discussed in Dawson (1968:238-239). An English translation by Tony Weir is now available: Wieacker (1995).

German scholars in time displayed a readiness and a willingness to submit to the dictates of an ever more perfect and more rigorous logic.

[215] It may be asked why this approach to law as a science by and large remained confined to Germany. Dawson in his classic oeuvre on *The Oracles of the Law* (1968:240ff) seeks an explanation in the authority of academic scholars. The *doctrine* is an authoritative source of law throughout the civil law. But, in addition, there developed the practice of "dispatching the record" *(Aktenversendung)* in Germany where the German courts would send the files of difficult cases to law faculties for a learned, detached opinion. The academics who received the file would write a collegiate opinion based on Roman law. Very little interest was shown in using local, customary law to assist in addressing legal issues. Often the law professors would be unfamiliar with local law and even though it could be submitted – technically – in evidence, it tended to be interpreted restrictively. A feeling existed, even among the litigants themselves, that to detach oneself from the local law was a virtue, and it was not uncommon for files to be sent to out-of-the-way law faculties deliberately.

[216] The practice of *Aktenversendung* acquired great prominence in the 17th century.[8] In that century (and the next) the Natural law school of thinking reached a climax. The significance of this observation lies in that natural law thinking reinforced the system-building approach to the law initiated by the post-glossators (Schlesinger 1988:273-274). In essence, the message of the Natural law school of thought was one of optimism: there is order in the world after all. This order was said to be brought about by a higher force (not God), and it could be detected through the application of reason, logic, and rationality. Major representatives of the Natural law school of thinking were Hobbes, Spinoza, and Pufendorf. French legal thinking was influenced by it as well. Broadly, Natural law was a crucial foundation stone upon which the 19th century codification movement was to build. Admittedly, at the beginning of the 19th century the Historical school of legal thinking reacted against the Natural law school and its "lifeless rationalism". The main representative of the Historical school in Germany was von Savigny (Zweigert and Kötz 1987 I:144-147; Schlesinger 1988:274-275). However, not even Savigny succeeded in effectively turning back the clock to ancient Roman or Germanic law.[9]

---

8   The replies from the law faculties were formulated in the form of draft decisions. In time they became more than merely advisory: they became the court decision itself. See Dawson 1968:261.

9   See [218] and [219] below.

[217] Codification in France preceded the enactment of the German civil code by nearly a century. In both instances the ideological impetus derived from the Natural law school of thought. But a more immediate trigger in France was the Revolution of 1789 followed by Napoleon Bonaparte's rise to power a decade later. The purpose of the French Revolution was to abolish the excesses of the *Ancien Régime*. To this effect a new legal order had to be established. Pivotal in this regard was the provision for the drafting of a *Code civil* for all French people in the Constitution of 1791. Three draft civil codes initially failed to obtain the approval of the legislature, however. All were rejected for being too long, too philosophical, or insufficiently revolutionary (West 1992:25). In 1799 Napoleon took (political) power and it was his perseverance that resulted in the promulgation of the *Code civil des français* in 1804. The actual text had been drafted by a commission of four distinguished judges (including Portalis) who drew heavily on the works of scholars, Pothier and Domat in particular. Even so, Napoleon – who had no legal training – insisted that the Code be drafted in language accessible to the ordinary citizen (Dadamo and Farran 1996:7-9; Dickson 1994:4-5).

[218] The idea of codification aroused scholarly interest in Germany throughout the 19th century. Under influence of the Natural law school of thought separate codes for Bavaria and Prussia had already been completed in 1756 and 1794, respectively. In the wake of the French *Code civil* of 1804, Professor Thibaut favoured the prompt adoption of a German code to facilitate the process of political unification. Ideally, the new law common to all German states should also be universally available and understandable; and not too much reliance should be placed on common law principles as they were historically determined in conditions different to the contemporary situation of the German states (Foster 1993:19). By contrast, members of the Historical school argued that a German code could not be adopted without extensive preliminary research into the (historical) development of German legal institutions. In the result the project of the civil code (*Bürgerliches Gesetzbuch: BGB*) became a mammoth task that did not eventuate until the end of the century. Ironically, only some members of the Historical school actually engaged in an historical investigation of indigenous, Germanic or customary law. Others, including Savigny himself, once again turned to classical Roman law. These legal scholars studied Roman law with the aim of discovering its "latent system" for purposes of adaptation to the needs of their own society. In the process, they brought the study of Justinian's *Digest* to its highest and most systematic level. A so-called Pandectist school grew out of the Historical school and it dominated legal scholarship in Germany when the preparation of the *BGB* began in 1874 (Glendon, Gordon, Osakwe 1985:52).

[219] In 1874 a first commission of 11 members (six judges, three civil servants and two law professors) was appointed and charged with producing a draft *BGB*. The first draft, published 13 years later, was severely criticised for being overly abstract and legalistic (Zweigert and Kötz 1987 I:148). Even though the composition of the commission was subsequently broadened to include several lay persons, the second (and final) draft remained essentially "pandectist" in language, method, structure and concepts (Dawson 1968:460). The *BGB*, promulgated in 1896 and in force since 1900, is a document by and for the law professional.

2.2 Developments at the Level of the European Community

(a) Formation of the European Community

[220] Roman law undoubtedly constitutes an important unifying factor in the historical formation of the European civil law. However, it is equally clear from the above discussion[10] that differences as regards the timing and the degree of penetration of Roman law in various parts of Europe resulted in a relatively high degree of diversity, especially when compared to the history of the common law in the English speaking world. Once the codification movement of the 19th century took hold, there occurred a more direct swing of the pendulum away from uniformity as the drafting of a code and the building of a (new) national identity often went hand in hand. The intervention of two World Wars during the first half of the 20th century, however, induced a rethinking of the concept of nation state and its limitations. A major factor contributing to the success of post-war attempts at the peaceful integration of Western Europe was the pragmatism displayed in the adoption of a staged approach to a united Europe. Specifically, unification of the national (economic) markets was viewed as a prerequisite for a fuller, political integration to be achieved at some later stage.

[221] In the first half of the 20th century Count Coudenhove led an active Pan-European movement (Zurcher 1958:X). He certainly was not the first person to call for European integration, and the expression "United States

---

10   See [211] ff above.

of Europe" is said to have been used as early as 1849 by Victor Hugo (Brugmans cited in Mathijsen 1995:12). But a more convenient starting point for a discussion of the origins of the European Community is 1945. The peaceful integration of Europe is after all a recent phenomenon and the end of the Second World War served as its direct trigger. Economically large parts of the "freed" as well as the "losing" countries were literally in ruins at that time. The political and military scene was not much better, and it is a fair observation that Western Europe came out of the war severely weakened. Unfortunately, there was precious little time to regain strength as the "real" war was soon to be followed by a "cold" war and, linked to this, fears grew for Russian expansionism. In the result, the so-called Allied Forces were not to stay allies for very long. A case in point is the position of occupied Germany and its post-war division into American, British, French, and Russian zones. Disagreement among these four allies meant that the first three zones were brought together in what became known as West Germany or the BRD (*Bundesrepublik Deutschland*), whereas the Russian zone formed East Germany or the DDR (*Deutsche Demokratische Republik*) in 1949. The war in Korea commenced a year later. Thus a near perfect scenario developed for a growing dependence of Western Europe on the United States of America. Expressions of this dependence can be found both in the economic and the political-military domains. Economically, the 1947 Marshall Plan resulted in the establishment of the Organisation for European Economic Co-operation in 1948. The OEEC is better known by its current name (since 1961) of OECD, ie the Organisation for Economic Co-operation and Development. But there is also the North Atlantic Treaty Organisation or NATO. The latter has been referred to as "[T]he umbilical cord that kept Western Europe attached to the United States long after the period of US economic dominance was over" (George 1991:38).

[222] To be fair, Europe had plenty of reasons to be grateful for the American assistance in re-building the continent.[11] But it must also be stressed that the American dominance in Western Europe provided an excellent backdrop for a range of proposals to try to strengthen Europe. The appeal of these proposals was directly linked to the perceived need for a Europe that could stand on its own feet.

---

11 A good example is the central library of the Catholic University of Leuven in Belgium. Twice it was destroyed by warfare this century. Twice it has been rebuilt with American funds.

[223] An early (post World War II) plea for "a kind of United States of Europe" came from Winston Churchill in a speech at Zurich University (Switzerland) in 1946. Even though Churchill was in political opposition at the time, it was clear that Britain at first did not see itself as becoming part of this unification exercise. On the one hand, the United Kingdom had suffered relatively little in the war when compared to the Continent, which may explain its less intense feeling of desperation. On the other hand Britain considered its real interests to lie in its colonies rather than on the Continent. Britain was prepared to participate, however, in a regional structure that involved no actual transfer of national sovereignty, and the Council of Europe was established in 1949. The Council's most renowned achievement to-date is the 1950 Convention on the Protection of Human Rights and Fundamental Freedoms. This European Convention provides for the establishment of a Human Rights Commission and a Human Rights Court based in Strasbourg (France).

[224] Of more direct relevance when tracing the origins of the European Community is a declaration by Robert Schuman, French Minister of Foreign Affairs, in 1950. Schuman echoed Churchill's call for a partnership between France and Germany when he made a specific proposal to merge the heavy industries of both countries (including any other country that wished to join). The proposal was for the production of coal and steel to be placed under the command of a joint High Authority, composed of independent persons and empowered to make decisions that would bind both member states and companies. Financial independence for this new supranational structure was to be provided through a levy on the production of coal and steel. The Treaty establishing the European Coal and Steel Community (ECSC) was signed in Paris in 1951 between France, Germany, the Benelux countries and Italy.

[225] The ECSC Treaty is significant for various reasons. Coal and steel had been instrumental in the previous war efforts and the Treaty was meant to act as a buffer against a revival of the German menace. The Treaty also tackled the existence of a political power vacuum in Europe, and the High Authority was seen as a governmental authority that could operate side-by-side with, and even instead of, the six national governments. Notwithstanding the many built-in safeguards, the Treaty indeed signalled a break with the classical pattern of establishing purely inter-governmental organisations at international law (Kapteyn 1989:8). Economic considerations played a rather subsidiary part at first. But the failed attempts at building upon the Schuman declaration via both a European Defence Community and a European Political Community led to a more "realistic" report prepared by the Belgian Foreign Minister Paul-Henri Spaak, in which the emphasis was on expanding economic integration beyond coal and steel. The Spaak report formed the basis for negotiations which led to the signing of two treaties in Rome on 25 March 1957. They are the Treaty establishing the European Economic Community (EEC) and the Treaty establishing the European Atomic Energy Community (EURATOM).

[226] Technically then there exist not one but three different European Communities. In practical terms, the European Economic Community has achieved the greatest prominence. It is currently known as the European Community, and this deliberate change of name – brought about by the 1992 Maastricht Treaty on European Union (TEU) – reflects a shift in focus away from the dominance of economic issues in the past. Under the Maastricht Treaty the European Community in turn constitutes the main (but not the sole) pillar in the constitutional structure of a new entity, the European Union. Other "pillars" of the European Union are, first, the so-called Common Foreign and Security Policy and, secondly, Cooperation in the fields of Justice and Home Affairs. To date the main legal (supranational) competences continue to be vested in the European Community pillar of the European Union.

(b) Impact of an expanding membership

[227] Significantly, the founding members of the ECSC, the EEC, and EURATOM – the Benelux countries, France, Germany and Italy – have legal systems that without exception belong to the civil law family. The civil law roots of the European Community have had a profound influence on the shaping of the new legal order within which the Community operates. The original framework of the European Community, ie the 1957 Treaty of Rome, bears a strong resemblance to a civil code: it contains a mere 249 provisions (Articles) in the form of relatively short one or more sentences. Specifically, the contents of the 1957 Treaty are rather abstract and general, with the required detail to be provided through a purposive interpretation by the various institutions set up under the Treaty.[12] The institutions themselves, especially the European Court of Justice and the auxiliary office of the Advocate General, bear the imprints of French administrative law (Borgsmidt 1988:106; Rasmussen 1983:156; Barav 1974:809). This French "reflex" was both deliberate and accidental. It was deliberate in that the European Court was designed as an administrative

---

12 Technically, the Treaty of Rome qualifies as a framework treaty (*traité cadre*). See the discussion in [326] below.

tribunal in essence and this is reflected in the text of the Treaty of Paris establishing the European Coal and Steel Community. It was accidental in that the dominance of French administrative law in the national legal scene of several West European nations predates the establishment of the European Coal and Steel Community.[13]

[228] The United Kingdom, Ireland and Denmark joined the European Community in 1973. Greece became the 10th member state in 1981. Spain and Portugal followed in 1986. The current membership is 15, Sweden, Finland and Austria having joined in 1995. In the result the European Community no longer is the exclusively civil law club it once may have been. The influence of European Community law on English law, in particular, has been the subject of comment in the past (Usher 1989:95). But the reverse is undoubtedly correct as well. A classical example as regards the influence of English law in the European Court of Justice is *Transocean Marine Paint* (case 17/74, [1974] ECR 1063). This case provides the first instance of the European Court drawing on English law, as suggested by its Advocate General, in the elaboration of general principles of European Community law to include the right to a hearing (audi alteram partem) (Hartley (1994:158). A more recent instance of English law shaping Community law is the case of *AM & S Europe* (Case 155/79, [1982] ECR 1575). In that case the English concept of legal professional privilege helped shape the decision of the European Court (Brown and Bell 1993:252). More generally, the law of the European Community is inevitably influenced by the legal traditions of its individual member states. As that membership becomes more diverse, the civil law dominance in law making within the European Community becomes less self evident.[14]

(c) Towards a new European "Ius Commune"?

[229] The substantive law itself of the European Community is ever-expanding and European Community law now regulates not only aspects of commercial law but, increasingly, social law, environmental law, and even consumer protection. The Maastricht Treaty on European Union has added education, culture, and public health as further areas of Community interest. Clearly, as European Community law becomes all encompassing,

---

13 Interestingly, all six founding members of the European Community at one time formed part of the Napoleonic empire: Brown and Bell 1993:252 and 262.

14 See the observations as regards Comparativism and the European Community in [123]ff above.

a new legal super structure that is shared by all member states reduces any existing legal diversity at the national level.

[230] The net effect of the European Community is that the distinction between civil law and common law is becoming more blurred. But it need not follow that law in Europe will turn into one big melting pot. According to Art 189 EC[15] European laws can take different forms. The legal technique of Directives, in particular, allows member states a choice as to how to implement any particular Community objective. Indirectly, at least, this allows for any difference in approach to law-making between civil law and common law countries to be continued. Secondly, the application and interpretation of all European laws is first and foremost a matter for the national courts of the member states, and the provision for so-called preliminary rulings in Art 177 reinforces this.[16] In essence, Art 177 EC stipulates that questions as regards the interpretation of Community law may be referred to the European Court by the domestic court, if the latter considers that a decision on the question is necessary to enable it to give judgment. Where the domestic court is the court of last instance in the case at hand, referral to the European Court is compulsory, but this is subject to the so-called doctrines of *acte éclaré* and *acte clair*. A fuller discussion takes place in Chapter 4 on the law-making process of the European Community.[17]

[231] A further obstacle to the establishment of a European *Ius Commune* is the notion of subsidiarity. Subsidiarity is a general principle of Community law. It can be found in Art 3b EC, as formally[18] inserted by the 1992 Treaty on European Union. Subsidiarity is a deliberately elastic concept. Under one interpretation it means that law making must take place at the level at which it can be done most effectively, even if this involves a devolution of powers to a level below the supranational level. As a practical matter this means that each (European) legislative initiative must be assessed on its own merits.[19] A competing and, for now at least,

---

15   Post Maastricht it has become common practice to use "EC" when referring to the Treaty of Rome, as amended.

16   Article 177 of the Treaty of Rome has been the subject of prolific legal commentary. A rich source of information is TMC Asser Instituut (1987).

17   See [439] – [442] below.

18   It is a matter of some controversy among scholars as to whether the application of subsidiarity to EC law-making, outside the area of environmental policy, pre-dates Maastricht. Compare and contrast Cass (1992) and Toth (1992).

19   In an apparent application of the subsidiarity principle a number of proposals for EC regulation have either been withdrawn or revised. Subsidiarity has also triggered a review of existing Community legislation: Delegation of the Commission of the European Communities to Australia and New Zealand (1994). For an application to the competition policy of the EC, see Idot (1994:37).

rather more popular interpretation appears to be, however, that law making best takes place at a level that is as closely as possible to the citizens of the European Union – thus favouring a decentralised approach to decision making in a much more general, principled, fashion. In this regard Lenaerts (1994:851) describes subsidiarity in terms of "a judicially enforceable mechanism of self-defence" against what some member states perceive as the risk of excessive use of (non-exclusive) Community powers.[20]

References

Barav, A, "Le commissaire du gouvernement près la cour de justice des communautés européennes", (1974) *Revue internationale de droit comparé* 809.

Bermann, GA, "Taking Subsidiarity Seriously: Federalism in the European Community and the United States", (1994) 94 *Columbia Law Review* 331.

Bermann, GA, "Subsidiarity and the European Community", (1993) 17 *Hastings International and Comparative Law Review* 97.

Borgsmidt, K, "The Advocate General at the European Court of Justice: A Comparative Study", (1988) 3 *European Law Review* 106.

Bronitt, S, Burns, F, and Kinley, D, 1995, *Principles of European Community Law. Commentary and Materials*, Law Book Co, Sydney.

Brown, LN, and Bell, JS, 1993, *French Administrative Law*, 4th ed, Clarendon Press, Oxford.

Cass DZ, "The Word that saves Maastricht? The Principle of Subsidiarity and the Division of Powers within the European Community", (1992) 29 *Common Market Law Review* 1107.

Coing, H, "The Roman Law as Ius Commune on the Continent", (1973) 89 *Law Quarterly Review* 505.

Dadamo, C, and Farran, S, 1996, *The French Legal System*, 2nd ed, Sweet & Maxwell, London.

David, R, and Brierley, JEC, 1985, *Major Legal Systems in the World Today*, 3rd ed, Stevens & Sons, London.

Dawson, JP, 1968, *The Oracles of the Law*, University of Michigan Law School, Ann Arbor.

Deak, I, and Rheinstein, M, "The Development of French and German Law", (1936) 24 *Georgia Law Journal* 551.

Delegation of the Commission of the European Communities to Australia and New Zealand, "Adapting Community Legislation to Subsidiarity", *Background Report*, June 1994.

Dickson, B, 1994, *Introduction to French Law*, Pitman Publishing, London.

---

20 The literature devoted to the question of how subsidiarity works in practice is both vast and conflicting. See Bronitt, Burns and Kinley (1995:127) and the references there. For a laudable attempt to use subsidiarity in a constructive manner, see also Bermann (1993:97) and (1994:331).

Foster, N, 1993, *German Law and Legal System*, Blackstone Press, London.

George, S, 1991, *Politics and Policy in the European Community*, 2nd ed, Oxford University Press, Oxford.

Glendon, MA, Gordon, MW, Osakwe, C, 1985, *Comparative Legal Traditions. Text, Materials and Cases*, West Publishing Co, St Paul.

Hartley, TC, 1994, *The Foundations of European Community Law*, 3rd ed, Clarendon Press, Oxford.

Idot, L, "L'application du « principe de subsidiarité » en droit de la concurrence", (1994) *Recueil Dalloz Sirey* 37.

Jolowicz, HF, 1952, *Historical Introduction to the Study of Roman Law*, 2nd ed, Cambridge University Press, Cambridge.

Kapteyn, PJG, and Verloren van Themaat, P, 1989, *Introduction to the Law of the European Communities. After the coming into Force of the Single European Act*, 2nd ed, Kluwer, Deventer.

Kuttner, S, 1983, *Gratian and the Schools of Law*, Variorum Reprints, London.

Lambiris, M, 1994, *Social Political and Constitutional Background to the Development of Roman Law 753 BC – 533 AD*, M Lambiris, Melbourne.

Lenaerts, K, "The Principle of Subsidiarity and the Environment in the European Union: Keeping the Balance of Federalism", (1994) 17 *Fordham International Law Journal* 846.

Mathijsen, PSRF, 1995, *A Guide to European Union Law*, 6th ed, Sweet & Maxwell, London.

Rasmussen, H, 1983, "The Court of Justice", in Commission of the European Communities, *Thirty Years of Community Law*, Office for Official Publications of the European Communities, Luxembourg.

Schlesinger, RB, Baade, HW, Damaska, MR, and Herzog, PE, 1988, *Comparative Law. Cases – Text – Materials*, 5th ed, Foundation Press, Mineola.

TMC Asser Instituut, 1987, *Article 177 EEC: Experiences and Problems*, Elsevier, Amsterdam.

Toth, AG, "The Principle of Subsidiarity in the Maastricht Treaty", (1992) 29 *Common Market Law Review* 1079.

Usher, JA, "The Impact of EEC Legislation on the United Kingdom Courts", (1989) 10 *Statute Law Review* 95.

Usher, "The Influence of National Concepts on Decisions of the European Court", (1976) 1 *European Law Review* 359.

Van Caenegem, RC, 1992, *An Historical Introduction to Private Law*, Cambridge University Press, Cambridge.

Von Mehren, AT, 1957, *The Civil Law System: Cases and Materials for the Comparative Study of Law*, Prentice Hall, Englewood Cliffs.

West, A, Desdevises, Y, Fenet, A, Gaurier, D, and Heussaff, MC, 1992, *The French Legal System: An Introduction*, Fourmat Publishing, London.

Wieacker, F, 1995, *A History of Private Law in Europe – with particular reference to Germany*, Clarendon Press, Oxford.

Wieacker, PRG, 1952 and 1967, *Privatrechtsgeschichte der Neuzeit*, Göttingen.

Zweigert, K, and Kötz, H, 1987, *An Introduction to Comparative Law*, Vol 1, Clarendon Press, Oxford.

Zurcher, AJ, 1958, *The Struggle to Unite Europe: 1940-1958*, Greenwood Press, Westport.

Chapter 3

Codes and Codification

3.1 The Concept of a Civil Code

(a) Codes and compilations

[301] It is no coincidence that the best-known civil codes, especially the French *Code civil* and the German *Bürgerliches Gesetzbuch*, all date from the 19th century. The very idea of a comprehensive, systematic statement of the law itself is a creature of "the Age of Reason", including its emphasis on logic and enlightenment. The civil codes are premised on the belief that life is not full of random events, but rather that there is order. More importantly, the concept of a civil code presupposes that the human intellect is capable of capturing this order as well as presenting it in a systematic and comprehensive fashion.

[302] It is sometimes suggested that the difference between contemporary civil law and common law does not concern the presence or absence of codified law. Instead, a more useful distinction is said to focus on the type of codification that may occur in various legal systems (Bergel 1988:1073). By distinguishing between substantive and formal codes the comparative researcher is thus able to go beyond the more traditional dichotomy of civil law and common law. To be sure, at the end of the day the result will probably still be that codes – substantive ones – prevail in the civil law but, the picture that is obtained undeniably is a much richer one. First, it must be appreciated that not every code in the civil law is the same. For instance, French administrative law has been codified but this particular exercise in codification was more in the nature of an American restatement and bears little, if any, resemblance to the French civil code proper. Secondly, some codes of the common law really deserve the label of code. A typical example is the American Uniform Commercial Code. Of course, what makes the UCC a particularly interesting example is that there was a clear European influence in its drafting process.[1]

---

1   Instrumental in the drafting of the UCC was Llewellyn. Karl Llewellyn spent his formative years both in the United States and Europe. For a detailed discussion see Herman 1982:1125.

[303] The above classification distinguishes codes from mere compilations and it is herein that lies its real significance. It also provides an excellent example of the functional (as opposed to the institutional) approach to comparativism as discussed in Chapter 1. But it would be wrong to attach any particular value judgment to the distinction. It does not necessarily follow that one type of code is "better" or "worse". Much ultimately depends on the purpose of codification itself. Where a primary consideration for any particular codification is to make the law accessible and/or to remove legal uncertainty, a compilation of the existing law may suffice. Famous examples from the history of the European civil law are the *Corpus Iuris Justinianis* and the codification of French customary law in the Middle Ages. More contemporary examples of formal codification in the civil law are the codes on labour law and social security law. In Belgium these are private initiatives – which is itself an indication as to the usefulness of compilations – in bringing together in one volume all the relevant texts of statutes and regulations in these fields of law. Compilations often show an attempt at ordering issues by subject matter. But they most certainly do not involve any rewriting of the law. Unlike substantive codes, they do not seek to break with the past. On the contrary, compilations reflect an attempt to capture the present.

[304] The 19th century codification movement represents a public initiative at revising the law so as to have a fresh start. This is most evident as regards the French *Code civil*. But codes need not be the product of a (violent) revolution. The German *BGB* probably is the most famous case in point, but several more contemporary examples can be given as well. The most recent and celebrated example of a successful codification in Western Europe is the promulgation of a new civil code in the Netherlands in 1992. This civil code, the *Nieuw Burgerlijk Wetboek (NBW)*, replaces the 1838 Dutch code which in turn replaced the first codification of 1809.[2] The highly pragmatic, gradual approach of the Dutch undoubtedly contributed in no small part to this result. Other European codifications in the post-World War II era took place in Greece and Portugal. The Greek civil code entered into force in 1946, but its formal promulgation dates from 1940.[3] In Portugal a new *Còdigo Civil* came into force in 1967. While noteworthy for its attention to foreign law, the Portuguese code ultimately is rather retrogressive and conservative (Zweigert and Kötz 1987 I:111-112). The

---

2   The 1809 codification was by order of King Louis Napoléon, brother of the French emperor.

3   The War was a major factor in this delay: Zweigert and Kötz 1987 I:161.

same is not true for the Dutch *NBW* which seems destined to follow in the footsteps of its illustrious French and German (or even Swiss) predecessors.

(b) Features of a civil law code

[305] The codes of the 19th century display certain distinguishing features as regards both their contents or subject matter; their manner of rule formulation; and their overall presentation or layout. They also claim to break with the past, display an air of permanency, and constitute authoritative statements of the law. Each of these characteristics requires some elaboration.

(i) Contents

[306] A fundamental division in all civil law systems is between private and public law. The distinction has its roots in Roman law, but there is no uniformity among countries as to its precise scope and effects. Private law is often used interchangeably with civil law. Strictly speaking, however, private law comprises two grand divisions of its own of which civil law is one and commercial law the other (Glendon 1985:256-259). Both the French *Code civil* and the German *BGB* are codifications of private law to the exclusion of commercial law. They comprise the legal rules that govern the relationship between private parties. The commercial activities of business people (*commerçant*; *Kaufmann*) are governed by a separate commercial code (*Code de commerce*; *Handelsgesetzbuch*). Interestingly, civil codes adopted during the 20th century tend to be less reluctant in incorporating commercial law. Examples are the Swiss civil code of 1907 (in force since 1912), the Italian civil code of 1942 and the Dutch *NBW* of 1992.[4]

[307] For the drafters of the French *Code civil* a direct relationship existed between their desire for legal certainty and the need to produce a comprehensive text.[5] The *Code civil*, as it stood in 1804, was certainly satisfactory from this point of view. Specifically, the law of persons (Book I) – including family law – and the law of things (*Biens*) – including property law (Book II) and (in Book III) the various ways of acquiring property (including contract, quasi contract, and tort) – were encompassed

---

4   See the discussion of the contemporary codification movement in [320] ff below.

5   "If the law should be clearly stated in a written document, this document should be complete, lest it be misleading": Tunc 1955:435.

within its 2281 provisions (*Articles*).[6] The German *BGB* is different from the French *Code civil* in its basic organisation, but its subject matter is essentially the same. The Dutch *NBW* of 1992 lays a similar claim to being comprehensive. Only, the proper scope of private law at the end of the 20th century now expressly extends to labour law and consumer protection, and this is reflected in the *NBW*. Procedural law, in line with tradition dating back to the French era, continues to form the object of a separate code (Hartkamp 1992:553).

[308] The real claim to fame of the civil law codes does not lie in the ability of their drafters to foresee all possible problems that may arise during the life-time of the code, however. Clearly, there was no way in which legal problems associated with the invention of the motorcar, for instance, could have been anticipated in 1804. Yet its eventuation was able to be accommodated by the *Code civil*.[7] The legal technique that made it possible is called statutory interpretation. The civil law approach to statutory interpretation is addressed later.[8] Suffice it to point out at this stage that a direct link exists between statutory interpretation and legislative drafting: any liberal, constructive approach to the interpretation of code provisions by the judiciary depends on the presence of a sufficiently high degree of generality and abstractness in the formulation of the legal rules and principles that are embodied in the code. The civil law drafting technique is discussed next.

(ii) Drafting technique

[309] The manner in which the legal rules in the code are formulated is said to be abstract, ie the code provisions reflect a relatively high degree of generality. By and large, the drafters of the 19th century codes mastered the skill of avoiding unnecessary detail without becoming overly abstract.[9]

---

6   Tunc (1955:435) notes that only one matter had not been dealt with in the *Code civil* that should have been: the law of mines which required special legislation as early as 1810.

7   Comprehensive legislation to compensate the victims of traffic accidents for personal injury was adopted in the late 20th century only. See Tunc (1983:489) for an excellent discussion of the background of the 1985 legislation.

8   See Chapter 4.

9   The need to get the balance right between specificity and generality is a concern that applies to the drafting of statutes outside the code as well. However, the result here has been varied in more recent times. The legislator is increasingly involved in reacting to particularised "crisis" situations instead of being able to legislate in a more pro-active manner as it used to be the case in the past. This appears to have a negative effect on drafting style. The same point is made in [317] below.

Of course, some variations exist between legal systems. When the French and the German codes are compared, it is hard to avoid the conclusion that overall the German code lacks the broad sweep displayed in the French code. In part, an explanation may lie in that the Napoleonic code was meant to be easily accessible to the average *citoyen*. The *BGB*, on the other hand, was designed as a code by lawyers and for lawyers; its abstract and technical style is therefore deliberate. Interestingly, the new Dutch *NBW* follows more closely the German than the French model in this respect.

[310] The Code provisions on the legally binding nature of contracts provide an excellent example to demonstrate the differences in drafting style between the *Code civil* and the *BGB*. Art 1134,1 *Code civil* stipulates that "Agreements that have been entered into lawfully constitute the law between those who entered into them". This may not be as striking or moving a formula as it is proclaimed by Zweigert and Kötz (1987 I:93), but it certainly is more elegant than the didactic instruction addressed to the legal profession contained in Para 241 *BGB* which reads that "by reason of the creditor – debtor relationship ... the creditor is entitled to demand performance from the debtor".

[311] Under influence of Napoleon the French code may once have been easier to read[10] but, some 200 years later, it no longer gives a full picture of private law in France as judicial glosses have become attached to the code provisions. A famous example is the law of tort as embodied in Arts 1382-1386 *Code civil*.[11] And, of course, not even the French got the balance between generality and specificity right for each and every provision of the civil code. An excellent instance of a timeless but not empty provision is Art 544 *Code civil* on real property:

> Ownership is the right to enjoy a thing (chose) and to dispose of it in the most absolute manner, provided one does not violate the statutes or regulations.

In direct contrast is Art 524 *Code civil* in which goods are termed immovable because of their purpose or destination. Article 524 deems immovable the things that the owner of a piece of agricultural land has placed on that land for the purpose of working the land. The drafters of the *Code civil* should have stopped there. Instead, that provision continues with an unnecessarily long-winded and outdated list of immovables that include not only farm animals or farm tools but also seeds given to leaseholders; pigeons in their cotes; rabbits in their rabbit shelter;

---

10 See [217] above.
11 A detailed discussion takes place in Chapter 6.

beehives; fish in lakes; equipment for extracting, boiling, distilling, etc; tools necessary to work in a forge, paper factory, or other factory; straw and manure; and those movables that their owner has attached to the land in a permanent fashion!

[312] At times the populist ambitions of the French *Code civil* have resulted in a product that, especially when compared to the German *BGB*, is unclear and imprecise. An example developed further in Chapter 5 of the book is the notion of *cause* (from the Latin: *causa*) in contract law. Article 1108 *Code civil* stipulates that a legitimate *cause* (*une cause licite*) is an essential condition for the valid formation of a contract. The same term is used in Art 1131 *Code Civil* where it is said that obligations entered into without *cause* or with a false or illicit *cause* (*sans cause, ou sur une fausse cause, ou sur une cause illicite*) can have no (legal) effect. However, the latter provision only makes sense if one is prepared to attach two different meanings to the same word. In Art 1108 as well as with respect to its first use in Art 1131 (*sans cause*), *cause* refers to the object of the obligation of the other party. On the other hand, this particular interpretation of *cause* is incorrect when used in connection with the second and third references to *cause* in Art 1131 (*une fausse cause ou une cause illicite*). For an obligation to be defective because of a false or illicit *cause* the word *cause* acquires the much broader meaning of the more general motivation for entering into that obligation.

[313] Unfortunately, this is by no means the sole instance of vague, imprecise and even incorrect use of terminology. In fact, it has been argued that it was the gaps and technical imperfections of the *Code civil* which gave the French courts their opportunity to develop the law (Zweigert and Kötz 1987 I:158). In Germany the courts have relied above all on the use of general clauses (*Generalklauseln*) by the drafters of the *BGB* to do precisely the same thing. These general clauses are said to have operated as a kind of safety valve, without which the rigidity of the *BGB* might have been unable to withstand the pressure of social change. The most important general provisions are Paras 138, 157, 242, and 826 *BGB*. To illustrate their drafting style, the reader is referred to their English translation in the Documentation section at the end of the book. The use of general clauses is by no means uniquely German, though.[12] A similar provision to the

---

12 Uniquely German is the expression "*Flucht in die Generalklauseln*" following a 1933 publication by Hedemann with this title as quoted in Dawson (1968:465). Dawson observes that the phrase has become a slogan in German literature to the extent of its now being in the public domain.

German requirement of good faith performance of contracts is embodied in Art 1134 of the French *Code civil*. Yet another example of a code basis for judicial creativity by legislative fiat is Art 1135 *Code civil*. That provision says that contracting parties are bound not only by the express terms of their contract but also by "all consequences triggered by equity, custom or the law ... depending on the nature of the particular obligations".

(iii) Overall lay-out and presentation

[314] The overall presentation of the 19th century codes is systematic. The main distinction in the French *Code civil* is between persons (*des personnes*) and goods (*des biens*). Book 1 on Persons covers aspects of what a student of the common law would expect to find in the subject of family law: marriage, divorce, adoption, guardianship, minors. But this first Book also contains provisions about citizenship rights (*droits civils*), thus demonstrating forcefully the nationalistic character of the Code even though the contemporary rules about the acquisition and loss of French nationality are now contained in special legislation. Also in Book 1 are provisions as regards the registration of legally significant events (births, weddings, deaths) in official records of civil status (*actes de l'état civil*) and domicile. The former especially have no place in the *BGB* but Zweigert and Kötz (1987 1:94) stress that their importance to the drafters of the French code following the secularisation of the family relationship and the separation of church and state were achievements of the Revolution. Book 2 deals with various aspects of property law and a rather large part of this Book is devoted to land servitudes.[13] A final Book 3 is a mixed bag comprising the basic provisions on contract and tort but also, among other things, the law of succession, matrimonial property law, the law of partnership, and rules for the priority payment of creditors.

[315] The drafters of the German civil code rejected the French (Roman-law inspired) classification as too simplistic. Instead, the *BGB* commences with a separate General Part (*Allgemeiner Teil*) in which general principles of law are stated that are to be used in the more specific parts (or books) of the Code. This first Book is a legacy of the Pandectist School which itself was an offshoot of the 19th century Historic School.[14] There are four

---

13 It will be remembered that the Industrial Revolution was late in coming to the Continent.

14 Foster 1993:20; Schmidt 1965:136; Zweigert and Kôtz 1987 I:150-153. The Pandectist School is named after the principal available source of classical Roman law, the Pandects (which is the Greek term for the Digest) of Justinian. Its most famous representative was von Savigny. See [218]-[219] above.

further books on Obligations, Property, Family Law, and Succession, respectively. The self-imposed rigidity and internal logic of its structure at times proves to be counter-productive and anyone searching the relevant *BGB* provisions on the contract of sale, for instance, needs to be aware that, conceptually, these provisions are present at three different levels of generality. In the result not just one but three Books of the *BGB* need to be consulted. Obviously, Book Two on Obligations is relevant. But contracts also rank under the general heading of juristic act (*Rechtsgeschäft*), ie an act with the intent to create legal obligations. The general provisions on juristic acts are comprised in the General Part of the *BGB*. Finally, Book Three on Property is relevant as it regulates the transfer-of-ownership aspect of the contract of sale. A similar, layered, approach to the organisational structure of the code has been adopted in parts of the new Dutch *NBW* of 1992. The Dutch approach is discussed later at [322-325].

(iv) Other features

[316] There are three further features of the 19th century codification movement. The codes represent a new start; they have an air of permanency; and they are authoritative. The break with the past was perhaps most dramatic in France where a French Revolution preceded codification which was personally supervised by Napoleon. The *Code civil* officially ended feudalism and substituted the basic principles of freedom of contract and a (quasi) absolute property right. But it is clear that pragmatism also featured highly in the approach of the drafters of the French code. Van Caenegem (1992:6-7) goes one step further and argues that the most important element in the *Code civil* is old law. Of course, it was never the intention of its drafters to re-establish the old legal order and abandon the advances made in the Revolution. In fact, the very principle of a codified legal system, uniformly applicable throughout France, was itself unique. But the *Code civil* has been written by legal practitioners who saw no benefit in forsaking – as a matter of principle – rules that had successfully withstood the test of times. One of the most influential authors of the Code was Portalis. His conservative convictions have been expressed in terms that leave no room for doubt: "it is useful to preserve everything which it is not necessary to destroy" and "a bold innovation is often no more than a glaring error" (Van Caenegem 1992:8; Merryman 1969:31; Bergel 1988:1078). By contrast the German *BGB* is the opposite of revolutionary in more than one way. First, it is not the product of a violent revolution as in France. Secondly, in terms of subject-matter, it is not a rejection of the past, but rather it seeks to preserve this past for the future

(Merryman 1969:33; Zweigert and Kötz 1987 I:149). In the result, notwithstanding a time difference in the drafting of the French and German codes of nearly 100 years, both codes can justifiably be called a product of the 19th century: the French 1804 code because of its forward-looking approach, and the 1896 German code because of its retrospective and reflective spirit. The drafters of the *BGB* certainly did not take much notice of the great social change which was occurring in Germany towards the end of the 19th century. In the view of Wieacker (1967:481) the *BGB* could not match Bismark's social security laws for the protection of workers as the *BGB* was primarily geared to the views of bourgeois society; hence the emphasis on the freedoms of contract, establishment, and competition (Riegert 1970:56; Zweigert and Kötz 1987 I:150).

[317] What distinguishes a true code from a mere compilation is that the former constitutes an original work.[15] Permanency is also an often admired feature of the 19th century codes. The French code was hardly modified at all during the first 100 years of its existence. One significant change to occur in the 20th century – both in France and Germany – concerned the reform of family law post-World War II. But, by and large, the *Code civil* and the *BGB* have withstood the test of time remarkably well. They were meant to last, which is in sharp contrast to contemporary legislation in both civil law and common law where the immediacy of the political response to any "crisis" that may arise from time to time can produce a backward rather than forward-looking approach to law making. Reactive as opposed to pro-active legislation is what often typifies contemporary legislation. Perhaps because of their almost visionary approach codes are also said to be authoritative in the sense of direction-giving. Technically the code is an Act of Parliament that requires no special majority for it to be amended, though. The authority of the code is therefore solely a reference to its superior moral as opposed to legal status.

[318] The above observations as regards the durability and moral superiority of the code have primarily the civil codes of the 19th century codification movement in mind. All in all, however, not less than five Napoleonic codes were adopted in the period between 1804 and 1811. Supplementing the *Code civil* are a separate commercial code, penal code, code of civil procedure, and code of criminal procedure. The same multiplicity of codes exists in Germany. These "supplementary" codes have proved less resistible to change. In France, the 1806 Code of Civil

---

15   See [301]ff above.

Procedure was replaced by a new Code of Civil Procedure in 1975; a 1958 Code of Criminal Procedure substitutes for its 1808 predecessor a new *Code pénal* entered into force on 1 March 1994.[16]

3.2 Circumstances Favouring Codification

(a) The 19th century codification movement

[319] It is no coincidence that the European codification movement took hold in the 19th century. Intellectual and political factors clearly favoured codification. On the one hand, the period of Enlightenment and the influence of the Natural law school of thinking provided strong incentives to break with the past and to substitute a new legal order based on "a few first principles, clear and unalterable, from which comprehensive schemes of social regulation could be deductively elaborated and applied – *more mathematico*" (Damaska 1983:357). On the other hand, the codification movement benefited from the absence of relatively sophisticated systems of parliamentary democracy as are in existence today, thus avoiding the need for "messy" (Damaska 1983:359) compromises. Equally beneficial, so it turned out, was the availability of learned jurists with the intellectual capacity and rigour to look beyond the narrow fields of their own specialisation – something which has become somewhat of a disease in the civil law of the late 20th century. Both the French and the German civil codes were the product of a small team of people. In France Napoleon appointed a commission of only four to draft the code, but it is probably the name of Portalis that will be remembered best. It was Portalis who, in his *Discours préliminaire*, laid down the ground rules for a code that needed to be both new and historical as to its contents, general and practical as to the type of its rule formulation (Bergel 1988:1081-1082).[17] In Germany there was the pervasive influence of Professor Windscheid and the 1888 draft *BGB* was occasionally referred to, not always without an element of cynicism, as the "Little Windscheid" or "Windscheid's book with additions".[18] The Swiss civil code is essentially the work of a single man, Professor Huber (Zweigert and Kötz 1987 I:173), and in the Netherlands it was the Project Meijers – named after an eminent scholar

---

16   See Fournier 1995:475 for an early discussion of the new French criminal code.

17   Technically, Portalis' *Discours préliminaire* did not make it into the text of the *Code civil*. There is a Preliminary Title but it comprises a handful provisions only.

18   The reference is to Windscheid's *Lehrbuch des Pandektenrechts*. See Schmidt 1965:136-137; Riegert 1970:53.

from Leyden University who had been entrusted with the task of drafting a new civil code in 1947 – that set the scene for a complete overhaul of the Dutch *Burgerlijk Wetboek* of 1838.

(b) The contemporary codification movement

[320] The European codification movement is not confined to the 19th century. But it is fair to say that there is hardly any civil code in force today that has not been influenced, directly or indirectly, by either the French *Code civil* or the German *BGB*. An exception must be made for the Austrian General Civil Code of 1811 which has been described as a work of great originality (Schlesinger 1988:546). This also goes for the Swiss civil code of 1907 which itself has acted as a source of inspiration for other legal systems. Most strikingly, the Swiss rejected the classic civil law distinction between commercial and non-commercial law that had been adopted by its French and German predecessors. The Swiss example was followed in the new Italian *Codice Civile* of 1942 and in the new Dutch *NBW* of 1992: both civil codes incorporate commercial law.

[321] The Swiss *Zivilgesetzbuch* (*ZGB*) had many admirers abroad. At one stage voices were raised in Germany in favour of an immediate repeal of the *BGB* and its replacement by the *ZGB*. Gorlé, Bourgeois and Bocken (1985:141) comment that the Swiss code has provided inspiration for all subsequent codification elsewhere, particularly in Turkey, Italy, Greece and the Netherlands. Especially attractive was that the *ZGB* managed to avoid all perceived "defects" of the *BGB*:

> The new (Swiss) Code was drafted in a popular and clear language, had an easily comprehended, relatively open structure, and instead of abstract casuistry which the BGB carried even into detail, made its statutory rules deliberately incomplete so that often it only sketched in an area within which the judge had to operate, using the standards of what was appropriate and reasonable and equitable (Zweigert and Kötz 1987 I:177-178).

Best known is Art 1 *ZGB*, the relevant part of which reads as follows:

> If no relevant provision can be found in a statute, the judges must decide in accordance with the customary law and, in its absence, in accordance with the rule which would, were they the legislator, adopt. In doing so attention must be paid to accepted doctrine and tradition.[19]

---

19 Translation in Zweigert and Kötz 1987 I:182 of the following text in French: "La loi régit toutes les matières auxquelles se rapportent la lettre ou l'esprit de l'une de ses dispositions. A défaut d'une disposition légale applicable, le juge prononce selon le droit coutumier et, à défaut d'une coutume, selon les règles qu'il établirait s'il avait à faire acte de législateur. Il s'inspire des solutions consacrées par la doctrine et la jurisprudence".

One, most respectable, commentator has complained that the Swiss approach amounts to an abandoning of responsibility by the legislature.[20] It must be appreciated, though, that this deliberate reliance on judicial activism in Switzerland is explicable in part by the presence of peculiarly local factors. In particular, lack of detail in the *ZGB* was the price that had to be paid in order to achieve the unification of private law in the wake of a long tradition of strong cantonal autonomy.[21]

[322] The Dutch *Nieuw Burgerlijk Wetboek (NBW)* of 1992 also deserves closer examination. Its predecessor, the civil code of 1838, was largely, and often literally, based on the 1804 *Code Napoléon*. By the middle of the 20th century the Dutch code had dated considerably. Efforts at rejuvenating the code had been made by both the legislature – in the form of separate statutes as well as partial amendments to the code itself – and the judiciary – especially in the field of tort law. But the overall result was not entirely satisfactory and complaints were made to the effect that Dutch (private) law had become "unsurveyable" (Hartkamp 1975:1061).[22] Work on a new code began shortly after the Second World War and it took nearly half a century to be completed. Initially known as the Project Meijers the successful completion of this huge task took place in various stages.[23] Meijers intended the new code to consist of nine books, preceded by a preliminary title. In the result a general part similar to the *Allgemeiner Teil* of the *BGB* was rejected. Book 1, on the law of persons and family law, came into force as early as 1970. Book 2, comprising the new laws on partnership and company law, took effect in 1976, and Book 8 on the law of transport in 1991. The core of the *NBW*, consisting of Books 3, 5, 6 and 7, have been in force since 1992. These books cover the general law of patrimony, property law, the law of obligations in general, and special contracts (including the law of sale), respectively. Book 4, on the law of succession, remains to be promulgated. The writing of book 9, on industrial and intellectual property rights, has not yet commenced.

[323] The new Dutch civil code has been described as "a monumental work" and "a major contribution to Western jurisprudence" (Whincup 1992:1210). The new Code did not intend to change fundamentally all

---

20 Rabels, "Streifgänge im schweizerischen Zivilgesetzbuch", (1910) 2 *Rheinische Zeitschrift für Zivil – und Prozessrecht des In-und Auslandes* 308 at 320, as cited in Zweigert and Kötz 1987 I:179.

21 A good introduction to Swiss law is by Dessemontet and Ansay (1995).

22 For a succinct review of the background to the Dutch recodification effort, see Hondius 1982:349-356.

23 The recodification of Dutch private law was not entirely uncontroversial: Hondius 1982:354; Hartkamp 1992:552.

existing law as developed by the legislature and the courts (Hartkamp 1975:1073). Yet, it is equally clear that the *NBW* is not a mere restatement either. Its contents, especially the law of obligations, has been influenced substantially by comparative law research. In the result Dutch (private) law has "floated away" (Hartkamp 1992:570) from its (almost exclusively) French origins. There continue to be strong influences – both old and new – from French and Belgian law (eg misrepresentation, undue influence, anticipatory breach: Hartkamp 1992:570). But uniform law has shaped the general provisions on contract formation and non-performance.[24] European Community law served as a source of inspiration for the Code provisions on product liability, sales agents and travel contracts. German influence is most pronounced in the area of good faith.[25] Also reminiscent of the *BGB* is the pattern of organisation of the *NBW*, especially in the parts on patrimonial law. The patrimonial law in Books 3 and following displays a layered structure. Specifically, the drafters of the *NBW* have organised its subject-matter in a logical manner, with general rules and concepts preceding the more detailed provisions. This organisational principle of moving from the general to the particular is apparent not only in the subject distribution among the various Books but also as regards the management of the Code provisions within each Book (Wessels 1994:170). A good example of this layered structure of the *NBW* is its coverage of the law of obligations. The law of obligations is contained in three Books. Book 6, comprising the general part of the law of obligations, precedes the more specific Books 7 and 8 on, respectively, special contracts and transport law. Title 1 of Book 6 regulates obligations in general, in principle regardless of the source of any particular obligation. The actual sources of obligations are dealt with in Titles 3 on tort, 4 on statute, and 5 on contract (Wessels 1994:171; Hondius 1982:360).

[324] Not surprisingly, perhaps, the comparative research basis of the *NBW* has a strong (but not exclusively) European focus.[26] The net result is a code that displays a style of its own, as it is based on a *ius commune* of continental Europe (Zweigert and Kötz 1987 I:105; Wessels 1994:198). It is still not a perfect code. Unlike the French and the Swiss civil codes, the *NBW* is not drafted in language that can be understood readily by laypeople. Even law professionals may find the extensive use of so-called

---

24   In particular, the 1964 and 1980 Conventions on the International Sale of Goods: Hartkamp 1992:570.

25   This is discussed further in Chapter 5.

26   The drafters of the *NBW* also consulted American, Canadian, South African and even Japanese legal materials: Wessels 1994:198.

linking provisions (*Schakelbepalingen*) problematic at first. A linking provision is a Code provision which confers a more general applicability to certain, specified legal rules, thus making these legal rules applicable to situations which fall outside their direct scope of application (Wessels 1994:187-189; Hondius 1982:360). Linking provisions are then a form of pre-approved (by the legislature) reasoning by analogy to facilitate cross-referencing between otherwise unrelated fields of law. The good faith provision of Book 6 on the law of obligations in general, for example, can be applied in the field of property law as regulated in Book 5, because of an express linking provision in Book 6.[27] Linking provisions may even lead to the (selective) application of Code provisions in areas of law that are not regulated by the *NBW* at all, eg tax law (Wessels 1994:189).

[325] Another feature of the *NBW* is its extensive reliance on judicial discretion (Hartkamp 1993:684 and 1992:551). This is both an element of weakness and a factor of strength. On the one hand, liberal use has been made of open-ended provisions and concepts by the drafters of the Code, and this can be perceived as frustrating the legitimate expectations of the Code users as regards legal certainty and predictability. The good faith provision, for instance, illustrates this concern rather well. One (common law) commentator observes that while good faith requirements are as typical of continental (contract) law as they are alien to the common, their latest formulation in the Dutch Code "seems almost alarmingly wide" (Whincup 1992:1209). The application of good faith in the European civil law of contract – including its Dutch exponent – is discussed in greater detail in Chapter 5 of this book. On the other hand, judicial activism is a prerequisite to keeping codes alive. The drafters of the *NBW* were very much aware of this need for a constructive relationship between the legislature and the judiciary. Hartkamp (1992:570) likens the Dutch approach to codification to that of the Swiss. Superficially, there may be significant differences between both civil codes because the *NBW* is more comprehensive and it employs a more technical language. But the relationship between codified and judge-made law, and notably the overt acceptance of the courts' task in interpreting and further developing the law, is essentially the same in both legal systems. The very promulgation of the *NBW* can then be viewed as a renewed commitment in principle not to let Dutch private law "slip" from a codified system to a mixed system – such as that of the Scandinavian countries – let alone a system of case law proper (Hartkamp 1992:552).

---

27   Article 6:216 *NBW*.

3.3 Legal Order of the European Community

[326] Similarities exist between the 1957 Treaty of Rome, by which the European Economic Community was established, and the 19th century codes, in particular the French *Code civil*. The Treaty is a framework treaty (*traité cadre*): it lays down a grand design only. Yet somehow the Treaty can make the same claim to comprehensiveness as a civil code. This is made possible by the insertion of provisions in the Treaty that allow for the development and growth of the Community's legal order from within. Two Treaty provisions that have proved to be especially useful in this regard are Arts 100 and 235 EC. Article 100 EC provides a legal basis for the adoption of Community laws for which a more specific Treaty basis is not available but that are nevertheless deemed necessary because the contemplated Community action brings about the harmonisation of domestic laws that "directly affect the establishment or functioning of the common market". Article 235 EC is even more open-ended in that it allows for Community action where no specific powers exist under the Treaty on the proviso that the Community action proves "necessary to attain, in the course of the operation of the common market, one of the objectives of the Community".

[327] Articles 100 and 235 EC, either individually or in combination, greatly facilitated the development of Community policies outside the purely economic domain prior to their express recognition as coming within the jurisdiction of the Community pursuant to the Single European Act (SEA) and the Maastricht Treaty on European Union (TEU). Prime examples include the enactment of EC laws in the areas of social policy – labour law and social security law, in particular – and environmental protection. As regards the latter, a new Title VII on Environment – consisting of Arts 130r, 130s, and 130t – was added to Part III of the Rome Treaty by Art 25 SEA. The social policy of the Community is discussed more fully in Chapter 7 of the book.

[328] Another feature of the Rome Treaty that contributes to its comprehensiveness is the abstract manner of its rule formulation. The 1957 version of the Treaty especially displays a clear preference for short and relatively general provisions.[28] But, in addition, the Treaty reads like a

---

28 See the examples in [329] below. Subsequent amendments by the SEA and the TEU have turned the text of the Treaty into a much more long-winded and intellectually bewildering document. This development is a reflection of the growing internal dissent among the member states.

series of (very broad and vague) policy statements. Noteworthy are the general aims and objectives as listed in the Preamble of the Treaty. They include, inter alia, a determination to lay the foundations of an ever closer union among the peoples of Europe and, as indicated already,[29] a desire to preserve and strengthen peace and liberty. More importantly, a first Part of the Treaty, entitled Principles, lists five general goals and two equally open-ended means to achieve these goals. The five goals of the Community are listed in the 1957 Treaty of Rome as follows: (1) the promotion throughout the Community of a harmonious development of economic activities; (2) a continuous and balanced expansion; (3) an increase in stability; (4) an accelerated raising of the standard of living; and (5) closer relations between the member states. The two means for achieving these (mainly economic) goals are the establishment of a common market and the progressive approximation of the economic policies of the member states.[30]

[329] Provisions of this nature encourage a purposive interpretation of Community law. The civil law approach to interpretation techniques is discussed in Chapter 4.[31] For now it may suffice to stress that this observation as regards the need for a liberal as opposed to a literal approach to interpretation permeates the entire Treaty text and it is not therefore confined to the objectives' clauses alone. Thus, for example, Art 8.1 EC states that the common market shall be established progressively during a transitional period of 12 years. Significantly, the meaning of "common market" is nowhere defined in the Treaty. Also, Art 9.1 EC declares that the Community shall be based upon a customs union which shall cover all trade in goods and which shall involve the prohibition (between member states) of customs duties on imports and exports "and of all charges having equivalent effect". Similarly, Art 30 EC prohibits quantitative restrictions on imports "and all measures having equivalent effect". The interpretation of the words in between the quote marks above has been the subject of numerous decisions by the European Court of Justice. This has also been the case with respect to the notions of public morality, public policy and public security. These latter general concepts feature in Art 36 EC and provide a justification for the

---

29   See [220]ff above.

30   The main amendments by the TEU are an express reference to the goal of achieving "a high level of employment and of social protection" as well as the insertion of one further means to achieve the Community's objectives, ie the establishment of an economic and monetary union.

31   See [415]ff and [434] ff below.

restrictions on the free movement of goods as proclaimed in Art 30 EC. Examples outside the economic domain can be found in the Treaty as well.[32]

[330] The overall lay-out of the 1957 Treaty of Rome is simple and logical. Of the six Parts in all, only four are of relevance for purposes of this book.[33] These four main arts of the Treaty resemble the Books of a civil code. Divided into Titles, Chapters, and Sections, they comprise – in addition to Part One on Principles as discussed above[34] – the relevant provisions on the foundations of the Community (in Part Two), its policies (Part Three), and its institutions (Part Five). The Community is founded on the so-called four freedoms of goods, persons, services and capital. The relative importance of the free movement of goods vis-à-vis the other three freedoms has been highlighted in the Treaty in that a separate Title One of Part Two of the Treaty is devoted to goods, whereas persons, services and capital have been grouped together in Title Three of Part One. At the insistence of France, agricultural goods feature in a separate Title Two of Part One even though, logically, the term goods is sufficiently broad to comprise agricultural produce. Still as regards the free movement of goods, the layout of the Treaty makes clear that this first freedom requires the establishment of a customs union (in Chapter One of Title One) as well as the removal of technical or non-tariff barriers to intra-Community trade; hence the provision for a Chapter Two in Title One to deal with the elimination of quantitative restrictions between member states (including measures that may produce the effect of quantitative restrictions, eg the discriminatory imposition of health or safety requirements).

[331] The substantive policies of the Community are governed by the provisions in Part Three of the Treaty. In 1957 these policies were confined to the Economic Policy (in Title Two of Part Two) and, to a lesser extent, the Social Policy (Title Three of Part Two) with various Common Rules embodied in Title One. Key provisions in this first Title are Arts 85 and 86 EC on competition within the Community. The text of these provisions has remained unaltered in the past four decades. In a nutshell, Art 85 EC prohibits concerted activities between two or more parties which may affect intra-Community trade and which have as their

---

32   Article 119 EC is one of five provisions on social policy in the 1957 version of the Treaty of Rome. It embodies the principle of "equal pay" for "equal work".

33   Not discussed here are Part 4 on Association of the Overseas Countries and Territories and Part 6 on General and Final Provisions.

34   See [328] above.

object or effect the prevention, restriction or distortion of competition. Listed in the text of the Treaty are the examples of, inter alia, price fixing, production controls and market sharing. To the same effect Art 86 EC prohibits the so-called abuse of a dominant position in the market by a single company or undertaking. A famous example is the *chiquita bananas* case (*United Brands v Commission*, case 27/76, [1978] ECR 207). In that case *United Brands* was held to be in breach of Art 86 EC even though, on the facts, the company controlled less than 50% of the market. A relevant consideration by the European Court of Justice was that the company's share of the market was several times bigger than that of its nearest competitor. Also, it was very difficult and costly for newcomers to enter the market. Most interesting, however, was the Court's definition of the relevant market. *United Brands* argued, unsuccessfully, that it was appropriate to consider the fresh fruit market without singling out one particular item of fruit. The Court disagreed and preferred to follow its Advocate General who produced a lengthy opinion to show that the inherent qualities of a banana – including its growing, harvesting, packaging and ripening methods – technically set it apart from other fresh fruit. A fuller discussion of Arts 85-86 EC takes place in Chapter 8.

[332] The SEA and the TEU have tended to complicate things considerably. Gone is the compactness of the 1957 version of the Rome Treaty. Gone also is much of the once appealing layout or structure of that Treaty. Overall, the total number of Parts to the Treaty establishing the European Community, as amended, remains at six. Only, a new Part Two on Citizenship of the Union has been inserted and the provisions on the four freedoms are now incorporated in Part Three on Community Policies. It is this Part Three especially that has become unwieldy with its seventeen Titles on, inter alia, Economic and Monetary Policy (Title 6); Social Policy, Education, Vocational Training and Youth (Title 8); Culture (Title 9); Public Health (Title 10); Consumer Protection (Title 11); Research and Technological Development (Title 15); and the Environment (Title 16). In one sense these new provisions on the substantive policies of the Community stand for a Community that is coming of age.[35] However, many of these provisions not only appear exceedingly vague but they also tend to be rather non-committal in terms of the actual powers conferred upon the Community. Illustrative are Arts 126, 128 and 129 EC on, respectively, education, vocational training and youth; culture; and public

---

35   See [229] above.

health.[36] The use of this type of Treaty provisions as a legal basis for Community action is hampered further by the elevation of subsidiarity to a general principle of Community law.[37]

[333] The practice of amending Treaty provisions by making use of letters as well as numbers commenced in the SEA. Thus, Arts 130a-e on economic and social cohesion, Arts 130f-g on research and technological development, and Arts 130r-t on the environment, were added to Art 130 which deals with the otherwise unrelated topic of the European investment bank. The TEU continues this practice. In addition, for reasons of political convenience, a number of provisions of the TEU remain outside of the EC Treaty of Rome entirely. They concern the common foreign and security policy of the European Union (Art J-J.11 TEU) as well as cooperation in the field of justice and home affairs (Art K-K.9 TEU). It has become fashionable to refer to them as second and third pillars of the European union, respectively, in addition to (but separate from) the first pillar comprising the European Community itself.[38]

[334] Equally lacking in transparency is the social policy component of the TEU. No fewer than 17 protocols have been attached to the TEU. One of these protocols is on social policy. It is the result of a political compromise, necessitated by the unwillingness of the United Kingdom to amend the social policy provisions in the Treaty of Rome. Under the Protocol on Social Policy the high contracting parties authorise all member states bar the United Kingdom to enter into an Agreement – the text of the Agreement is annexed to the Protocol – and to have recourse to the institutions, procedures and mechanisms of the EC Treaty in giving effect to the Agreement. Any EC laws adopted pursuant to the Agreement on

---

36 The relevant parts of these Treaty provisions read as follows:

Article 126. 1: The Community shall contribute to the development of quality education by encouraging cooperation between Member States and, if necessary, by supporting and supplementing their action, while fully respecting the responsibility of the Member States for the content of teaching and the organisation of education systems and their cultural and linguistic diversity.

Article 128. 1: The Community shall contribute to the flowering of the cultures of the Member States, while respecting their national and regional diversity and at the same time bringing the common cultural heritage to the fore.

Article 129. 1: The Community shall contribute towards ensuring a high level of human health protection by encouraging cooperation between the Member States and, if necessary, lending support to their action.

37 Subsidiarity features in Art 3b of Part One (Principles) of the EC Treaty. See also [231] above.

38 See [226] above.

Social Policy are not enforceable against the United Kingdom. A case in point is Directive 94/45/EC on European Works Councils.[39]

References

Bergel, JL, "Principal Features and Methods of Codification", (1988) 48 *Louisiana Law Review* 1073.

Damaska, M, "On Circumstances favouring Codification', (1983) 52 *Revista Juridica de la Universidad de Puerto Rico* 355.

Dawson, JP, 1968, *The Oracles of the Law*, University of Michigan Law School, Ann Arbor.

Dessemontet, F, and Ansay, T, (eds), 1995, *Introduction to Swiss Law*, 2nd ed, Kluwer, Deventer.

Foster, N, 1993, *German Law and Legal System*, Blackstone Press, London.

Fournier S, "Le nouveau code pénal et le droit de la complicité", (1995) *Revue de science criminelle et de droit pénal comparé* 475.

Glendon, MA, Gordon, MW, Osakwe, C, 1985, *Comparative Legal Traditions. Text, Materials and Cases*, West Publishing Co, St Paul.

Gorlé, F, Bourgeois, G, and Bocken, H, 1985, *Rechtsvergelijking*, Story-Scientia, Brussel.

Hartkamp, A, "Das neue niederländische Bürgerliches Gesetzbuch aus europäischen Sicht", (1993) 57 *Rabels Zeitschrift für ausländisches und internationales Privatrecht* 664.

Hartkamp, AS, "Judicial Discretion under the New Civil Code of the Netherlands", (1992) 40 *American Journal of Comparative Law* 551.

Hartkamp, AS, "Civil Code Revision in the Netherlands: A Survey of its System and Contents, and its Influence on Dutch Legal Practice", (1975) 35 *Louisiana Law Review* 1059.

Hawk, BE, "European Economic Community and United States Antitrust Law: Contrasts and Convergences", (1988) 16 *Australian Business Law Review* 282.

Herman, S, "LLewellyn the Civilian: Speculations on the Contribution of Continental Experience to the Uniform Commercial Code", (1982) 56:4 *Tulane Law Review* 1125.

Hondius, EH, "Recodification of the Law in the Netherlands. The New Civil Code Experience", (1982) 29 *Netherlands International Law Review* 348.

Merryman, JH, 1969, *The Civil Law Tradition*, Stanford University Press, Stanford.

Nicholas, B, 1982, *French Law of Contract*, Butterworths, London.

Riegert, RA, "The West German Civil Code, Its Origins and its Contract Provisions", (1970) 45 *Tulane Law Review* 48.

Schlesinger, RB, Baade, HW, Damaska, MR, Herzog, PE, 1988, *Comparative Law. Cases – Text – Materials*, 5th ed, Foundation Press, Mineola.

Schmidt, F, "The German Abstract Approach to Law", (1965) 9 *Scandinavian Studies in Law* 133.

---

39 See the discussion in Chapter 7, especially [740] ff.

Tunc, A, "The French Law of Traffic Victims Compensation: The Present and the Possible", (1983) 31 *American Journal of Comparative Law* 489.

Tunc, A, "The Grand Outlines of the Code Napoléon", (1955) 19 *Tulane Law Review* 431.

Van Caenegem, RC, 1992, *An Historical Introduction to Private Law*, Cambridge University Press, Cambridge.

Vranken, M, and Richardson, M, "Europe 1992: Past, Present and Future of European Community Law", (1992) 14 *Adelaide Law Review* 219.

Wessels, B, "Civil Code Revision in the Netherlands: System, Contents and Future", (1994) 41 *Netherlands International Law Review* 163.

Whincup, M, "The New Dutch Civil Code", [1992] *New Law Journal* 1208.

Wieacker, PRG, 1952 and 1967, *Privatrechtsgeschichte der Neuzeit*, Göttingen.

Zurcher, AJ, 1958, *The Struggle to Unite Europe: 1940-1958*, Greenwood Press, Westport.

Zweigert, K, and Kötz, H, 1987, *An Introduction to Comparative Law*, 2nd ed, Vol 1 Clarendon Press, Oxford.

Chapter 4

Life Beyond the Code

4.1 Role of the Legislature

[401] The European codification movement of the 19th century signalled a new beginning, a break with the past. But the 19th century codes also made a claim of comprehensiveness, of being all-inclusive. Clearly, the latter claim cannot be taken at face value. In the alternative, there would be no need for any further legislative activity once the code is in place; nor would there be any scope for judicial lawmaking. Neither of the above propositions holds true in the European civil law. There is life beyond the code. However, in order to appreciate fully the law-making process of the civil law, attention must be paid not just to its various contributors (including scholarship) but also to the interaction between legislature, judiciary, and *doctrine*.

[402] Not even the most perfect of codes can avoid ageing with the passing of time. Any large-scale revision of existing codes is difficult and the bulk of the provisions of the French and German civil codes are still in effect in their original form some 100 or 200 years later, notwithstanding the (abandoned) effort of an official Civil Code Reform Commission in France after the second World War (Tallon 1980:33). More successful, and widely used, has been the practice of enacting auxiliary legislation. These updating statutes do not aim at a wholesale revision of the codes. Rather they tend to focus on one or more specific areas previously covered or not yet covered by the codes. Auxiliary statutes are often required to respond to new social or technological developments not anticipated by the codifiers. Labour law and social security law are prime examples of growth in legislation subsequent to the 19th century codification movement. Since these new areas of law have little or no basis in the original codes anyway, it has been possible to develop and expand them outside of the civil codes without disturbing the overall structure and internal logic thereof. One side effect has been, however, that the specialist rules of the auxiliary legislation have to be read in conjunction with the more general rules of the civil code. Thus a dual source of regulation exists as regards the individual contract of employment because of its basis in contract law.

A parallel can be drawn in this regard between, on the one hand, the relationship between the code and legislation outside of the code and, on the other hand, the interaction between common law and statute law in the common law legal family. Quantitatively the growth of auxiliary enactments in civil law countries has been enormous and this development can be compared to the growth of statutory law in common law systems. But, the basic codes remain to the civilian what the common law is to the common law lawyer: they are the very core of the legal order (Schlesinger 1988:552).

[403] Occasionally it is possible to enact legislation that is formally incorporated in the code. An area of successful incorporation is French tort law, in the sense that the legislature succeeded in preserving the internal logic and structure of the Code. As discussed later,[1] French tort law is most famous for demonstrating judicial creativity in accommodating the theory of objective risk taking within a fault-based system of tort liability in the Code. However, legislative amendments of the core tort provisions in the Code also occurred. These amendments addressed the issue of liability for damage caused by fire. Interestingly, they have been drafted in such a manner as to make them an integral part of the Code itself.[2]

[404] In principle, it is preferable to attempt to integrate the auxiliary legislation in the code itself. In this manner the idea of the civil code as a comprehensive statement of the law is upheld. It is also a user-friendly approach as it reduces the number of reference sources to be consulted. In practice, the incorporation approach may often not work because of the sheer bulk of the average auxiliary statute. An example from the (French-based) Belgian civil code can be found in Title 18 of Book 3 on the regulation of priority rights among creditors. In 1851 an Act was passed to repeal the entire Title, encompassing Arts 2092 to 2203. Even though the original numbering system of the Code was adhered to by the Belgian legislature, the substituting provisions were simply too detailed and technical to uphold the general and abstract spirit of the Code. In the result any integration achieved is in form only and this part of the Code has itself been amended repeatedly.

[405] Where no attempt at incorporation is made, French publishing houses such as Dalloz simply reproduce the text of the supplementary legislation and insert it in between two code provisions where appropriate.

---

1   See Chapter 6 of the book.
2   New paras 2 and 3 were inserted in Art 1384 *Code civil* by the Act of 7 November 1922.

Examples are the special laws on intellectual property rights, inserted in the *Code civil*, in between Arts 543 and 544 on real property. Another example is the 1985 legislation on injury caused by road accidents, inserted immediately following Art 1384 *Code civil*. Especially popular among students and practitioners alike are the annotated versions of codes, whereby each code provision is accompanied by a (brief) discussion of the relevant case law. In Germany, these code commentaries (*Kommentare*) tend to be much more elaborate than in France.[3]

[406] The drafting style of contemporary civil law statutes ideally mirrors that of the classic codes. Perhaps it is an overstatement to suggest that all civil law texts "strike one as concise, straightforward and readable", whereas legislation in the tradition of the common law tends to be "long-winded, complex, indirect in approach and unreadable" (Dale 1981:141; Kötz 1987:1). At times prolixity, complexity, poor arrangement and excessive particularity are problems associated with statutes regardless of the civil law/common law divide. The difference between civil law and common law is then that the code's style has always been a conscious (and sub-conscious) reference point for drafters in the civil law, whereas the emphasis on plain English drafting in the common law is of a more recent origin (Bennion 1995:90). The absence of special parliamentary draftspersons in the civil law may also offer an explanation, at least in part, for the absence of the "opaque" style that can be found in the common law. Furthermore, legislative bills in the civil law are subjected to a two-fold process of revision after their initial drafting. Bills are first scrutinised by the *Conseil d'Etat* in France and by the Ministry of Justice in Germany. Next, they are revised in the Parliament before being debated. A Bill in the civil law is thus given a two-staged trial run before "the legislature launches it … on the nation" (Dale 1981:158).

4.2 The Judiciary and the Relationship between Law Enforcement and Law Making

(a) Court structure

[407] The court structure in the European civil law tends to be decentralised, specialised, and hierarchical. In France, matters of civil law

---

3   The *Münchener Kommementar zum Bürgerlichen Gesetzbuch*, for instance, published by CH Beck, is a multiple-volume *oeuvre* of some 10,000 printed pages and incorporating references to legal writing as well as to case law. See also [423] below.

or criminal law go in the first instance to one of 175 *tribunaux de grande instance* or, where the monetary value of the case is below a certain threshold, to a *tribunal d' instance* of which there are some 470 in total. Both are courts of general jurisdiction but, because of the emphasis on specialisation, their substantive jurisdiction is more limited than in the common law (Schlesinger 1988:371). When exercising their criminal jurisdiction, the *tribunal d'instance* and the *tribunal de grande instance* are referred to as *tribunal de police* and *tribunal correctionnel*, respectively. The *cour d'assises* hears the most serious of criminal offences (*crimes*). Separate courts (*tribunaux de commerce*) exist to determine commercial disputes, which typically involve litigation between merchants *(commerçants)* or litigation in relation to commercial activities (*actes de commerce*).[4] There are also specialist courts to deal with matters of labour law (*conseils de prud'hommes*), social security law and agricultural tenancy law. In Germany there exists in addition a separate tax court (*Finanzgericht*), but commercial cases are heard by the general court of first instance, ie the *Landsgericht* or, where small claims are involved, the *Amtsgericht*.

[408] It is a general feature of the civil law that appeals against first instance decisions are opportunities for the appellate court to try the case de novo. It does not necessarily follow, though, that on appeal every case is done all over again from scratch as the case file (*dossier*) accompanies the case at the appellate level. Court procedure is discussed in greater detail in Chapter 9. For now the following preliminary information may suffice. In France, appeals are heard by one of 30 *cours d'appel*, except for civil cases involving minor claims and criminal cases decided in the *cour d'assises* where the first instance decision is final.[5] In Germany, the specialist structure of the judicial system is carried through at the appellate level for matters of labour law and social security law as well. The administration of the German courts, both at the level of first instance and at the appellate level, is in the hands of the states *(Länder)*. Re-unification between East and West did not fundamentally alter the general structure of the German court system (Foster 1993:36).

[409] At the top of the court hierarchy are the French Court of Cassation *(Cour de Cassation)* and in Germany, the Federal Supreme Court

---

4   When only one of the parties to the dispute is a trader, the case must be tried in the ordinary courts if that trader is the plaintiff; if the trader is the defendant the plaintiff can choose the forum: West 1992:89.

5   West 1992:96. However, the matter may be brought before the *Cour de Cassation* by way of *Pourvoi en Cassation*. See [409]-[410] below.

(Bundesgerichtshof). The approach of both supreme courts differs in two major ways. First, in the *Cour de Cassation* appeal is available as of right, whereas in the *Bundesgerichtshof* leave to appeal needs to be obtained from either the appellate court or the supreme court itself.[6] In both legal systems the appeal is confined to points of law only. Secondly, the jurisdiction of the French court is generally limited to confirming or annulling the decision of the lower court, whereas the German court can go further and substitute its decision for that of the lower court. If the French supreme court decides to annul the decision of the appellate court, the case is referred to a different court of appeal for re-consideration. The latter court is not bound by the decision of the supreme court. It is therefore conceivable that the decision of the first appellate court is confirmed, which may trigger a new appeal to the supreme court. Following a second reference to the supreme court, any third appellate court that hears the case is bound by the decision in cassation. The situation in Germany is different. If, after an appeal on a point of law, the *Bundesgerichtshof* reverses a decision of the appellate court and sends the case for retrial before a lower court, the latter is bound by the ruling of the supreme court. In a sense this is an example of the application of precedent in the civil law. It would seem that the French system has been moving closer to the German model in recent years. In 1967 legislation was passed to allow a super-panel of the *Cour de Cassation* consisting of 25 judges (the *assemblée plénière*) to reverse decisions without having to refer them to another trial court for reconsideration. Since 1979 the French Code of Civil Procedure authorises the supreme court's ordinary panels, in their discretion, to do likewise. These legislative changes serve as an indication that, gradually, the traditional distrust of the judiciary because of abuses during the *Ancien Régime* has had to make way for the practical realities of contemporary France.[7]

[410] A special feature of French law is the so-called *pourvoi en cassation "dans l'intérêt de la loi"*. This procedural device allows for the *Cour de Cassation* to be approached even where the immediate parties themselves have not taken any such initiative. It reflects a concern to view court

---

6   In non-pecuniary cases plus pecuniary cases below a certain threshold leave is required from the appellate court; in other cases it is the *Bundesgerichtshof* which decides on leave: Markesinis 1994:6-7.

7   Note, however, the caution urged by Schlesinger (1988:466) who points out that the highest court of France continues to be called Court of "Cassation" (*casser* = to break or to quash). Schlesinger anticipates that, in light of its tradition, the Court will make use of its new power only sparingly.

decisions as not merely occasions to speak justice in the case at hand, but also as opportunities at which the law can be stated and clarified. Thus, even though the parties in a particular dispute may not seek to bring their case before the *Cour of Cassation*, the Public Ministry *(ministère public)* can do so whenever the case is perceived to raise important legal issues of principle. The outcome of any such *pourvoi* "in the interest of the law" leaves the position of the immediate parties untouched and the decision by the French Supreme Court only acts as a guide for future court cases that may be brought. This feature of the administration of justice in the civil law is uniquely French and it has no counterpart in the German legal system.

[411] A separate administrative court structure exists to deal with matters of administrative law. At the top of this separate court hierarchy are the French *Conseil d'Etat* and, in Germany, the *Bundesverwaltungsgericht*. In France, the political reason for this legal distinction was, once again, a distrust of the judiciary by the revolutionaries (Dadamo and Farran 1996:46; West 1992:23), although it has also been observed that the distinction between private and public law goes back to Roman law (Schlesinger 1988:300). Any conflicts of jurisdiction that may arise between the administrative courts and the "ordinary" courts are resolved by the *Tribunal des Conflits*. The *Tribunal* is composed of an equal number of representatives from the *Conseil d' Etat* and the *Cour de Cassation*, with any deadlock to be broken by the Minister of Justice (West 1992:105; Dadamo and Farran 1996:107). Under influence of Montesquieu's doctrine of separation of powers, it has become an established principle in most continental countries that, apart from criminal matters, the jurisdiction of the ordinary courts is limited to disputes governed by private law (Schlesinger 1988:300-301). In Germany, jurisdictional conflicts are largely regulated by the *Gerichtsver-fassungsgesetz* and a separate tribunal for the resolution of jurisdictional disputes does not exist.

[412] Constitutional complaints *(Verfassungsbeschwerde)* are brought before a separate constitutional court in Germany, the *Bundesver-fassungsgericht*, provided the complainant has exhausted any ordinary means of appeal first. German history, in particular the constitutional excesses which took place during the Weimar Republic and the Third *Reich*, places the German Constitutional Court in a strong (moral) position (Foster 1993:44). Legally, the Court's main function is that of guardian of the constitution *(Grundgesetz)*. It has powers to review federal and state legislation, and it can overrule laws found to be unconstitutional. The situation in France

provides a sharp contrast. Judicial review was not addressed in France until the 1958 Constitution of the Fifth Republic created a *Conseil Constitutionnel* (Constitutional council). The *Conseil* checks the validity of legislation before its promulgation only. French citizens have no rights to seek judicial review of the constitutionality of a statute once it has been enacted. Thus the principle of supremacy of statute law *(la souverainité absolue de la loi)* is upheld in France or, to use a less positive expression, the distrust of the judiciary is reinforced (Schlesinger 1988:378; Dadamo and Farran 1996:111-113; West 1992:106-107).

(b) Court personnel

[413] Judges in the civil law are civil servants who display a civil service mentality. Law graduates in the civil law tend to opt for a career in the judiciary soon after graduation. In France they attend a special school, the *école nationale de la magistrature*, and only a small proportion of judges are appointed directly from the bar. At the end of their training, during which a salary is earned, the new judges are appointed at the lowest level of the court hierarchy where they stay for the rest of their judicial career unless they move up through the ranks (West 1992:108-109; Dadamo and Faran 1996:143-144). In Germany, legal education itself is geared towards the judicial profession. Anyone who successfully passes two state examinations including a period of practical training (*Referendariat*) is deemed to possess the necessary qualifications to be appointed a judge. In reality, most law graduates subsequently go on to practise law in a law firm, become a notary public or choose to work in government administration (Zülch 1992:19; Foster 1993:65).

[414] Civil law features of the judiciary are collegiality and anonymity. Except for the lowest courts in the court hierarchy which comprise a single judge, cases are heard in panels of three or more. There is no scope for drafting a concurring or dissenting opinion (Zülch 1992:19; Foster 1993:65). It is occasionally suggested that the latter aspect leads to compromises among judges and that at times this detracts from the clarity of the reasons given in court decisions.

(c) Role of the judiciary in the Civil Law

(i) Application and interpretation of the law

[415] A comprehensive code ideally removes the need for any law making. Arts 4 and 5 of the French *Code civil* present an interesting challenge in this regard. On the one hand, the Code (including its auxiliary statutes) is meant to deal with all legal disputes that may arise. Thus, the judge should never have an excuse for refusing to decide a case under the pretext that the law is silent, unclear or inadequate (Art 4 *Code civil*). On the other hand, because of the division of labour between legislature and judiciary, it is the task of the legislature to legislate, whereas the judiciary supposedly applies the (written) law to the case at hand. According to Art 5 *Code civil*, it should never be necessary for the court to make law; all that is required is to find and apply the law. The Austrian General Civil Code of 1811 also states (in Section 12) that court decisions are not a source of law; however, the same Code acknowledges the limitations of the written law in deciding cases, and Section 7 makes express reference to courts being allowed to decide cases in accordance with the principles of natural justice. The Swiss civil code of 1907 goes one step further. While postulating that the Code governs all questions of law which come within the letter or the spirit of any of its provisions, Art 1 acknowledges openly that the Code may not give an answer to all questions that can arise. Swiss judges are expected to then decide the case in accordance with customary law and, failing that, "according to the rule which they would establish as legislator". Interestingly, the role of legal scholarship in guiding the judiciary in this exercise in legislative creativity is expressly stated in the Swiss code. By contrast the French and German civil codes do not contain express provisions as regards their own interpretation. In the result various schools of thought as to the proper relationship between legislature and judiciary have emerged during the past 200 years or so.

[416] A first school to become established in the wake of the 1804 code in France was the so-called literal or exegetical school of interpretation *(école de l'exégèse)* . This school demonstrated an obsession with the text of the legislation (code) that was remarkably similar to the prevailing approach to statutory interpretation in the common law world of the 19th century. Only, on the Continent a narrow reading of statutes was advocated out of distrust for the judiciary, whereas in the common law any distrust tended to be directed towards the legislature who was perceived to be encroaching upon the court's territory. The exegetical school of interpretation in essence seeks an answer to problems of statutory interpretation in the original intent of the legislator. This school has not disappeared from the current interpretative scene entirely. The emergence of techniques of interpretation such as the *a pari*, *a contrario* and *a fortiori* rules, to be applied to situations not covered by the letter of the statute, have their origin in the exegetical school. Put differently, the exegetical school adopts a "logical" approach to interpretation: law is viewed as an exact science

and susceptible to mathematical deduction.[8] However, since the text of the law is studied in splendid isolation, the exegetical school also reflects an approach to statutory interpretation that is fundamentally inward looking. Also the exegetical school does not specifically address the ever-changing environment that surrounds a particular legislative enactment.

[417] The promulgation of the German *BGB* in 1900 made apparent that the French Code of 1804 had aged. In part this problem of an ageing code was overcome by the passing of new legislation to supplement the *Code civil*. But there was also a need for a modern approach to statutory interpretation of the existing Code provisions. There emerged then a so-called scientific school *(école scientifique)* towards the end of the 19th century with Saleilles and Gény as first representatives. Under the scientific approach to statutory interpretation, successful interpretation is not about the revelation of the legislature's original intent. Rather, it is the goal or purpose of a particular legislative enactment that matters. The characteristics of this school are then in sharp contrast to those of the exegetical school. Whereas the latter could be viewed as being formalistic, the former fully subscribes to being realistic and liberal. The scientific school is "realistic" by acknowledging that legislation is not the sole source of law. It is "liberal" by preferring the development of the law by consensus in society at large (custom) over the dictate of the legislature. Gone is the idealistic world perception of the previous century when there was great appeal in the ideas of Rousseau who put it that all power emanates from the sovereign nation and is exercised via a democratically elected legislature. Gone also is the blind belief in the omnipotence of reason and logic as it finds expression in the Code.[9]

[418] A variation to the scientific school is the functional approach to interpretation. This approach stresses the imperfections of the statute as a vehicle for expressing the law. The continued usefulness of legislation is said to require that a "functional value" be built into the interpretation thereof. To this school of interpretation the social goal *(le but social)* of an enactment is a notion that allows for the required flexibility when interpreting legislation while yet avoiding excessive subjectivity.[10]

[419] The current civil law approach to statutory interpretation is one of the utmost flexibility. No single method of interpretation is advocated by

---

8   De Page 1962:11.

9   A parallel development in Germany was the school of free law finding *(freies Recht)*: Vranken 1991:36.

10   See the references in Vranken 1991:38.

legal scholarship as preferable under all circumstances. David (1972:166) has observed that contemporary French law knows no strict canons of interpretation. The German approach is essentially the same. Perhaps then it is not the interpretation techniques that matter so much as the fact that their results are "absorbed back into the code so as to form part of it thereafter" (Leser 1982:62). This is how the code remains relevant in the face of on-going change.

(ii) Judicial law making?

[420] A legal system that puts great emphasis on the primacy of written (ie statute) law and that refuses officially to acknowledge case law as a binding source of law, inevitably devotes a lot of energy to discussing the proper boundaries of statutory interpretation by the judiciary. Contemporary legal scholars – especially those who have had some exposure to common law – admit readily that, in reality, the courts never find law. Each time it is purported to apply a legal rule to a specific problem situation, the rule as it applies to the case at hand is formulated. This process of formulation is inevitably creative in the sense of being active and not merely passive. Van Gerven (1973:129) argues that legal rules, even when embodied in statutes, perform the function of guiding criteria or beacons. Unlike the approach of American legal realists, however, the value of these legal rules is not limited merely to predicting the outcome of cases to be decided in the future. Rather, legal rules do have a normative value in that one "feels" bound by them. But every legal rule also has to some extent an open texture, and no rule is ever truly complete: each time a rule is being applied to a particular problem, that rule is being built, perfected, added on to or changed. To obey the law requires then an act of respect, not submission.

[421] Legislative provisions, whether they occur in one of the classic codes or in statutes outside of the code, cannot be studied in isolation. A good example is the legal regime of tort law in the French and Belgian civil codes. On the surface, the relevant provisions are identical in both legal systems. However, diverging judicial glosses have made that the same code provisions of Arts 1382 ff now reflect a different legal reality in each country. In the next two chapters that follow below, prime examples of judicial creativity in the areas of contract and tort law are discussed which do not easily fit the label of statutory interpretation. Where the statutory "cord" is stretched beyond breaking point, it inevitably snaps. The judicial function of interpretation then turns from law finding to law making.

4.3 Role of Scholarship

[422] In the civil law legal family scholarship does not constitute an official source of law. Yet, its role has always been a crucial one. Immediately following the promulgation of the classic codes in the 19th century, it was the task of legal (mainly academic) commentators to guide the courts through the code, thus turning the code into a workable instrument for dispute resolution purposes. The above discussion of the various approaches to statutory interpretation can be seen in this light. In a more contemporary setting, it is scholars who draw the boundaries of what is acceptable in terms of creative judicial interpretation. Specific examples in the areas of contract and tort are discussed in Chapters 5 and 6, respectively. Furthermore, because of the relative terse format of civil law judgments, case notes or commentaries are vitally important for purposes of explaining the outcome in a particular case, including how the case can be fitted in the overall legal landscape of statute and case law. These academic commentators do not hesitate to adopt a critical stance where appropriate. Because of their involvement over time in both providing legal advice to the parties in dispute and the drafting of legislative bills, scholarship performs a vital link in the law-making process of the civil law.[11]

[423] Merryman (1969:59-60) argues that, if the common law is the law of the judges, the civil law is the law of the law professors. The importance of scholarship can be explained in historical terms.[12] But there is no doubt that to this day the authority of leading textbooks – in France: *Traités* – and code commentaries – in Germany: *Kommentare* – is considerably stronger than in the common law world, and the unflattering expression of "secondary authority" is simply unknown in the civil law (Schlesinger 1988:305). In Germany the names of Rabel, Kötz, and Larenz are familiar to all law students. The same goes for Carbonnier (who influenced the reform of family law in the 1960s and 1970s), Mazeaud and Tunc in contemporary France. The names of Dutch Professor Meijers and Swiss Professor Huber will be associated with the civil code of their countries

---

11 It does not follow, however, that all civil law courts make express reference to scholarship in their judgments. In this regard, a marked contrast exists between the French *Cour de Cassation* (which hardly ever openly discusses legal writings) and its German counterpart (which does so regularly): Kötz 1990:183. For a more sceptical review of the authority of American legal scholarship, compare Schauer 1991:1003.

12 In particular, the study of law at the medieval universities and, in Germany, the practice of *Aktenversendung*: [215]-[216] above.

forever, even though the latter scholar only got the project of the New Dutch civil code started. Interestingly, in the legal order of the European Community the Advocates General – some of whom are respectable academics in their home country – effectively function as privileged commentators when, in their written opinions (*conclusions*), they critically reflect upon legal developments in the Community, both as regards the case at hand and generally. The role of the Advocate General is discussed below.[13]

4.4 Law Making at the Level of the European Community

(a) Written law

[424] It has already been observed that the 1957 Treaty of Rome constitutes a framework treaty and that it resembles a 19th century code in that it is abstract and general.[14] As a practical matter, this meant that much Community law remained to be made at some later stage. The Treaty of Rome facilitates this dynamic approach to European integration. Article 189 EC stipulates that, in order to carry out their tasks, the Community institutions shall make Regulations, issue Directives, take Decisions, make Recommendations or deliver Opinions. A Regulation is stated to have general application; it is binding in its entirety and directly applicable in all member states. Regulations are therefore the functional equivalent of statutes in national legal systems. A Directive is binding as well, but only as to the result to be achieved. It is a type of EC law that leaves the national authorities the choice of form and method when implementing the Community objective(s) as embodied in the Directive. In the past, Directives have proved to be a popular legislative instrument for adopting EC laws in the social policy area. National implementation of social policy Directives can occur, for instance, by means of collective agreements negotiated by the so-called social partners, ie the collective representative organisations of employees and employers. A Decision is binding in its entirety in the same vein as a Regulation. Unlike Regulations, however, a Decision is binding only upon the specific parties to whom it is addressed. Finally, Recommendations and Opinions have no binding force at all.

[425] Because of the supranational nature of the EC legal order, the adoption of EC laws is the proper domain of the EC institutions and

---

13   See [434]-[435].

14   See [326]ff above.

individual member states have no discretion in deciding whether or not to be bound by any particular Regulation, Directive, or Decision. Because of the principle of supremacy of EC law, Regulations, Directives and Decisions prevail over any inconsistent national laws irrespective of whether the latter pre-date or post-date the relevant EC law. The non-implementation of a Directive may result in court action with the defaulting state as the defendant. Direct action before the European Court of Justice in Luxembourg can be brought by the Commission (on the basis of Art 169 EC) or, less likely, by another member state (on the basis of Art 170 EC). As a rule, private parties have no direct access to the European Court. However, national courts are expected to interpret domestic law so that it conforms with the terms of Community law. The legal basis for this "expectation" is Art 5 EC which states that member states shall facilitate the achievement of the Community's tasks. Under the so-called doctrine of direct effect member states can be required to compensate private parties for loss caused by the non-implementation of a Directive.[15]

[426] The official legislative body of the EC is the Council. The Council consists of a representative at ministerial level of each member state, authorised to commit the government of that member state (Art 146 EC). The current membership is therefore 15. Except where the Treaty provides otherwise, the Council acts by a majority of its members (Art 148 EC). Initially, majority voting was more the exception than the rule. Since the SEA and the TEU a greater balance exists between those occasions that call for unanimous decision making, qualified majority voting and voting by a single majority.[16] Under the SEA qualified majority voting proved a successful tool to speed up the completion of the internal (economic) market of the Community. However, initiatives under the TEU in the areas of the common foreign and security policy as well as co-operation in the field of justice and home affairs continue to be governed by the unanimity rule.

[427] The above Council must not be confused with the European Council. The ambitions for the establishment of a European Political Community (EPC) in the early 1950s were frustrated (Kapteyn 1989:9). Even so, the ultimate goal of the EC arguably has always been political. In

---

15 See the decision of the European Court of Justice in *Francovich*, case C-6/90 and 9/90, [1991] ECR I-5357. A summary of the current state of affairs can be found in Bronitt, Burns and Kinley 1995:128-146. See also Craig 1993:595 and the references there.

16 Where unanimity is required, abstentions do not prevent the adoption of the particular EC law at issue: Art 148, 3 EC.

the 1970s a practice developed whereby the heads of state and government meet in a so-called European Council to discuss matters of common concern without the need to worry about the jurisdictional constraints of the Rome Treaty on the formal institutions of the Community. The French president Giscard d'Estaing launched the idea in 1974. His aim was to have regular informal, high-level meetings. Ironically, perhaps, the meetings of the European Council have since developed into major media events. Before the SEA the European Council had no official status under the Treaty of Rome, and a rigid division was maintained between the activities of the Community institutions in the context of the EC and the meetings of the European Council for purposes of European political co-operation (Hartley 1994:23). The SEA acknowledges the existence of the European Council without, however, turning it into a Community institution proper. The emphasis in the European Council is on intergovernmental co-operation rather than supranational decision making, and the European Council escapes Community control exercised by the European Court of Justice. Maastricht did not fundamentally alter this situation.

[428] The European Council is the de facto key forum for the discussion of major issues regardless of whether they can be classified as strictly political in nature or rather whether they have a Community dimension in the proper sense of the word. Thus a consensus in the European Council has been necessary in the past to introduce direct elections in the European Parliament, to create the ECU and the EMS, and to hold the inter-governmental conferences that led to the SEA and the TEU (Weatherill and Beaumont 1993:75-76).

[429] The right of legislative initiative traditionally belongs to the Commission.[17] The Commission consists of 20 members, one national of each of the member states except for the five bigger countries who each can nominate two nationals. Significantly, the Commission acts in the general interest of the Community and it is completely independent in the performance of its duties. Specifically, it is stated in the Treaty that the members of the Commission shall neither seek nor take instructions from any government or from any other body in the performance of their duties. Similarly, each member state undertakes not to seek to influence the members of the Commission in the performance of their tasks (Art 157

---

17   Pursuant to Art 9 Merger Treaty, the Commission takes the place of the High Authority in the ECSC.

EC). Appointments to the Commission are for a period of five years, renewable (Art 158 EC).

[430] In the 1957 design of the Community the European Parliament was given a purely advisory role for purposes of EC law making. The classic scenario then was one whereby the Commission proposes, the Parliament advises and the Council decides. Attempts to tackle the democratic deficit in the Community resulted in the selection of the members of the Parliament by means of direct elections at five-year intervals. The first elections for the European Parliament were held in 1979. The SEA introduced a so-called co-operation procedure, which effectively amounts to a second reading stage for the consideration of legislative proposals by the Parliament. Specifically, legislative proposals of importance for the completion of the internal market continue to emanate from the Commission and the role of the Parliament during the first reading stage continues to be advisory only. But, under the co-operation procedure, the Council alone can no longer decide whether or not to legislate once it receives the opinion of the Parliament. Rather, the Council, acting by a qualified majority, must adopt a so-called common position. The Parliament has then three months within which to react. If the Parliament does not react, or its reaction is by way of approval of the common position, the Council is free to turn its common position into law. However, if the Parliament rejects the common position during the second reading stage, the proposal can only be adopted into law if the Council decides to do so unanimously. Alternatively, the Parliament may suggest amendments to the common position. These amendments are forwarded to the originator of the legislative proposal, ie the Commission. The Commission re-examines its original proposal in light of the proposed amendments but without being bound by them. In fact, the concern to uphold the right of initiative of the Commission is so strong that unanimity in the Council is required where the Council wants to adopt a text that is different from the re-examined text of the Commission (even if this means going against the wishes of the Parliament).

[431] The co-operation procedure sought to speed up the completion of the internal market by increasing the opportunities for the Council to adopt laws by a qualified majority instead of unanimity. Overall, this proved to be a successful exercise. However, in addition to speeding up the law-making process of the Community, the SEA also sought to make this process a more democratic one. The above discussion of the co-operation procedure shows that any increase in the powers of the Parliament has been very limited. The TEU goes some way towards correcting the democratic deficit, but it also resulted in complicating the law-making process of the Community even further. The so-called co-decision procedure of the TEU involves the establishment of a Conciliation Committee whenever the common position of the Council is about to be rejected by the Parliament. The Conciliation Committee comprises an equal number of members from the Council and the Parliament. The Committee is assisted by the Commission whose task it is to try to reconcile the position of both parties. A rejection by the Parliament of the common position following unsuccessful conciliation prevents the legislative proposal from becoming law. What makes this a co-decision procedure is the consideration that the Council cannot override the Parliament, not even by a unanimous vote. The co-decision procedure also reduces the Commission's right of initiative without, however, a corresponding strengthening of the right of the Parliament to propose legislation: once a Conciliation Committee has been set up, the Commission effectively looses control over its proposal; the Parliament, on the other hand, obtains a (negative) veto right at best.

(b) Case law

(i) Composition and structure of the European judiciary

[432] Two courts exist at the level of the European Community. They are the European Court of Justice and, since 1988,[18] the Court of First Instance. Strictly speaking the latter is not a Community institution in its own right, and Art 168a EC confirms that the Court of First Instance is merely "attached" to the European Court of Justice.[19] Geographically, the Court of First Instance is situated in Luxembourg and has its seat alongside the European Court of Justice. Its jurisdiction is limited to certain categories of cases only and a right of appeal exists to the European Court of Justice on points of law (Art 168a EC).

[433] The judges of the European Court of Justice are appointed by common accord of the governments of the member states for a renewable term of six years. They are chosen from persons whose independence is beyond doubt. They must possess the qualifications required for appointment to the highest judicial offices in their respective countries; alternatively, they must be "jurisconsults of recognised competence"

---

18   Council Decision 88/591 of 24 October 1988, *OJ* 1988 L319/1 and corrected in *OJ* 1989 C215/1. The Court of First Instance became operational towards the end of 1989.

19   See also Art 4 EC were the Community institutions are officially listed. The list does not comprise the Court of First Instance.

(Art 167 EC) which allows for the appointment of academic scholars to the bench.

[434] Cases are heard in panels (chambers) comprising an odd number of judges. In civil law tradition, the European Court of Justice acts as a collegiate body and its decisions are announced anonymously. There is no scope for the separate publication of concurring or dissenting opinions. It has been suggested that brief judgments that are obscure not infrequently serve as an indication of a lack of unanimity among the members of the European Court of Justice (Weatherill and Beaumont 1993:133). It is certainly correct to hold that decisions of the European Court of Justice typically lack the often prosaic style of judgments in the common law. But it is equally true that, while European case law may seem terse to someone steeped in the common law, the degree of reasoned detail resembles more closely German than French case law (Vranken 1993:433). Even so, one would be ill-advised to read the Court decision in any particular case in splendid isolation. In the civil law case annotations invariably provide invaluable insights both as regards the case at hand and the wider (legal) context. In this regard the opinions of the Advocate General occupy pride of place in European Community law.

[435] According to Art 166 EC Advocates General "assist the European Court of Justice in its task of ensuring that the law is observed in the interpretation and application of the EC Treaty". The task of the Advocate General goes beyond preparing a report for the trial stage of the court proceedings, though.[20] In a sense the opinion of the Advocate General can be likened to a first instance judgment with an immediate, automatic appeal to the European Court of Justice. The opinion actually proposes a solution to the issues at stake. In this the Advocate General sets out the facts of the case and expands the law in greater depth and (usually) with more clarity than the collegiate decisions of the European Court of Justice permit. The reasoned opinion of the Advocate General commonly refers to previous case law and it also contains prognoses for the future development of the law. On the other hand, the opinion of the Advocate General is not legally binding. A parallel can be drawn with the role of the *commissaire du gouvernment* in the judicial section of the French *Conseil d'Etat*, whose task it is to write a written opinion (*conclusions*) in the interests not of the parties but of the law (*la légalité*) (Brown and Bell 1993:101-103; Borgsmidt 1988:106; Barav 1974:809). Unfortunately, the European Court of Justice appears reluctant to enter into an open,

---

20   That is the function of the Reporting Judge.

constructive dialogue with the Advocate General and no meaningful references to the opinion of the Advocate General can be found in the Court's decisions. The net effect of all this is that valuable insights into the development of European Community law risk being foregone. (Vranken 1996:39).[21]

(ii) Role of the judiciary in the law making of the European Community

[436] The law-making function of courts in the civil law is not officially acknowledged. However, the various methods of statutory interpretation available to the courts often serve as a guise to do precisely this. The European Court of Justice is no different from other European civil law courts in this regard. The approaches available to the European Court of Justice can be categorised as literal, historical, contextual and purposive (Weatherill and Beaumont 1993:142). Because of the at times deliberate open-textured nature of both the EC Treaty and the secondary Community legislation, the literal interpretation technique tends to be of limited use in the European Court of Justice.[22] The preparatory materials of EC legislation, including the proposals of the EC Commission and the opinions of the Parliament, are published in the C-section of the *Official Journal*. However, the intent of the drafters is difficult to extract as the political negotiations that really matter in explaining how a particular piece of EC legislation came to be shaped are conducted in secret. In particular, the political give-and-take between the initiator of EC legislation – the Commission – and the ultimate decision maker – the Council – takes place in the Committee of Permanent Representatives (COREPER). That Committee consists of the permanent representatives (ambassadors) of the member states to the Community. Its deliberations, plus those of the Council of Ministers itself, are not open to the public nor are any minutes of meetings published.[23]

---

21 The status of Advocates General is largely the same as that of the Judges: the same conditions as regards their appointment, tenure and removal apply, and they also receive the same salary. In practice, several Judges and Advocates General are law professors.

22 The multi-lingual nature of Community law is yet another obstacle that makes the use of the literal method impractical: Weatherill and Beaumont (1993:143).

23 In the past the European Court of Justice has made but limited use of published *Travaux Préparatoires* in construing Community law: Weatherill and Beaumont 1993:145.

[437] Neither the literal nor the historical method of interpretation is particularly suitable in the context of the European Community. The drafting style of the Treaty of Rome has already been commented upon.[24] As for secondary Community legislation, Art 190 EC states that regulations, directives and decisions must give the reasons on which they are based, including a reference to any proposals or opinions which are required to be obtained pursuant to the Treaty. This facilitates a broad approach to interpretation that is schematic and/or teleological. By placing a particular legal provision in its context and by heeding the object or purpose of any particular piece of legislation, results can be achieved that have been called "very far-reaching, at least to the mind of a common lawyer" (Millett 1988-1989:172). A good example of contextual interpretation is the *Gingerbread* case in which the European Court of Justice held that Arts 9 and 12 EC have to be interpreted broadly (Cases 2 and 3/62, *Commission v Luxembourg and Belgium*, [1962] ECR 425). Article 9 EC prohibits the levying between member states of customs duties on imports and exports and of "all charges having equivalent effect". Article 12 EC adds that the prohibition in Art 9 extends to any new customs duties or "any charges having equivalent effect". In *Gingerbread* the Court made a special mention of both provisions being situated towards the beginning of the Part of the Treaty on (what was then called) the "Foundations of the Community". The Court also observed that Art 9 is placed at the beginning of the Title relating to "Free Movement of Goods" whereas Art 12 is similarly positioned at the beginning of the Section on "Elimination of Custom Duties". The Court inferred from this the essential nature of the prohibitions in Arts 9 and 12. Furthermore, the Court relied on the "general scheme" of these provisions as well as the Treaty as a whole. In the result the Court interpreted the expression "charges having equivalent effect" to constitute a catch-all concept covering not only charges of the same kind but all kinds having the same effect.[25] The classical example of teleological interpretation remains the case of *van Gend en Loos* (case 26/62, [1963] ECR 1). That case generally stands for the judicial confirmation of the supranational nature of the Community's legal order. The Court first observed that the objective of the EC Treaty was to establish a common market the functioning of which is of direct concern to interested parties in the Community. This implied that the Treaty represents more than an agreement which merely creates mutual

---

24   See [328]-[329] above.
25   Brown and Kennedy (1994:313) suggest that an English court might prefer a more restrictive approach to interpretation under the eiusdem generis rule.

obligations between the contracting states. The Court used the contextual and literal methods of interpretation to hold that its view was confirmed by the preamble to the Treaty which refers not only to governments but peoples. The Court concluded that "[T]he Community constitutes a new legal order of international law for the benefit of which the states have limited their sovereign rights, albeit within limited fields, and the subjects of which comprise not only member states but also their nationals" [1963] ECR 1 at 12). A purposive and contextual interpretation was also used in yet another classic case of Community law, *Costa v Enel* (Case 6/64, [1964] ECR 585) to the effect that Community law prevails over inconsistent national law.

[438] The distinction between statutory interpretation and judicial law making in the European Court is just as problematic as it is in the national courts.[26] A parallel can be drawn between the Rome Treaty and a civil law code, especially where the Treaty provisions are deliberately general – as in the case of Arts 9 and 12 above – or incomplete – the principles of supranationality and of the supremacy of Community law, for example. Some commentators argue that the legislative function of the European Court of Justice is inevitable (Brown and Kennedy 1994:296), appropriate even (Moens and Tzovaras 1992:76). Other scholars have been more critical (Hartley 1994:90; Rasmussen 1986). However, it is generally agreed that the European Court of Justice has played a major part in promoting European integration from the very beginning of the Community onwards.[27] It will be interesting to observe whether the largely unqualified pro-Community stance of the Court continues in the future. If it is true that the activities of the Court are subject to self-imposed constraints, including a concern for the perceived "expectations of its audience",[28] it may very well be that the insertion of the principle of subsidiarity in the EC Treaty at Maastricht results in a tempering of the European enthusiasm among all Community institutions including the Court.

(iii) Relationship with the national judiciary

[439] The establishment of a Court of First Instance in 1988 was an attempt to alleviate somewhat the workload of the European Court of Justice (Millett 1990; Kennedy 1989:7; Vandersanden 1991:56). The

---

26 See [420]-[421] above.
27 See the discussion in Vranken and Richardson 1992:225.
28 See the discussion of Bengoetxea (1993) in Bronitt, Burns and Kinley 1995:165.

jurisdiction of the Court of First Instance is exclusive rather than concurrent with that of the European Court of Justice except for appeals on points of law. Initially, the range of issues that trigger the competence of the Court of First Instance was defined narrowly to include, in essence, staff cases, ie disputes between the personnel of the Community and its institutions, certain competition cases and related damages claims. They are categories of cases that are deemed to be particularly time consuming because they tend to involve the close examination of often complex factual situations. On one estimate the transfer of cases to the Court of First Instance had the potential of reducing the workload of the European Court of Justice by one third. A Council Decision of 1993 has since expanded the jurisdiction of the Court of First Instance somewhat resulting in a transfer of all cases brought by private parties including, since March 1994, anti-dumping cases. In the result, it is now feared that the problem of case-overload has been shifted to the Court of First Instance (Brown 1995:748). At the same time, however, the average length of proceedings in the European Court of Justice continues to be relatively high.[29] As the substantive jurisdiction of the Community continues to expand, the pressure on the European Court of Justice is unlikely to ease in the immediate future. However, it ought not be overlooked that from the very inception of the Community provision has been made for the task of interpreting and applying EC law to be shared between the European Court of Justice and the national courts or tribunals in the member states. Without this provision – which is embedded in Art 177 EC – it would have been quite impossible for the European Court of Justice to service a Community of – in 1995 – some 370 million citizens.[30]

[440] Article 177 EC is generally known as the preliminary proceedings' provision. Specifically, where a question as to the interpretation or the validity of Community law is raised before any court or tribunal of a member state, the domestic court or tribunal may request the European Court of Justice to give a (preliminary) ruling. It is expected that the domestic institution will call for the assistance of the European Court of Justice whenever the former considers that a decision on a question of EC law is necessary to enable it to give judgment. It must be appreciated, though, that the procedure for preliminary rulings applies to cases that are

---

29 In 1994 the average length of proceedings involving requests for a preliminary ruling was 18 months. Direct actions, on the other hand, took 20.8 months on average to be decided.

30 A comprehensive review of Art 177 has been undertaken by the TMC Asser Instituut (1987).

(and remain) national court cases. Requests for preliminary rulings originate as well as end in the domestic court. Pending the interpretive ruling from Luxembourg, the national proceedings are temporarily put on hold. The Luxembourg ruling is binding, but only where the national judge decides to resolve the national case by reference to EC law. The net effect is then that the domestic courts and tribunals act as a filter that ideally avoids that the European Court of Justice becomes clogged unnecessarily with a high number of court cases. Even so, the number of cases that end up in the European Court of Justice has increased steadily over the years as indicated above.[31]

[441] In principle, no discretion to refer exists under Art 177 EC where the domestic court in any particular instance is the court of last resort under national law. An exception to this obligation of referral to the European Court of Justice has been created under the so-called doctrine of *acte éclaré*. Under this doctrine, where previous decisions of the European Court of Justice have already dealt with the point of law in question, the duty of the domestic court has been held to be without substance.[32] More questionable are attempts to expand the doctrine of *acte éclaré* to situations where the relevant provision of EC law is said to be clear so as not to require clarification by the European Court in the first place. The latter doctrine of *acte clair* as opposed to *acte éclaré* has the potential of undermining the need for a uniform interpretation of EC law throughout the Community. In the *CILFIT* case the European Court of Justice paid lipservice only to this doctrine by acknowledging its existence while yet attaching strict conditions to its application so as to render the doctrine of *acte clair* effectively inoperable.[33] The case involved an allegation by textile companies that certain duties, payable under Italian law, were in breach of EC law. The Italian government submitted that the Italian supreme court – the court of last instance under national law – did not need to refer the matter to the European Court of Justice since the answer to the question before the Italian court was obvious. As a general principle of interpretation, the doctrine of *acte clair* is recognised in most legal systems under the maxim: *in claris non fit interpretatio* (Toth 1990:10). At a more

---

31 See [439] above.

32 Da Costa, cases 28-30/62, [1963] ECR 31 at 38. It must be noted that, technically, the European Court of Justice is not bound by its own decisions.

33 The European Court of Justice held that no duty exists to refer questions to which the answer is "so obvious as to leave no scope for reasonable doubt". However, the European Court of Justice added that the national court must be convinced that the answer would be equally obvious to a court in the other member states and to the European Court of Justice itself: case 283/81, [1982] ECR 3415.

specific level, the procedure of Art 177 EC is derived from French law. Because of the duality of jurisdiction in the French legal system, a dispute may arise occasionally as to whether proceedings initiated in the civil courts can raise an issue that ought to have been brought more appropriately before an administrative tribunal or vice versa. A *question préjudicielle* is then said to exist, and the matter can be referred to the court of the relevant jurisdiction for determination unless the answer to the point raised is clear (Brown and Bell 1993:119).

[442] Two out of every three cases brought before the European Court of Justice are references pursuant to Art 177 EC. This category of cases has so far remained immune to the two-tier structure of the European judiciary because the power to entertain requests for preliminary rulings is expressly withheld from the Court of First Instance (Brown 1995:743; Vandersanden 1991:56-60). Article 177 proceedings are also known as indirect actions. Direct actions involving private parties as the plaintiff are discouraged.[34]

References

Barav, A, "le commissaire du gouvernement près la Cour de Justice des Communautés européennes", (1974) *Revue internationale de droit comparé* 809.

Bennion, F, "How they do Things in France", [1995] *Statute Law Review* 90.

Borgsmidt, K, "The Advocate General at the European Court of Justice: A Comparative·Study", (1988) 13 *European Law Review* 106.

Bronitt, S, Burns, F, and Kinley, D, 1995, *Principles of European Community Law. Commentary and Materials*, Law Book Co, Sydney.

Brown, LN, "The First Five Years of the Court of First Instance and Appeals to the Court of Justice: Assessment and Statistics", (1995) 32 *Common Market Law Review* 743.

Brown, LN, and Kennedy, T, 1994, *The Court of Justice of the European Communities*, 4th ed, Sweet & Maxwell, London.

Brown, LN, and Bell, JS, 1993, *French Administrative Law*, 4th ed, Clarendon Press, Oxford.

Craig, P, "Francovich, Remedies and the Scope of damages Liability", (1993) 109 *Law Quarterly Review* 595.

Dadamo, C, and Farran, S, 1996, *The French Legal System*, 2nd ed, Sweet & Maxwell, London.

---

34 Most direct actions are initiated by the Commission and they are directed at member states that fail to comply with their obligations under the Treaty (Art 169 EC). Member states can sue one another for failure to comply with EC law (Art 170 EC) but, understandably perhaps, they rarely will do so. Community institutions can also sue one another for alleged failures to act. Private parties can only institute proceedings against Community decisions that are addressed or "of direct and individual concern" to them (Art 173 EC).

Dale, W, "Statutory Reform: The Draftsman and the Judge", (1981) 30 *International and Comparative Law Quarterly* 141.

David, R, 1972, *French Law: its structure, sources, and methodology*, Louisana State University Press, Baton Range.

De Page, H, 1968 *Traité élémentaire de droit civil belge: principes, doctrine, jurisprudence,* 3rd ed, Vol 1, Brussels.

Foster, N, 1993, *German Law and Legal System,* Blackstone Press, London.

Hartley, TC, 1994, *The Foundations of European Community Law*, 3rd ed, Clarendon Press, Oxford.

Kapteyn, PJG, and Verloren Van Themaat, P, 1989, *Introduction to the Law of the European Communities. After the coming into force of the Single European Act,* 2nd ed, Kluwer, Deventer.

Kennedy, T, "The Essential Minimum: The Establishment of the Court of First Instance", (1989) 14 *European Law Review* 7.

Kötz, H, 1990, "Scholarship and the Courts: A Comparative Survey", in Clark, DS, (ed), *Comparative and Private International Law: Essays in Honor of John Henry Merryman on his seventieth birthday*, Dunker and Humblot, Berlin.

Kötz, H, "Taking Civil Codes Less Seriously", (1987) 50 *Modern Law Review* 1.

Leser, HG, 1982, "Legislation, Codification and Interpretation", in Horn, N, Kötz, H, Leser, HG, *German Private and Commercial Law: An Introduction*, Clarendon Press, Oxford.

Markesinis, BS, 1994, *A Comparative Introduction to the German Law of Torts,* 3rd ed, Clarendon Press, Oxford.

Merryman, JH, 1969, *The Civil Law Tradition. An Introduction to the Legal Systems of Western Europe and Latin America*, Stanford University Press, Stanford.

Millett, T, 1990, *The Court of First Instance of the European Communities*, Butterworths, London.

Millett, T, "Rules of Interpretation of EEC Legislation", [1988-89] *Statute Law Review* 163.

Moens, GA, and Tzovaras, T, "Judicial Law-Making in the European Court of Justice", (1992) 17 *University of Queensland Law Journal* 76.

Rasmussen, H, 1986, *On Law and Policy in the European Court of Justice: A Comparative Study in Judicial Policymaking*, M Nijhoff, Dordrecht.

Schauer, F, "The Authority of Legal Scholarship", (1991) 139 *University of Pennsylvania Law Review* 1003.

Schlesinger, RB, Baade, HW, Damaska MR, Herzog, PE, 1988, *Comparative Law. Cases – Text – Materials*, 5th ed, Foundation Press, Mineola.

Tallon, D, "Reforming the Codes in a Civil Law Country", (1980) 15 *Journal of the Society of Public Teachers of Law* 33.

TMC Asser Instituut, 1987, *Article 177 EEC: Experiences and Problems*, Elsevier, Amsterdam.

Toth, AG, 1990, *The Oxford Encyclopaedia of European Community Law. Volume 1 Institutional Law*, Clarendon Press, Oxford.

Vandersanden, G, "A Desired Birth: The Court of First Instance of the European Communities", (1991) 21 *Georgia Journal of International and Comparative Law* 51.

Van Gerven, W, 1973, *Beginselen van Belgisch Privaatrecht. I. Algemeen Deel,* Standaard, Antwerpen.

Vranken, M, "Role of the Advocate General in the Law Making Process of the European Community", (1996) 25 *Anglo American Law Review* 39.

Vranken, M, "The Relevance of European Community Law in Australian Courts", (1993) 19 *Melbourne University Law Review* 431.

Vranken, M, and Richardson, M, "Europe 1992: Past, Present and Future of European Community Law", (1992) 14 *Adelaide Law Review* 219.

Vranken, M, "Statutory Interpretation and Judicial Policy Making: Some Comparative Reflections", (1991) 12 *Statute Law Review* 31.

Weatherill, S, and Beaumont, P, 1993, *EC Law. The essential Guide to the Legal Workings of the European Community*, Penguin Books, London.

West, A, Desdevises, Y, Fenet, A, Gaurier, D, and Heussaff, MC, 1992, *The French Legal System. An Introduction*, Fourmat Publishing, London.

Zülch, C, "Legal Education in Germany", (1992) 5 *Society of Public Teachers of Law Reporter* 19.

Part B

Substantive Law

Chapter 5

The Law of Contract

5.1 Purpose and Outline of the Chapter

[501] This chapter has a double purpose. It seeks to discuss the notion of freedom of contract as it applies at the close of the 20th century. But it also aims at building upon the conceptual framework sketched in the earlier part of he book. Specifically, this chapter serves as an illustration as to the nature and the extent of judicial activism in the civil law. A further opportunity to demonstrate the creative use of code provisions by the courts arises in Chapter 6. Interestingly, each time this judicial creativity has been encouraged and guided by legal scholarship.

[502] As a practical matter, three lines of inquiry will be followed. First, the French law of contract formation will be studied. Attention will be paid to the doctrine of defects in the consent *(vices du consentement)*. What makes this doctrine an attractive tool for judicial activism is its relatively subjective nature, particularly as far as the notion of mistake is concerned. Also, the rigidity of the remedy of rescission exists in form only: far from limiting the options to either affirming or annulling the contract, under this doctrine the court retains a power to balance the interests of the contracting parties by ordering the "innocent" party to pay additional damages where appropriate.[1] The second line of inquiry focuses on the requirement for contracts to be performed in good faith. The emphasis is on the *Treu und Glauben* provision of para 242 *BGB*. Finally, an outline is given of recent EC initiatives at consumer protection. Product liability is discussed in Chapter 6.

---

1   The legal basis for ordering the payment of damages in addition to the annulment of the contract is the precontractual liability for fault *(culpa in contrahendo),* whether intentional or not, whereby one party causes harm to the other party: Ghestin 1993:558. Interestingly, in France this is a tort-based type of liability: see [504].

5.2 Contract Law in Context

(a) The law of obligations

[503] Conceptually, the starting point for a discussion of the civil law of contract is the law of obligations. The latter concept covers a much wider (legal) reality than the law of contract. Specifically, obligation acts as an umbrella concept for the study of not only contract but also tort and even the law of restitution.

[504] The term "obligation" broadly refers to a legal duty. This duty may arise out of an agreement between the parties but it may be triggered by other (legally relevant) factual situations as well. The first type of situation concerns obligations or legal duties that come about before parties have formally entered into an agreement. Typically, the construct of *culpa in contrahendo* has the net effect of imposing a duty of care, or even an obligation of good faith, in the pre-contractual stage. Thus if a civil law court were to be confronted with a problem of unconscionable conduct similar to that which the Australian High Court in *Walton Stores (Interstate) Ltd v Maher* (1988) 164 CLR 387 had to address, it is likely that the civil law court would award damages on the basis of a fault committed in the pre-contractual stage.[2] Von Jhering, who is generally regarded as the father of the doctrine of *culpa in contrahendo*, favoured contract as the legal basis for the establishment of liability in the pre-contractual phase.[3] However, legal systems that follow the French model generally reject contract as the legal basis for *culpa in contrahendo* in favour of the general tort provisions of Arts 1382 and 1383 *Code civil* (Schmidt-Szalewski 1995:127).[4]

[505] A second type of non-contractual obligation arises in situations where no legal effect whatsoever is intended nor anticipated. Rather it is the mere act of someone – the debtor – that triggers the legal duty. The French refer to these areas of law as *délit*, *quasi délit* and *quasi contrat*. As discussed in Chapter 6, the first two concepts are a direct reference to the common law equivalent of tort, whereby *délit* covers instances of

---

2 The High Court of Australia invoked the concept of equitable estoppel to ensure that Walton Stores could not deny the existence of a binding contract.

3 Parties are assumed to have entered into an (implicit) agreement (*Zielvertrag*) to exercise appropriate care in their negotiations for a contract. See the discussion in Freriks 1992:1187 at 1215-1217.

4 The origins of the doctrine of *culpa in contrahendo* and its application in France and Germany is discussed in Mirmina 1992:79-89. For an application of the doctrine to the (pre-contractual) duty of disclosure in France, see Legrand 1991:318.

intentionally inflicted harm and *quasi délit* comprises negligence. The expression of *quasi contrat* is misleading, because any link with contract is a legal fiction: the legal consequences of a particular, non-contractual, situation are dealt with as if they concern a matter of contract law. A most famous example of quasi-contract is *negotiorum gestio*. According to Art 1372 *Code civil*, where someone voluntarily looks after the property of someone else – regardless of whether this is done with or without the owner's knowledge – that someone is under a legal duty (*obligation*) to continue to look after the property until such time the owner is in a position to resume control. Significantly, Art 1372 adds that "that someone takes on the same obligations as if there had been an express mandate or agency agreement". The origins of *negotiorum gestio* can be traced to Roman law. Yet another example of quasi-contract, reminiscent of the common law of restitution, is unjust enrichment. Interestingly, classical Roman law knew no general remedy for unjust enrichment (Gallo 1992:438). Similarly, the text of the French *Code civil* confers a right to restitution only in very particular circumstances. (Dickson 1995:112) and the existence of a general remedy for unjust enrichment is the result of judicial creativity (*Affaire Boudier*: Cass, 15 June 1892, *DP*, 1, 596). In contrast, the writings of von Savigny were largely instrumental in persuading the drafters of the *BGB* to deal with unjust enrichment (*ungerechtfertigte Bereicherung*) in general terms (Para 812 *BGB*; Gallo 1992:440-442).[5]

[506] Contract and tort are the two most common applications of the law of obligations. Even in the field of contracts, however, obligations can arise without the existence of a corresponding legal duty for the party to which these obligations are directed. Donations, for instance, are an exception to the principle of contract formation by mere consent: the preparation of an official document by a notary public is an additional requirement for the valid formation of this solemn contract (*contrat solemnel*). Significantly, the obligation of the donating party arises by reason of a unilateral undertaking, given gratuitously. Put differently, there is an obligation to give but merely an entitlement rather than a corresponding duty to receive. Any objections as to the lack of consideration by a common law observer are no obstacle to the labelling of gifts as contracts in the civil law.

---

5   Gallo (1992:441) argues that the German jurists, apparently unable to "manage" the general principle, have subsequently tried to delineate particular grounds of unjust enrichment. See also Zimmermann 1995:403.

(b) Juristic acts

[507] The importance of the concept of juristic act lies in that it allows for a link to be made between the rather general notion of obligation and the more specific notion of contract. Juristic act (*acte juridique* or *Rechtsgeschäft*) is in essence a creation of 19th century German scholarship and, unlike the concept of obligation, it has no real basis in Roman law. The influence of the German scholars on French legal thinking is especially evident in the writings of Saleilles where juristic acts are defined as a manifestation of the human will with the intent to produce a legal effect.[6] In between obligation and juristic act stands the category of legal act (*Rechtshandlung*). In contrast to "juristic" acts, "legal" acts cover both the intended and unintended legal effects of legally relevant facts. Moving from the general to the specific, the relationship between the various concepts can be presented in the following table (Van Gerven 1973:281):

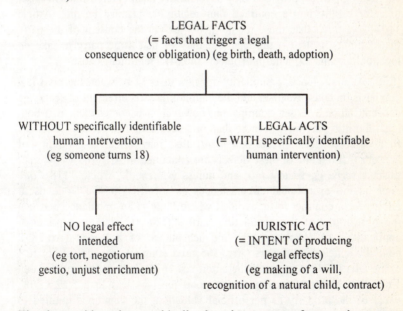

LEGAL FACTS
(= facts that trigger a legal
consequence or obligation) (eg birth, death, adoption)

WITHOUT specifically identifiable
human intervention
(eg someone turns 18)

LEGAL ACTS
(= WITH specifically identifiable
human intervention)

NO legal effect
intended
(eg tort, negotiorum
gestio, unjust enrichment)

JURISTIC ACT
(= INTENT of producing
legal effects)
(eg making of a will,
recognition of a natural child, contract)

The above table makes graphically clear that contracts form a sub-category of obligations. Significantly, they also form a sub-category of juristic acts and the latter depend for their legal effect upon the intention of the acting

---

6   Saleilles, 1929, *De la déclaration de volonté. Contribution à l'étude de l'acte juridique dans le code civil allemand,* as cited in Zweigert and Kötz 1987 II:4.

party. It follows that contracts can be invalidated because of a defect in that intent. French courts and doctrine make maximum use of this emphasis on the consensual aspect of contract law in order to correct perceived excesses of contractual freedom, as discussed below.

5.3 Conditions for the Valid Formation of a Contract under French law

(a) Consent

[508] Article 1101 of *Code civil* defines a contract as an agreement (*convention*) by which one or more persons commit themselves vis-à-vis one or more other persons to do, not to do, or to give something. Article 1134, para 1, stipulates that contracts constitute the law as between the contracting parties, provided they have validly been entered into. In order to enter validly into a contract, four requirements must be met. Article 1108 *Code civil* lists these requirements as: (1) the consent of the party that commits itself; (2) the legal capacity of that same party to take on legal obligations; (3) a definite object; and (4) a legitimate cause.

[509] At first glance, a similarity appears to exist between the civil law emphasis on consensualism and the common law requirement of reality of consent. Upon a closer examination, however, it becomes clear that both legal families part ways at more than one occasion. The French Code lists four defects (*vices du consentement*) that may affect the validity of consent. All but one of these defects are contained in Art 1109 *Code civil*: mistake (*erreur*); fraud (*dol*); and duress (*violence*). Article 1118 *Code civil,* in the exceptional circumstances as specified in the Code itself, allows for a contract to be avoided where there is an imbalance between the obligations of the contracting parties (*lésion*). The three principal applications of *lésion* concern the acceptance of a legacy (Art 783), contracts entered by minors (Art 1305) and contracts for the sale of real estate (Art 1674). As regards the latter, Art 1674 *Code civil* stipulates that when the vendor of an immovable good receives less than 5/12 of the value of the property as per official valuation, the vendor is entitled to have the sale made undone. The underlying rationale for this pro-vendor stance by the drafters of the Code is the (irrebuttable) presumption that, if vendors stand to lose that much, there must have been something wrong with their consent.

[510] Of greater practical relevance than *lésion* are the three other concepts of mistake, fraud and duress. They constitute the classical vices of the consent in French contract law.[7] Nicholas (1992:76) argues that mistake, fraud and duress have more in common in the civil law than the corresponding notions in the (English) common law. Specifically, these three concepts are said to share a "fundamental unity of substance", meaning that all three concepts in French law are approached from the same angle. The question each time is whether they induced the party affected by the vice to enter into the contract. When the answer is in the affirmative, the legal effect is identical in all three situations: the contract is affected by a relative nullity ab initio. The contract can be rescinded upon application to the court, and the legal effects of the rescission apply retroactively. It is perhaps because of this common approach to the various defects in the consent that the practice of the French courts reveals no rigid distinction between the three concepts of mistake, fraud and duress. But it may still be preferable to discuss each of the three *vices du consentement* separately, both for pedagogical purposes and because it clearly also is in line with the original intent of the drafters of the Code.

(i) Mistake

[511] Article 1110 *Code civil* draws a distinction between mistake as to substance (*erreur sur la substance*) and mistake as to the identity of the other contracting party (*erreur sur la personne*). Nullity is a sanction that attaches only to mistakes about the substance of the matter that is the object of the agreement: *"L'erreur n'est une cause de nullité de la convention que lorsq'elle tombe sur la substance même de la chose qui en est l'objet"* (Art 1110, 1 *Code Civil*) By contrast, a mistake as to the identity of the other party does not usually lead to rescission, except for instances of contracts that have been entered into *intuitu personae*. The only major category of contracts of the latter type are individual employment contracts, at least as far as the person of the employee is concerned. More problematic is the determination of the so-called substance of the contract (Malinvaud 1972:215). Unlike the treatment of mistake at common law, the French courts by and large prefer a wide, flexible interpretation. And these courts are typically placed at the lower end of the court hierarchy (*le juge du fond*). In principle, the meaning of "substance"

---

7   *Lésion* became a general doctrine in Europe during the Middle Ages but few modern legal systems have retained this generalised notion. A notable exception is Art 1448 of the Italian Civil Code: Angelo and Ellinger 1992:474-475.

is a matter of law, but the French Court of Cassation in practice happily accepts that the meaning of substance can only be understood properly by reference to the plaintiff, ie the party seeking to obtain nullification of the contract. Put differently, the meaning of substance is not determined in the abstract. Instead, the courts are expected to ascertain what it was that the plaintiff consented to when entering into the contract. That, in the opinion of the *Cour de Cassation*, is an issue of fact to be decided on a case-by-case basis by the trial judge.

[512] A determination of the meaning of substance by reference to one of the contracting parties entails the risk of promoting a rather uncertain approach to the doctrine of mistake. And, undoubtedly, the French approach is relatively subjective when compared to the common law. Substance is an elastic concept and, for instance, even where there is no mistake as to the materials of which a particular object is composed, French courts have found in favour of *erreur sur la substance* on the basis that the mistake concerned an essential quality of the matter which is the object of the transaction. Many cases involve the genuineness of antiques or the authenticity of works of art . But the principle of the "essential quality" has been applied in other, less discreet contexts as well (Nicholas 1992:86-90). Examples are contracts for the sale of secondhand cars involving a mistake by the purchaser as to the year of manufacture or cars that subsequently turn out to be the subject of a security interest of a third party. In the latter instance the buyer arguably is interested, not just in the technical qualities of the vehicle, but also in obtaining exclusive, peaceful enjoyment. Where the consent of buyers can be said to have been determined by a false idea as to the extent of the rights they are acquiring, a successful action for the rescission of the contract on the basis of Art 1110 *Code civil* can be brought.

[513] The civil law does not worry unduly about the finer points of any distinction between common, mutual or unilateral mistake. Some commentators have been quite critical, though. Malinvaud (1972:215) puts it bluntly that the subjective approach to mistake has gone too far and that the notion of substance has lost direction entirely: "*Avec la conception subjective, on est tombé d'un excès dans l'autre; [L]a notion de substance a complètement perdu son sens*". But it does not follow that the security of transactions is of no concern at all. A three-fold qualification of the otherwise subjective approach to mistake ensures that contracts continue to be a relevant tool for organising human inter-action in France. First, the mistake may not be inexcusable. Furthermore, there is a need for the other

party to have been aware that it was the mistake that triggered the consent of the mistaken party. And finally, mistake as to substance does not extend to mistake as to value. Each of these three qualifications needs some further elaboration.

[514] What is or is not inexcusable depends on the knowledge and the expertise (or lack thereof) of the mistaken party. The focus of this first qualification thus remains squarely on the plaintiff. Clearly, mistakes as to the genuineness of antiques, the authenticity of works of art, or the essential qualities of second hand cars will be judged more harshly when the buyer is the *musée nationale* or a professional car dealer. Contract avoidance is refused on the grounds of *erreur inexcusable* whenever the plaintiff's conduct at the time of the contract was "simply negligent" or "faulty", and negligence in this context consists most often of not seeking enough information about the contract (Schmidt-Szalewski 1995:88). But the burden of proof is on the defendant and the common law principle of *caveat emptor* or buyer beware has traditionally been applied in France in a heavily modified format only. In fact, the emphasis of the civil law is more on the reverse, ie on the entitlement of the weaker party to receive information. To be clear, no general provision in the *Code civil* exists that obliges parties to exchange information that is useful for the formation or performance of contracts. Even so, the trend in recent years has been to increase the instances of judicially imposed entitlements to information.[8] These concerns about the need for informed decision making and a meaningful freedom of assent have also resulted in legislative intervention for the protection of the consumer. In 1804 already the *Code civil* made sellers strictly liable for latent defects in the goods they sell, whether the buyer is a consumer or not (Arts 1641-1649 *Code civil*). A century later, a statute of 1905 imposed criminal liability on persons who use fraud when selling food.[9] Renewed legislative activity since the 1970s has resulted in the regulation of door-to-door sales by providing for a cooling-off period of seven days,[10] the prohibition of deceitful advertising (*la publicité trompeuse*),[11] the protection of consumers purchasing goods on credit and

---

8   See the interesting discussion in the context of Belgian contract law by Freriks 1992:1187. A systematic, early account for France is by Juglart 1945:1 and, more recently, by Legrand 1991:318.

9   The statute has since been extended to cover many other products and services: Dickson (1994:149).

10   The Act of 22 December 1972 is now Art L 121-23 of the Consumer Code.

11   See Art 44 of the so-called *Loi Royer* of 1973.

a new law on unfair contract clauses (*clauses abusives*).[12] Finally, a statute of 26 July 1993 makes provision for the existing statutory measures to be consolidated in a consumer code (*Code de la consommation*).[13]

[515] By and large, the French approach to consumer protection is a balanced one. On the one hand, French law favours a liberal interpretation of the term consumer.[14] In fact, protection against uninformed consent is available to anyone who enters into a contract outside of the normal scope of their professional activity.[15] Thus, a real estate company can be a consumer for purposes of questioning an allegedly unfair clause in a contract for the installation of an alarm system at its business premises.[16] On the other hand, the duty to inform of the professional party in a consumer contract does not wholly exempt consumers from any obligation to inform themselves. A recent example is the signing of a contract whereby (adult) children personally guaranteed the payment of money owned to the bank by their father up to a maximum of 1.5 million francs. A bank claim for payment was met with a refusal by the children on the grounds that the bank allegedly had failed to tell the children of two bank loans

---

12 Both Acts date from 10 January 1978 and they are known as the *Lois Scrivener*. Several of the above subject matters are now also governed by EC law. See [552]ff.

13 This Code comprises five books of which Book 1 deals with consumer information and the formation of consumer contracts. Other books deal with the quality and safety of goods and services (Book 2); consumer credit (Book 3); consumer organisations (Book 4); and various government institutions concerned with consumer matters (Book 5, incomplete). Article L. 111-1 of the Consumer code comprises a new general obligation of information which was first introduced in consumer contracts by an Act of 18 January 1992. It provides that professional sellers of goods or providers of services must, before the conclusion of the contract, "allow the consumer to know the essential characteristics of the goods or services". No specific sanctions have been made available by the 1992 legislature and the general rules of contract law must therefore be applied. It follows that a breach of the 1992 statute may trigger a court acton for rescission on the basis of vitiated assent: Schmidt-Szalewski 1995:94.

14 No statutory definition of consumer exists.

15 Contrast the EC Directive of 5 April 1993 on unfair clauses in contracts concluded with consumers. Article 2b of the Directive defines consumer as any natural personal who, in contracts under its scope, acts for non-professional purposes: see [561] below. French consumer law benefits natural and legal persons alike: Schmidt-Szalewski 1995:91.

16 Cass civ 1st, 28 April 1987, *JCP* 1987 II, 20893, note Paisant; *D* 1988, I, note *Delebèque*. The Court held invalid a clause to the effect that the contractual obligation of the burglar alarm company constituted "*une obligation de moyens et non de résultat*".

previously granted to the father that had remained unpaid. It was held that, because of the magnitude of their commitment, the children ought to have informed themselves about the nature and the extent of their commitment before signing the contract. Specifically, the *Cour de Cassation* ruled that the validity of a personal guarantee cannot be challenged on the basis of a mistake as to the solvability of the principal debtor, unless it can be shown that this was a precondition for the signing of the guarantee. The issue of proof is a matter for determination by the trial judge (Cass civ 1st, 19 March 1985, *Bull civ* – I, n 98).

[516] A second qualification as regards the subjective approach to mistake concerns the need for the other party to have been aware, actually or constructively, that the mistake triggered the consent of the mistaken party. Once again, there is room for judicial discretion and the principle is easier to state than to apply. Problems arise because of the need to distinguish between a mistake as to substance and a mistake as to motive. It is only the former type of mistake that leads to nullification of the contract. But the applicable test is the same each time, because the emphasis is on the state of mind of the plaintiff at the time of contracting. In essence, the difference between substance and motive is then one in degree of subjectivity only. For instance, it may be possible to obtain rescission of a contract in which one buys a napkin that the purchaser mistakenly believes to have once belonged to King Louis Sixteenth (Nicholas 1992:91). But it is unlikely that one will be able to convince the French courts to be released from a contract for the purchase of a house which the purchaser believes to be the ideal place for raising a family even though a medical examination subsequently reveals that neither of both spouses is biologically able to produce an offspring. In the first instance, the reason for wanting to buy the napkin – the motive – is a desire to possess a relic that once belonged to a member of the French royalty. In the second instance, the motive for purchasing the house is a personal desire to live there with one's spouse and numerous children in spacious accommodation and close to all the "right" schools. Assuming that the vendor knew in both cases about the reason for the purchase of the napkin/house, it is only in the first case of the napkin that this knowledge is held against the vendor. The explanation is that a sufficiently close link exists between the essential quality of the napkin as a relic and any personal reason for wanting to purchase it for the mistake to qualify as "*une erreur sur la substance*". By contrast, any link between the desire to buy a family home and the quality of the house itself

is much more difficult to argue, and it is likely to be rejected as a mistake as to motive only.[17]

[517] A third, and final, qualification of the subjective approach to mistake can be made. A mistake as to substance must be distinguished from a mistake as to value. If one recalls the narrow approach of the drafters of the Code to *lésion*,[18] this distinction makes perfect sense. On the other hand, the very reason for anyone seeking to bring an action on the basis of mistake as to substance is often precisely the loss the mistaken party stands to make if no rescission is granted. There is likely to be a clear difference in value between, for instance, antique and contemporary items of furniture, original works of art and copies, recent and old second hand motor vehicles, etc. The difference between mistake as to substance and mistake as to value is then difficult to apply in practice because it effectively presupposes that one is able to isolate cause and effect. An example is where party A agrees to rent a villa at the *Côte d'Azur* during the summer. The rent is steep, but A believes that in this way a relaxing holiday in comfort can be assured. Unfortunately, it turns out that there is a gross imbalance between the price paid and the goods received: the house is much smaller than what A had hoped for; there is only the tiniest of gardens at the back of the house; the plumbing is disastrous and there is hardly any furniture. On the facts of the case, there were in addition indications that the letting agency had contributed to the (mistaken) belief by the plaintiff that the enjoyment of a luxurious holiday was a legitimate, reasonable expectation.[19] But the issue of fraud or induced mistake is discussed later. The court preferred to address this particular case from the perspective of mistake alone. Specifically, a distinction was made between

---

17 Psychological motivation is not taken into account: Cass civ, 1 March 1853, *DP*, 1853, I, 134. Technically, it may be possible to obtain rescission on the basis of Art 1131 *Code civil* by claiming that the obligation to purchase was undertaken for a false, ie erroneous cause (*une fausse cause*). Schmidt-Szalewski (1995:118) cites the example of Cass civ 1st, 6 October 1981, *Bull civ,* I, n 273, involving French television station *Antenne Deux*. The television station had started broadcasting a new television programme in which viewers had to guess the identity of a person on the basis of being shown bits and pieces of "cut up" faces. When another company claimed to have invented this particular game, *Antenne Deux* initially agreed to pay for the right to use the concept in its programmes. However, *Antenne Deux* subsequently learnt that the game method did not constitute a work (*une oeuvre*) for purposes of French intellectual property laws, and thereafter it refused to pay. The Court accepted the submission by *Antenne Deux* that its agreement to pay had been entered into for no cause or for a false cause.

18 See [509] above.

19 Cass civ, 29 November 1968, *Gaz Pal*, 1969, 1, 63, as discussed in Nicholas 1992:90-91.

a mistaken valuation pure and simple, on the one hand, and, on the other hand, a mistaken understanding of the facts upon which that valuation is based. Provided these facts concern the "substantial qualities of the thing that is the object of the obligation", it is possible to find in favour of *une erreur sur la substance*! *In casu*, the Court of Cassation ruled that, in view of the price paid, those aspects of the accommodation that were the subject of the complaint could justifiably be considered to be substantial qualities.[20]

[518] In addition to the three-fold qualification of the subjective approach to mistake, the French courts impose a heavy burden of proof on the mistaken party in an apparent move to compensate for any self-induced undermining of the principle of certainty of contract (Malinvaud 1972:217). The plaintiff must be able to satisfy the trial judge that a particular aspect of the contract was considered to be "of substance" (*un caractère substantiel)* whereas this particular aspect was in reality not present at the time of contracting. That same plaintiff must also show that the presumed existence of that particular aspect of the contract determined the consent of that party. Needless to say that to establish this double state of mind is often not possible without the making of assumptions. Judicial discretion is no idle concept in this area of law.[21]

(ii) Fraud (dol)

[519] In the above example of rental accommodation at the *Côte d'Azur*[22] the letting agency knew that what was required was not so much a holiday without more but rather a holiday "in style". On the facts of the case there even were indications that the agency had contributed to the mistaken belief of the plaintiff. At common law, this type of situation is likely to raise the issue of misrepresentation. As any student of the common law is aware, the legal construct of misrepresentation is not without problems of its own. Specifically, the question arises as to whether or not any misrepresentation is merely innocent since this affects the available remedy. And a preliminary issue always is whether it can be said that a

---

20 By contrast, the French Court of Cassation has refused to annul a sale of shares on the basis of an alleged mistake as to their value: Cass com 26 March 1974, *Bull civ*, IV, n 108.

21 See Cass civ 1st, 26 February 1980, *Bull civ* I, n 66 for an example where the plaintiff was successful and Cass civ, 24 March 1987, *Bull civ* I, n 105 for an example of an unsuccessful plaintiff. The latter case is also discussed in *Rev tr dr civ*, 1987, 741, n 2, *obs* Mestre.

22 See [517] above.

misrepresentation occurred in the first place. A crucial distinction in this regard is between representations of fact and representations of opinion. By contrast, in the French courts there is no need for there to have been a fraudulent misrepresentation for the contract to be set aside. In fact, it is not even relevant that a representation has been made. Article 1116 *Code civil* instead requires the occurrence of the rather vague concept of "*manoeuveres*".

[520] The term *manoeuvres* suggests positive acts of fraud with the intent to mislead. But the current application of Art 1116 *Code civil* has evolved towards the prohibition, more generally, of a mere bad faith in the exploitation of the other party's spontaneous mistake (Ghestin 1993:542; Schmidt-Szalewski 1995:88). When compared to the situation at common law, several interesting features emerge. First, mere advertising puff (*dolus bonus*) is insufficient a ground for avoiding the contract in both legal families. By contrast, for the establishment of a *dol*, the occurrence of illicit conduct is required and, thus, a mere innocent misrepresentation will not do. Also, *dol* is not confined to instances of misrepresentation. Rather, what matters is the state of mind of the *dol*-feasor. In fact, it can even be argued that state of mind is just as important, if not more important, than the nature of the fraudulent act itself. In this regard, case law shows that even silence may constitute "*manoeuvres*" for purposes of Art 1116 *Code civil* (Cass civ 3, 15 January 1971, *Bull civ*, III, n 38; *D*. 1971, *som* 148; *Rev tr dr civ*, 1971, 839 note Loussouarn, Y). The technical French expression for this type of fraud is *réticence dolosive* or *dol par réticence*. Significantly, the term *réticence* is best translated to mean "not telling" rather than "keeping silent", because this type of *dol* arises only in situations where a duty to speak or inform exists in the first place.[23] Ghestin (1993:535) gives the example of the well-informed professional who otherwise may feel tempted to take (unfair) advantage of the ignorance by the other party. But the case law is by no means limited to professionals only. A by now classic example concerns the sale of a house in the countryside to a city dweller without informing the buyer about plans for the establishment of a pig farm next door in the near future (Cass civ 3, 2 October 1974, *Bull civ*, III, no 330, 251; *D*, 1974, *inf rap* 252). There is also the case where the purchaser of land mistakenly believed that the land was suitable for building purposes (Cass civ 3, 7 November 1984, *JCP*, 1985, IV, 27). Arguably, these examples are manifestations as to the

---

23   It will be recalled that the *Code civil* does not contain a general duty for the contracting parties to speak, whereas the more recent *Code de la consommation* does so with respect to contracts for the sale of goods or services: see [514] above.

existence of a general duty of good faith or fair dealing during the contract formation stage in contemporary French law and it has been judicially created to supplement Art 1134 *Code civil* as regards the good-faith performance of contracts. This emphasis on a duty to inform enables the courts to sidestep the need to find an intention to deceive (Nicholas 1992:103). What can not be sidestepped, however, is the requirement for the plaintiff to show that, but for the induced mistake, no contract would have been entered into (*dol principal*). Proof that the contract would have been assented to albeit under different conditions, will trigger an entitlement to damages only (*dol incident*). The notion of *dol incident* is alive and well in Belgium. In France, by contrast, legal scholars are divided as to the usefulness of the distinction with *dol principal*. Ghestin (1993:557), in particular, interprets a decision by the Court of Cassation in 1984 as having abolished the difference between both types of fraud (Cass com, 2 May 1984, *Bull civ*, IV, no 45, 123; *JCP* 1984, IV, 218). To be clear, the mistake component of the *dol* concept need not be a mistake as to the substance. Thus, a mistake as to value or as to simple motive may not be sufficient to warrant annulment of the contract on the basis of Art 1110 *Code civil*, but it can suffice for purposes of Art 1116 *Code civil*.

(iii) Duress (violence)

[521] The practical relevance of *violence* in contemporary France is limited, even though its application is by no means restricted to instances of physical abuse (Ghestin 1993:561). The historical significance of *violence* can be inferred from the fact that the drafters of the *Code civil* devoted no fewer than five provisions to this concept. The potential field of application is wide in that, in contrast with fraud, Art 1111 *Code civil* provides that duress need not emanate from the party that stands to benefit from the contract. Similarly, duress need not necessarily be directed against the innocent contracting party: Article 1113 *Code civil* expressly stipulates that the latter party's spouse, descendants or ascendants may also be the victim of duress. On the other hand, in common with the concept of mistake, not just any instance of duress leads to nullification of the contract. Article 1112 *Code civil* requires that the duress is such as to impress upon reasonable persons, so as to make those persons fear for their physical or economic wellbeing: *"de nature à faire impression sur une personne raisonnable, et qu'elle peut lui inspirer la crainte d'exposer sa personne ou sa fortune à un mal considérable et présent"*.

[522] Two observations are in order. First, notwithstanding an express reference to the "reasonable person" approach, there is no total objectivity

here as the drafters of the Code stress that account must be taken of age, gender, and the condition or state of the person subjected to duress in determining whether the duress did in fact constrain that person. In the result, each case is decided on its own merits. For instance, the sale of all her belongings by a sick and elderly woman in exchange for a commitment by the purchaser to look after her was annulled on the basis of *violence* (Cass civ 3, 19 February 1969, *Bull civ*, III, 119). On the other hand, a claim for annulment by an employee was rejected because it was deemed that someone in the position of personnel manager ought to have been able to properly assess the consequences of the employment contract that had been entered into (Cass soc, 5 January 1984, *Bull civ*, V, no 6, 4). A second observation as regards the person of the victim is embodied in Art 1114 *Code civil*. Specifically, it is stipulated that mere fear for one's parents, out of respect (*la crainte revérencielle*), does not normally constitute duress. The contemporary significance of Art 1114 lies in that it provides an argument *a contrario* to avoid that duress is invoked in instances other than instances of illegitimate pressure. Clearly, it would make little sense to grant an application for the annulment of a mortgage agreement, for instance, simply because the creditor threatens legal action if no repayments are made. Entirely different is the situation where the exercise of the rights of the creditor is in a manner that amounts to an abuse of law. The doctrine of abuse of rights (*abus de droit*) is based on the premise that only certain legal entitlements or rights can be exercised in an entirely discretionary manner and that, increasingly, rights are functional. If rights serve a certain function, anyone who turns a legal entitlement away from its particular function, abuses this right. The legal basis for this doctrine of abuse of rights is, in Germany, Para 226 *BGB*. In France, no express basis exists in the Code. Even so, the tort provisions of Arts 1382 and 1383 *Code civil* are generally invoked in support of the doctrine. Recently, the *Cour de Cassation* had an opportunity to state the relationship between the doctrine of *abus de droit* and duress in the following terms:

> The threat to exercise one's rights under the law does not amount to duress for purposes of Articles 1111 ff *Code civil* unless these rights are exercised in an abusive manner by reference to their purpose or to obtain a promise or an advantage that bears no relationship to or is out of proportion to the primary commitment (*La menace de l'emploi d'une voie de droit ne constitue une violence au sens des articles 1111 et suivants du Code civil que s'il y a abus de cette voie de droit soit à la détournant de son but, soit en en usant pour obtenir une promesse ou un avantage sans rapport ou hors*

de proportion avec l'engagement primitif (Cas civ 3, 17 January 1984 *Bull civ*, III, no 13, 10, confirming the appellate court's decision of Paris, 8 July 1983, *D*, 1983, 473, note Landraud).[24]

(b) Object and cause

[523] Article 1108 *Code civil* lists *objet* and *cause* (from the Roman *causa*) as two separate requirements for the valid formation of a contract. In practice, however, the distinction is not always easy to make and, when looking at the French law of contract through common law eyes, it may be tempting to lump both concepts together by using the quasi-mathematical formula of object plus cause equals consideration. The civil law is, unfortunately perhaps, somewhat more complex than this equation suggests. Not even among civil law commentators is the usefulness of having two separate requirements entirely without controversy, though. On the one hand, there is no concept in the common law which corresponds to the French *objet*. On the other hand, civil law commentators of especially the German legal systems at times question the significance of *cause* as well and no such concept is provided for in the *BGB*. The new Dutch *NBW* also omits *cause* as a separate requirement for the valid formation of a contract.[25]

[524] Logically, object and cause are separate requirements because each concept serves a different function. In simple terms object answers the question as to what it is one commits oneself to. By contrast, the notion of cause reveals information as to why one legally commits oneself in the first place. For example, in a contract for the sale of a car the vendor agrees to hand over the vehicle because the purchaser agrees to pay for it and vice versa. In civil law terms, the "object" of the obligation of one party constitutes the "cause" of the obligation of the other party. Of course, this line of reasoning only holds true for bilateral contracts containing reciprocal obligations that are – roughly – equal. As discussed below, it is more difficult to equate the concepts of object and cause in other types of contract.[26]

[525] One complicating factor is the confusion triggered by the multiple meanings of both object and cause as used in the *Code civil*. The drafters

---

24 A general discussion of the doctrine of abuse of law can be found in Ghestin and Goubeaux 1994:747.

25 Not all traces of the concept of *cause* have been removed, though. See the discussion in Van Dunné 1993:210.

26 See the discussion of unilateral contracts and aleatory contracts in [528] and [529] below.

of the *Code civil* have used the same term of *objet* in three different contexts. At times *objet* is used by reference to the contract in general, but it is also used by reference to the main obligation(s) which that contract creates. And the same term of *objet* can even refer to the performance (*la prestation*) that arises from the obligation. For example, in a contract for the sale of a car, the notion "object" consists of both the car, *and* the obligation to convey the car, *and* the actual act of conveying itself (Ghestin 1993:654; Nicholas 1992:114). These distinctions are not very significant in practice, however.

[526] Of greater practical significance is the double meaning of *cause*. The concept of internal *cause* seeks an answer to the question as to why one party legally commits itself in the commitment of the other party to the contract. Thus, the *cause* of the obligation of the vendor in the above example of car sale is the object of the obligation of the purchaser. The concept of external *cause* goes beyond this as it puts emphasis on the overriding purpose or the motivating reason that triggers the legal commitment of either party. A parallel can be drawn with mistake as to substance. However, in the context of *cause*, motivation does matter because the *Code civil* states expressly that illicit cause is a ground for cancellation of the contract.[27]

[527] It is the external *cause* concept that provides the strongest argument in favour of the object/cause distinction to date. Unfortunately, perhaps, the external *cause* concept is also a rather more subjective notion than internal *cause*. A first type of situation involves bilateral contracts where the reciprocity of the parties' obligations is less than perfect. Secondly, the *cause* of the obligation of the party that commits itself in a unilateral contract is necessarily external only. And finally, the *Code civil* outlaws bilateral contracts with a so-called illicit *cause*. Each type of situation is further explained below.

[528] The principle of contractual freedom cannot guarantee a perfect equation between the obligations of the contracting parties. Because of the narrow approach to *lésion* in the *Code civil*, it was not anticipated by the drafters of the Code that the courts would often have to concern themselves with the value of contracts for the various parties. The Code even makes express provision for so-called chance or aleatory (*alea* is Latin for chance) contracts which are valid provided the *alea* can be said to be genuine (Arts 1104 and 1964 *Code civil*). Article 1964 *Code civil* defines aleatory contracts as contracts whereby the effects for one or more

---

27   See [530] below.

of the parties, in terms of profit and loss, depend upon an uncertain (future) event. Put differently, a contract is aleatory when the extent of one party's performance depends on some future uncertain event and the other party's performance does not vary correspondingly (Nicholas 1992:45). A typical instance of aleatory contract is the so-called *rente viagère* whereby one party hands over certain property rights in return for periodic payments by way of income support for the remainder of the first person's natural life. A variation are the so-called *baux à nourriture* involving a promise to provide board, lodging and care instead of a life annuity. The element of *alea* or chance consists of the uncertainty as to when the relevant party will die. Suppose an elderly woman agrees to transfer the property rights of her house to a neighbour, who happens to be both a friend and a nurse, in exchange for an undertaking of care for as long as she lives. Suppose also that the woman dies within a few weeks of having entered into the contract. Her heirs, who may wish to challenge the deal, are unlikely to be able to argue successfully that the contract is void for lack of *objet*. After all, the obligation of each party has a perfectly valid object constituted by the house – as far as the woman is concerned – and by the home care – as for the nurse. *In casu*, the woman received homecare albeit not for very long. The object of the obligation of the nurse may therefore have been trivial or insubstantial, but it nevertheless was real. The *Code civil* does not require the object of obligations to be substantial. Since the obligation of the nurse has an *objet*, it would be difficult for the heirs to argue that the woman's obligation lacks (an internal) *cause*. But they may wish to argue that, using the concept of external *cause*, the motivating reason or overriding purpose of the deal was for the woman to be cared for for more than a few weeks only. Aleatory contracts involving a life annuity are the subject of express regulation in the *Code civil*.[28]

[529] The concept of external cause is also useful in gratuitous contracts. In agreements to make a gift, there simply fails to exist an internal cause that can correspond to the obligation of the donating party. The beneficiary is under no duty to receive. Even so, the contract is not normally struck down for lack of cause. Only, it is the intention to be generous,

---

28 According to Art 1974 *Code civil* life annuity contracts are void if the beneficiary of the annuity dies the very day the contract is entered into. Article 1975 *Code civil* extends this rule to sick people who die within 20 days of the date of the contract. The courts at time do not hesitate to apply Art 1975 beyond the 20-day deadline: Ghestin, 1993:863-864; A Bénabent, note under Cass civ 3, 6 November 1969, *JCP*, 1970, II, 16502.

gratuitously (*animus donandi; l'intention libérale*), that constitutes the (external) cause of the obligation of the donating party.

[530] A third and final category of contract where use is made of the concept of external cause concerns obligations entered into with an illicit cause. According to Art 1131 *Code civil* any such obligation shall have no effect. A classic example is a contract for the lease of a house for purposes of operating a brothel. The *objet* of the obligations of the parties is, for the lessor, to give vacant possession and, for the lessee, to pay the rent. Both are perfectly legitimate activities in their own right. Rather, it is the motivating reason for taking out the lease that is illicit. Only the concept of external cause can therefore assist in striking down the contract on the basis of Art 1131 *Code civil*.

[531] The origins of the external cause concept is said to lie in canon law. Canon law sought to build upon the perceived imperfections of Roman law as the latter recognised the legal enforceability of certain specified categories of contract only. The Catholic Church found this situation unacceptable on moral grounds. Specifically, a desire existed to operate on the basis of a more general *pacta sunt servanda* principle. However, the canonists were sufficiently realistic to appreciate that some qualification of the principle of the legal enforceability of obligations was appropriate. The qualification put forward was that all obligations require a legitimate *causa*, which was broadly understood to mean the motivating reason or purpose of the obligation.[29]

[532] The above discussion has managed to expose the tip of the proverbial iceberg only. As it has been put eloquently by Litvinoff (1987:3), the doctrine of cause has had a most eventful existence:

> It has been praised as the quintessence of wisdom, deprecated as a truism, and blamed as a nebulous abstraction. It has also been made to reflect all kind of changing philosophies ranging from the natural law ideas of the canonists, through the liberalism that inspired the redaction of the Code Napoleon, the first Civil Code, and to the socio-economic approach of some contemporary doctrine.

Writing from a common law perspective, Markesinis (1978:54-55) describes the French approach as "invariably, neater and more convincing". Notwithstanding the self-criticism of some French legal scholars including Ghestin, it is a fair prediction that the concept of *cause* is likely to remain an integral part of French law for now.

---

29   The history of the concept of *causa* prior to the Napoléonic code is discussed in *Ghestin* 1993:821ff.

5.4 The German Doctrine of Good Faith at the Contract Performance Stage

(a) The BGB and the formation of the contract

[533] The German *BGB* was enacted some 100 years after the French *Code civil*. Even so, both codes are products of the 19th century and bear the marks of its liberal individualism. At the end of the 20th century the basic premise of contractual freedom continues to hold true, including the underlying assumption that individual well-being inevitably leads to general well-being and that the legal protection of individual self-interest is therefore legitimate. However, throughout this century attempts have been made to curb and control any perceived excesses. The issue has been tackled in Germany – as in France – not just by the legislature but also by the judiciary. The discussion below is then a prime example of judicial creativity in the civil law as applied to the German law of contract. However, whereas the French put heavy emphasis on the consensual element of contract, invoking various defects of the consent to attack the validity of the contract at its formation stage, judicial activism in Germany has tended to focus more readily on the performance stage of the contract. Certainly, the *Treu und Glauben* (good faith) provision of Para 242 *BGB* has proved to be most "useful" in effectively allowing the judicial rewriting of contracts where to do so is deemed appropriate. Paragraph 242 has also been the subject of scholarly attention internationally,[30] and a major part of this section of the book is therefore devoted to this provision of the German civil code.

[534] It would be wrong to assume, though, that issues of contract formation, including consent, are wholly irrelevant in German law. In fact, the *BGB* contains several provisions that are framed in terms that are sufficiently broad so as to allow for leeway in their (judicial) interpretation. Particularly significant are Paras 119, 123 and 138 *BGB* on, respectively, mistake, fraud and usury. A brief discussion is warranted.

[535] Paragraph 119, II *BGB* allows for the rescission of contracts affected by a defect in the consent (*Willensmangel*) because one party is mistaken as to an essential characteristic (*Eigenschaftsirrtum*). A parallel can be drawn with the concept of mistake as to substance in French law. Only, the German notion of *Eigenschaftsirrtum* also covers what is

---

30   A most prolific writer on this subject has been Dawson. See, in particular, Dawson 1934:171, 1976:1041, and 1983:1039.

referred to as *erreur sur la personne* in French law.[31] A person's essential characteristics can be age, reliability, criminal record or political views. An example is the rescission of the employment contract of a cashier with a record of theft (Foster 1993:207).[32] Most importantly, mistake in German law is less subjective than its French counterpart. Specifically, a characteristic is essential if it has an objective importance to the contract. The German courts have defined "essential characteristic" to include only the "factual and legal qualities of things which specifically characterise them", excluding "factors which only have an indirect effect on their value" (BGHZ 6, 54, 57, as cited in Foster 1993:207). A mistake as to motive, for instance, is considered to be an outside factor which therefore clearly cannot lead to rescission. Similarly, authenticity is regarded as an essential quality but mistakes as to value remain without a remedy unless they can be linked to an essential quality (BGHZ 6, 371 as cited in Foster 1993:207).

[536] Instances of induced mistake are governed by Para 123 *BGB*. According to this provision someone who "makes a declaration of will" through fraud or illegally through duress can avoid the declaration. As in French law, the fraud or deceit must be intentional, which increases the burden of proof of the innocent party since proof of gross negligence by the other party is not enough. German law does not use the expression of *"manoeuvres"* and fraud can be made out both in instances of action and inaction by the defendant. Foster (1993:207) gives the example of a prospective purchase of a second hand car and the duty of the dealer to provide information, upon request, about the accident record of the vehicle.

[537] Freedom of contract has been elevated to a fundamental right in the post-World War Two Constitution (*Grundgesetz*) of Germany (Brox 1990:20). Everyone is entitled to develop their personality (*Persönlichkeit*). But this freedom is not absolute and limitations are the rights of others, public order and morality (*"soweit er nicht die Rechte anderer verletzt und nicht gegen die verfassungsmässige Ordnung oder das Sittengesetz verstösst"*: Article 2 *GG*). Contracts that are contrary to public policy or morals are void as provided in Para 138, I *BGB*. Even more striking is Para 138, II *BGB*. It declares void transactions where there

---

31   See [511] above.

32   Thus the application of the German dismissal laws may be avoided. A question arises, though, as to whether the employer has not only a right but also a duty to ask questions when interviewing prospective employees, eg for security-sensitive jobs. See Weiss 1994:64.

has been a striking disproportion between the performance of both parties and one party has exploited the need, inexperience, lack of sound judgment or a significant weakness of will of the other party. A similar provision features in the Swiss Code of Obligations (Taisch 1992:529).

[538] The law of contract is in constant evolution, and the German legal system is no exception. It is not always possible to detect a clear direction in which the law is developing. However, it is clear that the German law of contract throughout the 20th century has been typified by judicial activism for the protection of the weaker party (Medicus 1993:22: *"zum Schutz des typischerweise Schwächeren"*). But, overall the appeal of the *BGB* provisions on contract formation, especially those Paragraphs as regards defects of the consent, has been limited. Either there is something seriously wrong with the consent of one of the parties, in which case grounds for rescission (*Anfechtungsgrunde*) exist and the contract is deemed void ab initio, or, in the absence of any such *Willensmangel*, the contract stands. The general clauses of the *BGB* proved to be more useful in this regard.[33] At the contract performance stage, the *Treu und Glauben* provision of especially Para 242 *BGB* allowed for much more flexibility in "adjusting" the relationship between the contracting parties.[34]

(b) Paragraph 242*BGB*

[539] The establishment of a general law of contract based on consensus is the result of a long process. Under Roman law contractual obligations could arise out of four types of consensual arrangements only: sale (*emptio venditio*), lease (*locatio conductio*), mandate (*mandatum*) and partnership (*societas*). An agreement that did not fit into one of these categories was not actionable. The existence of non-enforceable contracts (*pacta nuda*) was attacked on a principled level by the canon lawyers. A "decisive breakthrough" was brought about by the natural lawyers (Zimmermann 1990:544). Grotius, in particular, has been credited with the proposition that it is good faith (*fides*) that forms the basis of justice. Hence, promises must be kept, whether they have been couched in a specific form or not.

[540] To the natural lawyers contract was an essential tool for the regulation of human affairs. From there it followed that all contracts (*pacta*) must be binding. Once this principle had gained general

---

33   See the discussion in [539] ff below.

34   Even among German scholars it is generally agreed that the literature on Para 242 is *"fast unübersehbar"*. Most textbooks on *Schuldrecht* contain a section on the good faith clause. See eg Schlechtriem 1994:68ff; Brox 1990:50ff.

acceptance, the significance of *pacta sunt servanda* shifted from formalism to consensualism. The maxim came to imply that contractual promises must be honoured under all circumstances (Zimmermann 1990:576). The attitude prevailing in the 19th century was that everyone was free to decide whether to enter into a contract or not (*Abschlussfreiheit*). Also, it was up to the parties to determine the content of their transaction (*Inhalts-freiheit*).[35] Provided that the content was not illegal or immoral, there was to be no judicial interference. In particular, the validity of a contract could not depend on the adequacy of consideration. It was for the parties to make their bargain, not for the courts. The courts were to be merely concerned with the fairness of the bargaining process.[36]

[541] The principle of *pacta sunt servanda* was never applied without exceptions, not even in Roman law. Even so, the correcting doctrine of *rebus sic stantibus* did not originate in Roman law. Rather, moral philosophers were the first to draw attention to the injustice of insisting on the performance of contracts where there had been a change of circumstances from those which existed at the time of entering into the contract.[37] By the end of the 15th century its field of application was described in the broadest possible terms. The doctrine reached its peak in popularity during the 17th century, especially in the field of public international law. But in the area of private law its fame ultimately began to fade away and 19th century legal science was predominantly hostile to it. With the benefit of hindsight, the underlying idea was to have lost its attraction only temporarily, though.

[542] To be sure, the drafters of the *BGB* had considered but rejected the doctrine of *rebus sic stantibus* for lack of precision and for, potentially, undermining the need for legal certainty. In fact, the *BGB* clearly intends to let risks lie where they fall. Specifically, Para 275 *BGB* stipulates that unexpected, unforeseen circumstances – even where they are beyond the control of the parties – have no effect on the contract except where such performance has been rendered (literally) impossible and not just extremely onerous. But it was the sheer magnitude of the problem of changed circumstances for the performance of long-term contracts in the

---

35   Scherrer W, *Die Geschichtliche Entwicklung des Prinzips der Vertragsfreiheit*, 1948, at 31 as cited in Zimmermann 1990:577.

36   Hence, for instance, fraud, misrepresentation and duress were the only defences recognised under Roman law.

37   Zimmerman 1990:579-580 cites Seneca, Cicero, St Augustine, St Thomas of Aquinas, Bartolus and Baldus.

aftermath of the First World War that forced the hand of legal writers and courts alike in developing a solution *extra legem*.[38]

[543] The First World War triggered a massive inflation on a scale beyond comprehension. In the course of a few years only, the purchasing power of the *Reichsmark* (RM) became one billionth of its value immediately before the war. The repercussions were severe, especially as regards (long-term) contracts that had been entered into before the war but that required performance after the war had ended.[39] For instance, a stipulated price per barrel of 5 RM might have been reasonable at the time of the formation of contracts for the supply of beer immediately before the war. But, after the war was over, the purchasers would have been able to buy the entire stock of their supplier at that price. Thus breweries effectively could be forced to go out of business, because they would only be able to replace their stock at a production cost that was a million times one million higher than before the war. Needless to say that to insist on performance of the contract in these circumstances amounted to a huge transfer of wealth. Most importantly, this gross distortion of pre-existing relationships had nothing to do with the normal assumption of risk by the contracting parties. Eventually, the German legislator stepped in but it proved to be a classic case of too little too late. The Revalorisation Act of 1925 contained specific provisions for the revalorisation of certain contracts only. A whole series of transactions were effectively left out, in that the courts were instructed to work out a solution by application of "the general principles of law" instead. Also, statutory intervention came about some seven years after the war had ended. During the intervening years court cases were introduced and needed adjudication. German scholars as well had set their minds to work long before the action taken by the legislature. And this scholarship displayed no lack of creativity unhampered, apparently, by the young age of the *BGB*.[40]

[544] The adoption of a narrow approach to frustration by the drafters of the Code has already been alluded to.[41] In effect, their approach was not only more narrow than the medieval canon of *rebus sic stantibus*, it was also more restrictive than the common law concept of frustration. Even so, German scholars argued, both before and after the enactment of the *BGB*,

---

38 The qualification of "extra legem" is by Zimmermann 1990:582. Its literal meaning is "outside of" the law and not "against" it.

39 See the excellent discussion in Dawson 1934:171.

40 The *BGB* came into effect on 1 January 1900. By the time the First World War was over, the *BGB* was thus not even two decades old!

41 See [542] above.

that a person's will is formed on the basis of certain suppositions and, if these suppositions turn out to be wrong, it is not always fair to hold people to their word. Of course, the promisor's interest in having the contract set aside must be balanced against the interest of the community at large in certainty of the law. Windscheid is a 19th century scholar whose suggested criterion for balancing private and public interest did not go unnoticed. His doctrine of tacit presupposition (*Voraussetzungslehre*) did not commend itself to the drafters of the *BGB*, however. The 20th century argument for the recognition of a variation to the principle of *rebus sic stantibus* by Krückmann proved equally unsuccessful. More persuasive was Paul Oertmann who developed his doctrine of the collapse of the foundation of the transaction (*Wegfall der Geschäftsgrundlage*) in the early 1920s.[42] In fact, it has been observed that, well over half a century later, the German courts have hardly moved away from the Oertmann doctrine to the extent of seemingly ignoring any later developments in German scholarly thinking ("*Versuchen wir ein Resümee zu ziehen, so ist wohl vor allem hier bemerkenswert, wie die Rechtsprechung, einmal von der Oertmannsche Formel inspiriert, von den weiteren Entwicklungen in der Literatur nicht oder kaum mehr Notiz nahm*": Diesselhorst 1980:168). That same author also comments that law and morality have become intertwined, the law of contract in particular ("*Eine weitere Entwicklung wird an unserem Thema deutlich: Die Ethisierung des Rechts, insbesondere des Vertragsrechtes*": Diesselhorst 1980:169).

[545] To Oertmann the foundation or the basis of the contract does not refer to the actual terms of the contract itself. Rather, the reference is to certain assumptions as to the existence of fundamental – objective – circumstances which form the basis of the transaction for one or both parties: "*die beim Geschäftschluss zutage getretene Vorstellung der Beteiligten über das Bestehen gewisser für ihren oder einen ihrer Willen massgebenden Umstände*".[43] In the 1920s the required change of circumstances was found to exist in the radical change in the economic balance of the relationship between the contracting parties due to the de facto collapse of the German national currency. Interestingly, the courts not only went along with the reasoning by Oertmann, they even took his doctrine one step further. Specifically, whereas the Oertmann design allowed for the rescission of contracts only, in time the courts started effectively to rewrite the contract. Furthermore, this judicial revision of

---

42 All three scholars are discussed in Dawson 1983:1039.

43 Oertmann, P, 1921 *Die Geschäftgrundlage. Ein neuer Rechtsbegriff*, as cited in Esser and Schmidt 1976:268-269.

contracts was limited initially to instances where rescission would have been the alternative. But at a later stage any reference to rescission was abandoned and the legal basis of Para 242 *BGB* was invoked to justify the "rebuilding" of contracts whose foundation had simply been "impaired" rather than destroyed.

[546] The acceptance of the Oertmann doctrine by the courts implied an acceptance of the need for a (modified) *clausula rebus sic stantibus*. As envisaged by Oertmann the limited applicability of the doctrine was itself a safeguard against an excessive undermining of legal certainty. However, the much wider application of the Oertmann doctrine by the courts in the post-World War One years requires further justification. Two major explanations as offered by the Germans courts themselves can be identified (Dawson 1983:1039). The first justification may sound familiar to a common law readership. In essence, the German courts claim to involve themselves in the construction of the contract for purposes of not interfering in but reinforcing the private autonomy of the parties. A classic illustration is the so-called *Volkswagen* case, concerning purchasers of cars who had placed their orders before the (Second World) War and who sought to enforce the contract after the War even if that meant that the court had to fill in certain vital details including price, model, year of production, dates for payment and delivery. The German supreme court ruled that even a major revision of the contract is justified in instances of collapse of the foundation of the transaction:

> The courts can adjust the contractual obligations of the parties in a major way in instances of collapse of the foundation of the transaction. They can do so when necessary to obtain the performance of the contract in a manner that does justice to the legitimate interests of both parties. (*Die Gerichte können bei einem Wegfall der Geschäftsgrundlage die Vertragspflichten rechtsgestaltend sehr erheblich ändern, wenn dies geboten ist, um zu einer Leistungsfestsetzung zu gelangen, die den beachtlichen Interessen beider Parteien gerecht wird*) (BGB 23 October 1951, (1952) 7 *JZ* 145 at 146, note G Kegel).

The legal basis for any such judicial intervention is the principle of *pacta sunt servanda*:

> Legally, the basic premise is that contracts must be performed (*Rechtsgrundsätzlich is davon auszugehen dass Verträge zu halten sind*) (at 146).

[547] It follows from the above that the German courts are prepared to use para 242 *BGB* as the legal basis for filling gaps and rewriting even essential terms of the contract. Initially, the parties became actively involved in this business of rewriting the contract. Thus it was not unusual for the former *Reichsgericht* to appoint a college of experts to assist in the revalorisation of money debts after the First World War. The names of these experts were typically put forward by the parties themselves. Later on, this practice of party involvement was discontinued. Nowadays, the courts no longer ask for the parties' agreement with the rewritten contract and such agreement is no longer assumed either. As a practical matter, the net effect of judicial rewriting tends to favour one party at the expense of the other. Hence it would appear futile to invite or expect the agreement of the parties. Of course, under these circumstances it becomes increasingly difficult to justify judicial intervention on the basis of reinforcing party autonomy.

[548] In the so-called *metalscrap* case the court ruled that contemporary Germany is not a free but rather a social market economy. The plaintiff – a dealer in scrap – was said to be a member of a community that makes it possible for that party to conduct its business unmolested. In exchange, the court held that the plaintiff owes a corresponding duty to society not to be greedy or selfish in fixing its prices (OLG Bremen, *NJW* 1963, 1455; Dawson 1983:1094). Clearly, the court here is no longer involved in gap-filling so as to better reflect the parties' intent. Instead, a second rationale for the judicial rewriting of contracts has emerged, ie the need to enforce the social function of contract, even if it means that contract escapes private autonomy to some extent.

[549] Medicus (1993:70) gives a further explanation for the continued attractiveness of Para 242 *BGB*. A new function for Para 242 has been triggered by the new (post-World War Two) German constitution. Specifically, Para 242 has become a much preferred vehicle for the introduction of the values of the *Grundgesetz* in the civil code.[44] A recent example is the 1993 decision of the Federal Constitutional Court (*B VerfG*) which starts from the premise that the courts must respect the constitutional guarantee of private autonomy whenever they apply such general clauses as Para 242 *BGB*. According to the Constitutional Court this duty implies an obligation for the court to scrutinise the contents of "contracts that carry an unusually heavy burden for one of the parties and that are the result of a structural bargaining inequality" (*"Verträgen die einen der beiden Vertragspartner ungewöhnlich stark belasten und das Ergebnis strukturell ungleicher Verhandlungsstärke sind"*).[45]

---

44   An English translation of the German Constitution can be found in Currie 1994.

45   *B VerfG* 19 October 1993, (1994) 89 *Entscheidungen des B VerfG*, 214, no 18, with a critical note by K Adomeit in (1994) *NJW* 2467. For an earlier, critical review of the alleged social function of contract law in Germany, see Schmidt, 1976:381.

[550] In 1976 special legislation was adopted to protect consumers that are party to standard contracts. The new Act on Standard Contract Terms (*Gesetz zur Regelung des Rechts der Allgemeinen Geschäftsbedingungen – AGB Gesetz)* of 9 December 1976 has been in force since 1 April 1977. In essence, the Act entails a codification of pre-existing case law. This is true especially as regards the control of the contents of standard terms in accordance with the *Treu und Glauben* requirement of the *BGB* (von Marschall 1979:287; von Caemmerer 1975-1977:244).[46]

[551] The idea that contracts perform a social function which places limits on the private autonomy of the parties is by no means confined to Germany. In Belgium recent case law shows a rapid increase in importance of the good faith principle which is no longer limited to constituting a device for the interpretation of contracts but has become, effectively, a prescriptive norm (De Bondt, Bocken, Geers and Van Heuverswyn 1994:146). A turning point in this regard was a 1983 decision by the Belgian *Cour de Cassation* (Cass, 19 September 1983, *RW*, 1983-84, 1982). Similarly, the concept of good faith permeates all branches of the new Dutch law of obligations and contract (Hartkamp and Tillema 1994:48). Even more significant developments have taken place at the supranational level of the EC in recent years. These are discussed next.

5.5 Consumer Protection at the Level of the European Community

(a) Introduction

[552] One of the earliest manifestations of an interest by the EC in consumer protection is a declaration by Sicco Mansholt in 1961. The then Vice-President of the EC observed that the general interests of consumers were not represented to the same extent as those of producers in the common market (Kendall 1994:7 Lewis 1992:139). In 1969 a special consumer affairs unit was set up within the Directorate General for Competition. This forerunner of DG XI on the Environment, Consumer Affairs and Nuclear Safety had as its task the examination of all legislative proposals for their impact on consumers. At their Paris Summit of October 1972 the Heads of State/Government openly acknowledged that social

---

46   According to one Dutch commentator, the legislature sought to build upon earlier judicial activism in that it was felt that the political climate was ripe for a fuller and more direct law on consumer protection: Molenberg 1995:348-349.

integration was an important goal in its own right and thus it was no longer to be simply the by-product of any initiatives in the economic domain. The Paris Summit expressly referred to consumer protection and the EC Commission was asked to formulate a comprehensive social programme including measures in the consumer area. The first consumer protection and information programme was adopted by the Council of Ministers in 1975. This programme set out five basic consumer rights: protection of health and safety; protection of economic interests; the right of redress, information and education; and the right of representation. The main focus of the discussion below is on the so-called right to the protection of economic interests, in particular the protection against abusive practices like misleading advertising and unfair contract terms. The regulation of contracts negotiated away from business premises and distance selling are also touched upon. Consumer safety, especially the liability of manufacturers for defective products, is discussed in Chapter 6.[47]

[553] The 1975 programme was followed by two further consumer programmes in the 1980s. These programmes in turn led to the adoption of two three-year action plans for the periods of 1990-1993 and 1993-1995, respectively. The first action plan included a limited number of legislative measures aimed at harmonising national law. Interestingly, it also stated that the effective management of consumer policy must be achieved at individual member state level (Kendall 1994:10). EC legislation adopted during the first action plan includes Directive 90/88/EEC amending Directive 87/102/EEC concerning consumer credit (*OJ* 1990 L61), Directive 90/314/EEC on package travel, package holidays and package tours (*OJ* 1990 L158), Directives 90/496/EEC, 91/72/EEC, 91/238/EEC and 92/11/EEC on the labelling and presentation of foodstuffs intended for the final consumer (*OJ* 1992 L276, *OJ* 1991 L 42, *OJ* 1991 L 107 and *OJ* 1992 L 65), Directive 92/59/EEC on general product safety (*OJ* 1992 L 228); Directive 93/13/EEC on unfair terms in consumer contracts (*OJ* 1993 L 95).

[554] Lane (1993:959) argues that, the above achievements notwithstanding, consumer protection has never been a high priority of the Community. It was only given formal recognition in the EC Treaty through the insertion of Art 100A by the SEA. According to Art 100A EC the Commission must take as a base a high level of consumer protection when proposing internal market legislation. Before the SEA, all initiatives had to

---

47   See Reich (1992:23) for a general overview of the EC approach to the protection of the consumers' economic interests.

be taken, from the 1975 consumer policy programme onwards, on the basis of general provisions in the Treaty, such as Art 2 (improvement of living conditions), Art 100 (functioning of the common market) and Art 235 (subsidiary provision). However, the main advantage of the SEA, ie its provision for a qualified majority voting system, remained limited to issues of internal market completion rather than consumer protection as such (Goyens 1992:74-75). Since Maastricht, consumer protection has been raised to the level of a full Community policy.[48] It would appear that the fear for a negative impact of the subsidiarity clause in the TEU on the Community's consumer protection policy has thus far been unfounded (Kendall 1994:25).

(b) Community legislation

(i) Advertising

[555] The first Community legislation on misleading advertising dates from 1984 (Directive 84/450/EEC, *OJ* 1984 L 250/17). It was the direct, but much delayed, result of the first consumer programme adopted in 1975 (Kendall 1994:163). The need for Community intervention in this area arose out of an awareness that advertising, in an internal market, reaches beyond national borders and differing (national) rules pertaining to misleading advertising may hinder intra-Community trade (Lewis 1992:157). As it can be inferred from its Long Title, the Directive relates to the approximation of the laws, regulations and administrative provisions of the member states concerning misleading advertising. In essence, the Directive aims at protecting the general public, including consumers, from misleading advertising and its negative consequences. The member states are required to ensure that effective means exist for the control of misleading advertising as well as opportunities for redress. Article 3 provides a definition of what can constitute misleading advertising. Specifically, account must be taken of all features of the advertising, including the information it contains regarding the characteristics of the goods or services being advertised (eg their nature, composition, method or date of manufacture), the price of the goods or services (which may include the manner in which the price is calculated), and the nature, attributes and rights of the advertiser (eg identity, assets, qualifications). The Directive does not prohibit the voluntary control of misleading advertising by self-regulatory bodies. Also, the member states are free to adopt (or retain) more stringent provisions with a view of consumer protection. In 1991 the

---

48   This is the combined effect of Arts 3S and 129a TEU.

Commission proposed to extend the application of the Directive to comparative advertising (*OJ* 1991 C 180/14). Under the proposal comparative advertising would be permitted, provided it does not mislead consumers or discredit or denigrate competitors. Following amendments to the original proposal in 1994 a common position was reached in the Council of Ministers on 19 March 1996 (*OJ* 1996 C 219/14).

[556] Separate Directives regulate the advertising of foods, (Directive 79/112/EEC, *OJ* 1979 L 33/1) medicines (Directive 92/28/EEC, *OJ* 1992 L 113), but not tobacco products.[49] Advertising and sponsorship on television comes within the scope of Directive 89/552/EEC (*OJ* 1989 L 298). This so-called Broadcasting Directive came into force in October 1991. It requires that commercials are clearly advertised as such. They must be kept separate from other parts of the programmes by visual means or recognisable sounds. The objective is to remove subliminal or surreptitious advertising: it must be obvious that an advertisement is just that (Kendall 1994:165). A related requirement is that commercials may only be shown between programmes or at natural intervals during programmes. Works such as feature films or films made for television may be interrupted once for each completed period of 45 minutes. News and current affairs programmes, documentaries, religious programmes and children programmes may not include an advertisement break if their duration is less than 30 minutes. Television advertising must not exceed 15% of the daily transmission time, but this may be increased to 20% under certain circumstances. Typically, member states are empowered to set stricter standards should they wish to do so.

(ii) Doorstep and distance selling

[557] The Doorstep Selling Directive (Directive 85/577/EEC, *OJ* 1985 L 372) aims to protect the consumer in respect of contracts negotiated away from business premises. As it is stressed in the preamble to the Directive the main difference between doorstep sales and in-store sales lies in that the former tend to be initiated by the trader in a situation where the consumer is generally unable to compare the quality and price of the goods or services on offer. According to Art 5 of the Directive consumers have the right to cancel contracts for the provision of goods or services within a

---

49   The original proposal for a Directive to restrict the advertising of tobacco products dates from the late 1980s. The original proposal (*OJ* 1989 C124) has been amended repeatedly. Apparently, the issue is an emotive one: Kendall 1994:173.

period of one week.[50] The cooling-off period commences upon receipt by the consumer of a notice issued by the trader informing the consumer of this right of cancellation. Consumers cannot waive their rights (Art 7). Member states are free to adopt more favourable consumer protection laws.[51]

[558] The Doorstep Selling Directive was the first to employ the technique of a compulsory cooling-off period. The technique has proved successful in that it provides consumers with some protection in situations in which "surprise is the essence of the act of the vendor" (Lewis 1992:166). The same technique is also used in the proposed regulation of distance selling.[52] According to Kendall (1994:99), the proposal is linked to the internal market of the European Community in which the telephone, fax machine, mail, television and computer are increasingly important vehicles in the formation of contract for the supply of goods and services. In a unified economic market consumers can make purchases across national boundaries, but they may experience vastly differing degrees of protection from national legislation. There are problems with, inter alia, lack of information, terms of delivery, and length of the cooling-off period (if available at all: Kendall 1994:99). In 1992 the Commission issued a Recommendation on codes of practice for the protection of consumers in respect of contracts negotiated at a distance (Recommendation 92/295/EEC of 7 April 1992, *OJ* 1992 L156/21). This was followed by a proposal for a Directive in that same year (*OJ* 1992 C156/142). The Council adopted a common position on 29 June 1995 (*OJ* 1995 C288/1).[53]

(iii) Unfair contract terms

[559] The Directive on unfair terms in consumer contracts was adopted on 5 April 1993 (Directive 93/13/EEC, *OJ* 1993 L95/29). It has been heralded as a most important piece of Community legislation because of its far-reaching effect upon the national law of contract. Specifically, it makes a core element of the private law of the member states a matter of EC law

---

50 The Directive does not apply to all contracts for the provision of goods or services. Important exemptions are, for instance, contracts for the construction, sale or rental of real estate, insurance contracts and contracts for securities: see Art 3.2 of the Directive.

51 Article 8. Consumers are defined in Art 2 as natural persons who act for purposes which can be regarded as outside their trade or profession.

52 See also the 1992 proposal of Directive on timesharing.

53 The adoption of the Directive itself is imminent: on 7 February 1996 the Commission issued its opinion on the amendments by the Parliament to the Council's common position: COM (96) 37.

and, thus, a matter for the final interpretation by the European Court of Justice (Lewis 1992:166; Lewis in Legrand 1992:283-285).

[560] The gestation of the 1993 Directive was not entirely uneventful. As early as 1984 the Commission published a consultation paper on "Unfair Terms in Contracts concluded with Consumers".[54] The paper was circulated widely and it triggered intensive opposition from business organisations throughout the Community because of its allegedly overprotective nature (Lockett and Egan 1995:14). Having considered the issue, the European Parliament accepted the need for increased consumer protection. It was even suggested at one stage that any EC legislation to curb the imposition of unfair contract terms be made applicable to not only consumers but more generally so as to cover other instances of inequality in bargaining strength between the parties as well. However, this suggestion did not survive in the final text of the Directive. Even so, in mid-1986 the Council adopted a Resolution calling for proposals under the "New Impetus for Consumer Policy". Attempts at using the SEA to ensure a speedy enactment of the draft Directive failed, in part because of doubts by the United Kingdom as to whether the single market, in itself, was sufficient to justify the proposed EC legislation. Significantly, the UK's Department of Trade and Industry also expressed misgivings due to the fact that the proposed legislation was substantially broader than existing UK legislation (Lockett and Egan 1995:14). The Directive on Unfair Terms in Consumer Contracts was adopted on 5 April 1993 (Directive 93/13/EEC, *OJ* 1993 L95/29) by a qualified majority vote pursuant Art 100A EC. It required the member states to comply with the new EC law before 1 January 1995. All contracts concluded from that date onwards are affected.[55]

[561] *Ratione personae* the Directive applies to contracts with consumers as one of the parties. Consumers are defined in terms that are identical to those of the doorstep selling Directive.[56] They are natural persons who, in contracts concluded with a seller or supplier, act for purposes which are outside their trade, business or profession. In a discussion of the initial proposal of Directive this limitation of the Directive's applicability to so-called consumer contracts only has been criticised as a strict distinction between consumer contracts and other types of contracts risks introducing

---

54   Technically, the Commission document took the form of a Communication to the Council: Com (84) 55 final, in *EC Bull*, Supp 1/84.

55   For an overall picture of the Directive, see Hondius 1994:34.

56   See [557] above.

a division into the law of contract which was hitherto unknown in the member states and which is reminiscent of the socialist legal systems (Brandner and Ulmer 1991:648). Clearly the drafters of the final text of Directive decided not to take this criticism on board. On the other hand, *ratione materiae* the Directive differs from the first proposal of 1990 in that individually negotiated contract terms have been excluded from its application. The Directive thus heeds earlier criticism of unnecessarily restricting the freedom of contract if the EC law would have applied not only to standard contracts but to all types of consumer contracts, regardless of whether they are widespread and regardless of the circumstances of their conclusion.[57] According to Art 3.2 of the Directive a contract term should always be regarded as not individually negotiated where it has been drafted in advance, and the consumer has therefore not been able to influence the substance of the term – particularly in the context of a pre-formulated standard contract. The burden of proof is on the seller or supplier who claims that a standard term has in fact been negotiated individually.

[562] The preamble of the Directive instructs the member states to ensure that unfair terms are not used in consumer contracts. If such terms are used nevertheless, they are said not to bind the consumer. A term is regarded as unfair if, contrary to the requirement of good faith, it causes a significant imbalance in the parties' rights and obligations under the contract, to the detriment of the consumer (Art 3.1 Directive). Article 4 of the Directive specifies that the unfairness of a contract term must be assessed broadly. Account must be taken of the nature of the goods or services for which the contract was concluded. Also, reference must be made to all the circumstances pertinent to the conclusion of the contract. Finally, the other terms of the contract and even other contracts on which the consumer contract depends, must equally be taken into account. An Annex to the Directive contains a "gray" list of terms which may be regarded as unfair. The list is purely indicative and non-exhaustive. The ultimate responsibility for drawing up the actual list of prohibited unfair contract terms rests with the member states (Art 6.1 Directive).

[563] The member states of the EC retain the discretion to implement the Directive by means of national legislation which treats terms that fall within the grey list of the Annex as fair. Of overriding importance,

---

57 "[T]he consequence would be that in the field of consumer contracts the results of contractual negotiations would to a great extent be replaced by pre-established statutory or judicial provisions. The economic functions of the freedom of contract on an individual and general level would thus be considerably restricted": Brander and Ulmer 1991:652.

however, remains the fairness test of the Directive itself (Lockett and Egan 1995:33). As part of the test of (un)fairness the Directive uses the concept of good faith. This need not surprise anyone since the Directive is seemingly based on the German Standard Contracts Act of 1976.[58] Good faith undoubtedly is a familiar concept in civil law systems generally. But differences in approach between countries mean that it may be difficult to interpret the good faith requirement of the Directive by simple reference to national law alone. Some guidance is offered in the preamble of the Directive where it is stipulated that particular regard must be had to the bargaining strength of the parties. Also relevant in making an assessment of good faith is whether the consumer had an inducement to agree to the potentially unfair term(s) as well as whether the goods or services are sold or supplied to the special order of the consumer. On the other hand, the preamble considers that the requirement of good faith may be satisfied where the seller or supplier deals "fairly and equitably" with the other party whose "legitimate" interests the seller or supplier has to take into account. As a practical matter, the most crucial consideration in applying the fairness test is whether the contractual term in issue causes a significant imbalance in the parties' rights and obligations (Lockett and Egan 1995:23). Not surprisingly, perhaps, the expression "significant imbalance" has not been defined in the Directive. However, when the text of the Directive is compared to the initial draft of 1990, it would appear that the emphasis is on the rights and duties of the parties at the formation and not at the performance stage of the contract.[59]

[564] Important exclusions from the scope of the 1993 Directive are, inter alia, employment contracts and – partially at least – insurance contracts. The former category of contract has expressly been listed in the preamble. The partial exclusion of insurance contracts derives from the fact that Art 4.2 of the Directive excludes terms describing the subject matter of the contract and/or the quality/price ratio of the goods supplied or services rendered from the (un)fairness test. Thus, terms which define and circumscribe the insured risk or the insurer's liability escape scrutiny.[60]

---

58 See [550] above; Dean 1993:584. An amendment to the 1976 Act, further implementing the Directive, came into effect on 25 July 1996.

59 According to the 1990 draft Directive a term would also be unfair if it causes the performance of the contract to be unduly detrimental to the consumer: Brandner and Ulmer 1991:658.

60 Lockett and Egan 1995:20-21. Note, however, that because of the requirement of intelligibility – ie written contract terms must be drafted in plain English – unclear or ambiguous terms are interpreted in favour of the consumer: Article 5 of the Directive.

[565] The 1993 Directive on unfair contracts terms was implemented in France by Act no 95-96 of 1 February 1995.[61] Title I of the Act is entitled *Clauses abusive et présentation des contrats*. An assessment by the distinguished Professor Ghestin concludes that the net result, in terms of additional consumer protection, is limited (Ghestin and Marchessaux-Van Melle 1995:275, no 3854). Clearly, the 1995 Act does not aim to remove any of the – relatively high – consumer protection devices that were in place already.[62] An example of improved consumer protection is the express statutory provision that ambiguous contract terms must be interpreted in favour of the consumer or, more generally, in favour of the non-professional party (New Art L133-2 *Code de la consommation)*. Previously, the unwritten principle of *contra proferentem* was sometimes invoked by the French courts to produce the same effect (Cass civ, I, 4 June 1985, *Bull civ*, I, no 175; Mestre 1986:49).

References

Angelo, AH, and Ellinger, EP, "Unconscionable Contracts: A Comparative study of the Approaches in England, France, Germany, and the United States", (1992) 14 *Loyola of Los Angeles International and Comparative Law Journal* 455.

Brandner, HE, and Ulmer, P, "The Community Directive on Unfair Terms in Consumer Contracts: Some Critical Remarks on the Proposal submitted by the EC Commission", (1991) 28 *Common Market Law Review* 647.

Brox, H, 1990, *Allgemeines Schuldrecht*, 18th ed, Verlag CH Beck, München.

Calais-Auloy, J, "L'influence du droit de la consommation sur le droit civil des contrats", (1994) *Revue trimestrielle de droit civil* 239.

Currie, DP, 1994, *The Constitution of the Federal Republic of Germany*, University of Chicago Press, Chicago and London.

Dawson, JP, "Judicial Revision of Frustrated Contracts: Germany", (1983) 63 *Boston University Law Review* 1039.

Dawson, JP, "Unconscionable Coercion: The German Version", (1976) 89 *Harvard law Review* 1041.

Dawson, JP, "Effects of Inflation on Private Contracts, Germany 1914-1924", (1934) 33 *Michigan Law Review* 171.

Dean, M, "Unfair Contract terms: The European Approach", (1993) 56 *Modern Law Review* 581.

---

61 *JO* 2 February 1995, 1755. The text of the Act has been reproduced in (1995) 4 *Actualité législative Dalloz* 119.

62 Mestre (1995:351 at 361) complains that some judges got carried away a bit in their pursuit of consumer protection under the pre-1995 Act: *"On le voit, certains juges n'hésitent pas à faire de la lutte contre les clauses abusives un véritable sport, et peuvent même à certains égards sembler un peu trop emportés par leur élan!."* For a general discussion, see Calais-Auloy 1994:239.

de Bondt, W, Bocken, H, Geers, I, van Heuverswyn, C, "*Kroniek van het Belgisch privaatrecht* 1991-1992", (1994) 11 *Nederlands Tijdschrift voor Burgerlijk Recht* 146.

Dickson, B, 1994, *Introduction to French Law*. Chapter 8: Contract Law, Pitman Publishing, London.

Diesselhorst, M, Die Geschäftsgrundlage in der neueren Rechtsentwicklung, in Immenga, U, (ed), 1980, *Rechtswissenschaft und Rechtsentwicklung,* Verlag Otto Schwartz & Co, Göttingen.

Esser, J, and Schmidt, E, 1976, *Schuldrecht. Allgemeiner Teil. I*, 5th ed, CF Müller Verlag, Heidelberg.

Foster, N, 1993, *German Law and Legal System*, Blackstone Press, London.

Freriks, D, "Onderzoeks-en mededelingsverplichting in het contractenrecht", (1992) 29 *Tijdschrift voor Privaatrecht* 1187.

Gallo, P, "Unjust Enrichment: A Comparative Analysis", (1992) 40 *American Journal of Comparative Law* 431.

Ghestin, J, and Marchessaux-van Melle, I, "L'Application en France de la directive visant à éliminer les clauses abusives après l'adoption de la loi no 95-96 du I février 1995", (1995) 25 *La Semaine juridique* 275.

Ghestin, J, and Goubeaux, G, 1994, *Traité de droit civil. Introduction générale*, 4th ed, LGDJ.

Ghestin, J, 1993, *Traité de droit civil. Les obligations: La formation du contrat*, 3rd ed, LGDJ, Paris.

Goyens, M, "Consumer Protection in a Single European Market: What Challenge for the EC Agenda?", (1992) 29 *Common Market Law Review* 71.

Hartkamp, AS, and Tillema, MMM, 1994, "Netherlands", in Herbots, J, (ed), "Contracts", in Blanpain, R (gen ed), *International Encyclopaedia of Laws*, Kluwer, The Hague.

Hondius, E, 1994, "EC Directive on Unfair terms in Consumer Contracts: Towards a European Law of Contract", (1994) 7 *Journal of Contract Law* 34.

Juglart, "L'obligation de renseignement dans les contrats", (1945) *Revue trimestrielle de droit civil* 1.

Kendall, V, 1994, *EC Consumer Law*, Chancery Law Publishing, London.

Lane, R, "New Community Competences under the Maastricht Treaty", (1993) 30 *Common Market Law Review* 939.

Legrand, P, Jr, "Information in Formation of Contracts: A Civilian Perspective", (1991) 19 *Canadian Business Law Journal* 318.

Legrand, P, Jr, "Judicial Revision of Contracts in French Law: A Case-Study", (1988) 62 *Tulane Law Review* 963.

Lewis, X, "L'européanisation du common law", in Legrand, P, (ed), 1992, *Common law, d'un siècle l'autre*, Blais, Montréal.

Lewis, X, "The Protection of Consumers in European Community Law", (1992) 12 *Yearbook of European Law* 139.

Litvinoff, S, "Still Another Look at Cause", (1987) 48 *Louisiana Law Review* 3.

Lockett, N, and Egan, M, 1995, *Unfair Terms in Consumer Agreements*, Wiley & Sons, Chichester.

Malinvaud, P, "De l'erreur sur la substance", (1972), *Recueil Dalloz Sirey*, Chronique, 215.

Markesinis, BS, "Cause and Consideration: A Study in Parallel", (1978) 37 *Cambridge Law Journal* 53.

Marsh, PDV, 1994, *Comparative Contract Law, England, France, Germany*, Gower, Aldershot.

Medicus, D, 1993, *Schuldrecht I. Allgemeiner Teil,* 7th ed, Verlag CH Beck, München.

Mestre, J, "Jurisprudence française en matière de droit civil. Obligations en général", (1995) 94 *Revue trimestrielle de droit civil* 351.

Mestre, J, 1986, "L'évolution du contrat en droit privé français", in Journées R Savatier, *L'évolution contemporaine du droit des contrats*, PUF, Paris.

Mirmina, SA, "A Comparative survey of Culpa in Contrahendo, focussing on its Origins in Roman, German, and French Law as well as its Application in American Law", (1992) *Connecticut Journal of International Law* 77.

Molenberg, LJH, 1995, *Het collectief actierecht voor consumentenor-ganisaties op het terrein van de algemene voorwaarden*, Gouda Quint, Arnhem.

Nicholas, B, 1992, *The French Law of Contract*, 2nd ed, Clarendon Press, Oxford.

Reich, N, "Protection of Consumers' Economic Interests by the EC", (1992) 14 *Sydney Law Review* 23.

Schlechtriem, P, 1994, *Schuldrecht.Allgemeiner Teil*, 2nd ed, JCB, Tübingen.

Schmidt, J, "Ein soziales Obligationsmodell im Schuldrecht? Gedanken zur Neuauflage des Esserschen Lehrbuches", (1976) 176 *Archiv für die civilistische Praxis* 381.

Schmidt-Szalewski, J, 1995, "France", in Hebots, J, (ed), Contracts. Volume I, in Blanpain, R, (gen ed), *International Encyclopaedia of Laws*, Kluwer, The Hague.

Taisch, F, "Unconscionability in a Civil Law System: An Overview of Swiss Law", (1992) 14 *Loyola of Los Angeles International and Comparative Law Journal* 529.

Treitel, GH, 1988, *Remedies for Breach of Contract. A Comparative Account*, Clarendon Press, Oxford.

Van Dunné, JM, 1993, *Verbintenissenrecht. Deel I. Contractenrecht*, 2nd ed, Kluwer, Deventer.

Van Gerven, W, 1973, *Beginselen van Belgisch Privaatrecht. Algemeen Deel*, 2nd ed, Standaard, Antwerpen.

von Caemmerer, "Standard Contract Provisions and Standard Form Contracts in German Law", [1975-1977] *Victoria University of Wellington Law Review* 235.

von Marschall, WF, "The New German Law on Standard Contract Terms", (1979) *LLoyds Maritime and Commercial Law Quarterly* 278.

von Mehren, AT, 1992, "The Formation of Contracts". Chapter 9 of Volume VII on Contracts in General, *International Encyclopaedia of Comparative Law*, JCB Mohr, Tübingen, and Martinus Nijhoff, Dordrecht.

Weiss, M, 1994, "Germany", in Blanpain, R *International Encyclopaedia of Labour Law and Industrial Relations*, Kluwer, Deventer.

Zimmermann, R, "Unjustified Enrichment: The Modern Civilian Approach", (1995) 15 *Oxford Journal of Legal Studies* 403.

Zimmermann, R, 1990, *The Law of Obligations. Roman Foundations of the Civilian Tradition*, Juta & Co, Cape Town.

Zweigert, K, and Kötz, H, 1987, *An Introduction to Comparative Law*, Vol 2, Clarendon Press, Oxford.

Chapter 6

The Law of Tort

6.1 Introduction

[601] The essence of the French law of tort is captured in five short provisions of the *Code civil*. Together Arts 1382-1386 *Code civil* constitute a perfect example of what civil codes have come to represent, ie a comprehensive and compact but therefore also rather sweeping statement of the law. The tort provisions of the *Code civil* have stood the test of time extremely well.[1] Only two major parliamentary updates have been required in the past two centuries. A first legislative update took place towards the turn of the 19th century, involving the adoption of special legislation to cover industrial accidents.[2] Some hundred years later special legislation was enacted to deal with traffic accidents.[3] Particularly interesting from a common law point of view is that this legislation, adopted to "update" the Code, was by no means revolutionary in that it did not really break any new ground. Rather, both in 1898 and in 1985 the legislature effectively built upon a judicially initiated – and backed by *la doctrine* – shift away from a purely fault based system of tort liability. The discussion of the French law of tort in this chapter focuses on the manner in which the courts have adopted a gradual, incremental approach to this particular instance of judicial law making. Developments in the German law of tort provide an intriguing contrast in this regard. Clearly, case law is also important in explaining the German state of affairs as regards tort law. But traditionally a greater reluctance has existed in Germany to use the courts in moving away from the fault-based approach to tort in the *BGB*.

---

1   For some reflections on the reasons for the persistence in contemporary law of this pattern of a wide standard of liability in the civil law as compared to a "pigeonhole" system of nominate torts in the common law, see Rudden 1991-92:105.

2   Initially, the workmen's compensation legislation of 1898 applied to work accidents (*accidents du travail*) in certain industries only. Gradually, its scope of application has been extended to cover all work-related accidents including certain types of professional illness.

3   The Act 85-677 of 5 July 1985, not unlike the workmen's compensation legislation of 1898, aims at improving the situation of the victim.

This tradition of reliance on parliamentary initiatives at establishing selective regimes of strict or quasi-strict liability predates the 1896 Code.[4]

[602] Following an analysis of tort law in general, this chapter pays special attention to the issue of product liability. Product liability is a subject which has increased in importance significantly during the latter half of the 20th century. This area of law is permeated with developments at the level of the European Community. It is equally clear, however, that these supranational developments took place against a backdrop of consumer protection initiatives in the member states' domestic laws. The dividing line between contract and tort as the legal basis for the regulation of product liability is not a clear-cut one in this regard.

6.2 Judicial Creativity and the Role of Fault in French Tort Law

(a) Tort law in the 1804 *Code civil*

[603] The basic rule (*règle générale*) of French tort law is contained in Art 1382 *Code civil*. It is stated there, in terms that are undeniably straightforward, that anyone who causes harm to someone else because of the fault (*faute*) of the former is liable to pay compensation. The preparatory works of the *Code civil* confirm that fault is the primary basis of the French law of tort. The term "fault" is not defined in the Code itself. However, the follow-on provision of Art 1383 makes clear that this concept is sufficiently broad to cover instances of negligence (*négligence* or *imprudence*) as well as intent.[5] Liability attaches in the first instance to the person inflicting the harm. But Art 1384(1) introduces also various instances of vicarious liability. Specifically, Art 1384 (1) *Code civil* stipulates that one is liable not only for injury caused by one's own act, but also for injury caused by the act of persons or things under one's guard ("*des personnes dont on doit répondre ou des choses que l'on a sous sa garde*"). The actual categories of personnes "*dont on doit répondre*" have been specified in Art 1384 itself. Included in the list are the liability of parents for their children, of employers for their employees, and of

---

4   For a list of French legislation introducing no-fault liability outside the areas of worker compensation and traffic accidents, see Roland and Boyen 1988:21-25.

5   Technically, French tort law has adopted Art 1382 as the legal basis for damage caused with intent (*responsabilité délictuelle*), whereas Art 1383 covers instances of harm that has been inflicted unintentionally (*responsabilité quasi délictuelle*).

teachers for their pupils. To prevent Art 1384 from becoming too long and therefore aesthetically less appealing, the drafters of the Code opted for a specification of the types of things (*choses*) alluded to in Art 1384(1) in the separate provisions of Arts 1385 and 1386. Accordingly, Art 1385 *Code civil* lists the liability in tort of guardians of animals that cause havoc and Art 1386 does the same with respect to guardians of collapsing buildings. The relative specificity of Arts 1385 and 1386 is for reasons that are purely historical. At the time of drafting of the *Code civil*, falling debris from buildings in a state of poor repair or construction and animals – the latter were the main means of transport of persons as well as goods – constituted two major causes of injury without it always being easy for the victim to establish fault. Articles 1385 and 1386 effectively reflect an early concern for the plaintiff in tort actions. The manner in which both provisions have been phrased, however, does not make it entirely clear how the burden of proof is to be shared between the parties. Under one interpretation it remains for the plaintiff to show a prima facie case of liability. Alternatively, Arts 1385 and 1386 arguably establish a presumption of liability that is to be rebutted by the defendant. Unfortunately for the victim, the only explicit provision for a (rebuttable) presumption of liability is Art 1384(5) as regards parents and teachers.

(b) Judicial evolution towards a dual basis for tort liability

(i) The case of Montagnier

[604] Under the traditional approach to tort liability in the *Code civil* fault constituted the sole legal basis for liability. This approach was said to be morally justified in that it was considered improper to condemn the "innocent" to repair damage caused without that person's fault.[6] Thus, when a mule – owned and under the guard of the defendant – dislodged several stones of a wall, thereby hitting the plaintiff who was seated at the base of the wall, no one showed great surprise when the trial court rejected a claim of liability on the basis of Art 1385 *Code civil*. Conventional wisdom was indeed that Art 1385 had to be interpreted by reference to Arts 1382 (intentional infliction of harm) and 1383 (negligence). On the facts of the case the defendant had taken care at all material times. Rather, what had happened was that the mule had unexpectedly bucked, as mules tend to do from time to time for no apparent reason. Even so, the *Cour de*

---

6   Ripert, *La règle morale dans les obligations civiles*, no 121; Mazeaud and De Juglart, *Leçons de droit civil*, Part II, Vol 1, no 375 at 343; Rodière in Beudant, *La responsabilité civile*, no 1405 (all authors as cited in Roland and Boyer 1988:19).

Cassation in *Montagnier*[7] ignored four of its previous decisions to the contrary in quashing (*casser*) the decision of the lower court. It effectively announced a change in policy by ruling that Art 1385 establishes a presumption of fault that can only be rebutted by proof of an unforeseeable event (*cas fortuit*) or of a fault committed by the injured party.

[605] No careful reading of the *Montagnier* (announcement of) decision provides an explanation for this major shift in policy by the highest French court. More elaborate, and informative, is the report of the reporting judge. According to this report the plaintiff's argument was based on the premise that statutory provisions must be read in such a way as to make sense (Tomlinson 1988:1316ff). Specifically, it was argued that there would have been no point in having Art 1385 on the statute books if all that that provision achieves is to repeat what Arts 1382 and 1383 already hold. Therefore, if Arts 1382 and 1383 establish fault as the basis for tort liability, it necessarily follows – so ran the plaintiff's argument – that Art 1385 must mean something different. Allegedly, the minimal effect of Art 1385 was to shift the burden of proof to the defendant. However, there could be no doubt that the guardian of the animal had exercised due care. Therefore, in order for the claim to be successful, the plaintiff's argument had to be taken one step further. The plaintiff thus argued – successfully – that Art 1385 introduces a presumption of liability that is rebuttable under the strictest conditions only.

[606] The above submission by the plaintiff is less far fetched than it may seem. Drawing upon previous decisions of trial judges as well as scholarly writings the plaintiff displayed both a reasoning *a contrario* and a reasoning by analogy. The former type of reasoning centred around Art 1384(5), whereas the latter was based on Art 1733 *Code civil*. First, counsel for the plaintiff drew attention to the fact that Art 1384(5) exonerates parents and teachers who show due care but it does not expressly do the same with respect to employers. Previous case law was invoked where it had been accepted that, since they are not mentioned in Art 1384(5), employers cannot avoid liability by showing proper care had been exercised. Expanding this argument *a contrario*, the plaintiff in *Montagnier* submitted that, since guardians of animals do not feature in Art 1384(5) either, they can not exonerate themselves by showing due care. Secondly, according to Art 1733 *Code civil* tenants are liable for damage caused by fire unless they can show that the fire took place

---

7   Cass civ, 27 October 1885 and reproduced – in English translation – in Tomlinson 1988:1365.

without their fault. Even though Art 1733 concerns an instance of contractual liability rather than liability in tort, several learned writers had argued that the same legal regime ought to apply to guardians of animals. Some lower courts had already accepted this argument in the past. The victorious plaintiff brought all of the above to the attention of the *Cour de Cassation* and concluded with a general plea for "justice" to be done.

[607] The significance of *Montagnier* lies in the fact that it cut the link between Art 1385 and Arts 1382-1383 *Code civil*. As discussed earlier, the existence of such link originally had been accepted throughout most of the 19th century. Because of the (formal) absence of a doctrine of binding precedent in the civil law, the practical relevance of the decision in *Montagnier* could only become apparent later. But subsequent decisions of the *Cour de Cassation* confirmed the stance taken in 1885. Moreover, legal scholars commented approvingly, no doubt in part because they could not fail to see the attractions of moving away from an exclusive reliance on subjective fault towards a system of objective risk creation.[8] The theory or doctrine of objective risk creation had the potential of being applied profitably in an industrial context including instances of motor car accidents. More generally, today's era of consumer protection and product liability makes very plain the limits of a system of liability based on subjective fault alone.

[608] In principle, civil law courts do not make law. Thus a statutory basis for this new theory of risk allocation had to be found. Because of its express reference to animals, Art 1385 *Code civil* could only provide a rather narrow basis. Similarly, the proper scope of application of Art 1386 comprises – on the face of its text – buildings and not, for example, pieces of industrial equipment or motor cars. The courts therefore "found" a more suitable legal foundation in Art 1384(1). Only, a succession of cases was needed to reach this result. They are discussed next.

(ii) The case of Jand'heur

[609] It will be recalled that the drafters of the *Code civil* intended Art 1384(1) to be purely a transitional provision.[9] The case of *Jand'heur* (Cass civ, 21 February 1927, *D*, 1927, I, 97; Cass (*chambres réunies*), 13 February 1930, *D*, I, 57) has been identified as the main decision of the

---

8   Roland and Boyer (1988:29) note that one or other form of risk doctrine has been advocated from the late 19th century onwards with Saleilles as one of its main promoters.

9   See [603] above.

Cour de Cassation to bring about a "career turn" for Art 1384(1) *Code civil* (Tomlinson 1988:1337). A proper understanding of *Jand'heur* requires a brief discussion of two intermediate decisions in *Teffaine* (Cass civ, 16 June 1896, *D*, 1897, I, 433) and *Résine de Bordeaux* (Cass civ, 16 November 1920, *D*, 1920, I, 169) as well. All three cases are analysed below.

[610] In *Jand'heur* a young girl had been run over by a delivery van. On the facts of the case nothing wrong had been found with the mechanics of the truck and the vehicle was in a perfect running order. The *Cour de Cassation* used Art 1384(1) as the legal basis for its decision to impose a presumption of liability upon the defendant which was held to be rebuttable on the most narrow of grounds only. In order to enable an interpretation of Art 1384(1) in this manner, two problems needed to be overcome. Both problems originated in the actual choice of words in the *Code*, including the traditional interpretation of these words in the past. Specifically, a first problem to arise was whether a delivery van can qualify as a "thing" (*chose*) for purposes of Art 1384(1). A second, more problematic issue concerned the meaning of the word "act" (*fait*) in the same Article, because of its repercussions for any attempts at reconciling the new doctrine of assumption of risk with the 1804 system of subjective, fault-based liability. In this regard it became crucially important to know where to draw the line between, on the one hand, the act of human beings or Art 1382-1383 type situations, and, on the other hand, the act of things to be governed by Art 1384(1) *Code civil*. Put differently, the question was where the act of things (*fait de la chose*) starts and, therefore, where the act of persons (*fait de l'homme*) stops. The decision in *Jand'heur* was issued on the supposition that both issues had been settled by two earlier decisions referred to above,[10] ie *Teffaine* and *Résine de Bordeaux*.

[611] The case of *Teffaine* is noteworthy because it cut the link between Art 1384(1) and Arts 1385-1386 *Code civil*. The traditionally narrow interpretation of "things" in Art 1384(1) by reference to, exclusively, animals (Art 1385) or buildings (Art 1386) was discontinued at the end of the 19th century. The facts of the case were that a mechanic on a tug boat was killed when the ship's defective boiler exploded. As in *Montagnier*, the *Cour de Cassation* adopted a seemingly simple syllogistic reasoning involving a *major*, a *minor* and a conclusion. In the *major* part of its decision, the Court bluntly stated that the liability of the guardian of the boiler is governed by Art 1384(1) *Code civil*. In the *minor*, it was held that

---

10   See [609] above; Tomlinson 1988:1322.

the injury had been caused by the "act" of a thing, ie the explosion of the defective boiler. The "inescapable" conclusion reached by the Court was therefore that, as this was not a case of *force majeure* or *cas fortuit*[11] (which would have required, inter alia, the intervention of a force external to the boiler), the defendant could not escape liability by invoking the exoneration provision of *Montagnier*.

[612] *Teffaine* is an important decision, because it stands for the "discovery" of Art 1384(1) by the courts as a provision in its own right. The case confirms that Art 1384(1) no longer needs to be given meaning by reference to Arts 1385-1386. In *Jand'heur* the *Cour de Cassation* would make active use of this new interpretation of the *Code civil*. But there was a second hurdle that remained to be addressed. *Teffaine* involved a defect in the boiler. This reduced its precedental value in that an important category of accidents, eg traffic accidents, tend to occur without the motor vehicle being defective. The interpretation of Art 1384(1) in *Teffaine* was therefore of little use when accidents take place due to driver fatigue, speeding (the heavy-foot syndrome!), etc. A quarter of a century after the decision in *Teffaine* the *Cour de Cassation* resolved that a thing may be said to "act" even though it reveals no internal defect. The relevant decision is the case of *Résine de Bordeaux*.[12]

[613] In *Résine de Bordeaux* vats filled with resin were stored on a train in the French port of Bordeaux. For some unknown reason the resin ignited. The fire spread to neighbouring properties. The *Cour de Cassation* used Art 1384(1) as the legal basis for holding the railway company liable because of the mere fact that it was the guardian of the resin. Put differently, the interpretation of the "act" of a thing was held not to be limited to defective things. At the time the decision was a most controversial one. On the one hand, there had been no internal defect in the resin, and thus the defendant could not be held liable by applying the legal reasoning in *Teffaine*. On the other hand, the Court also noted that this was not a case involving an external force beyond anyone's control either. Had the resin been struck by lightning, for instance, the defendant could have been exonerated. Instead, the cause of the resin igniting was simply

---

11 The concepts of *force majeure* and *cas fortuit* are regularly used interchangeably by the French courts. Both are characterised by the occurrence of an event that normally is unforeseeable, inevitable and external to the thing causing the damage. A succinct discussion of these features can be found in Roland and Boyer 1988:278-283. The exonerating effect of *force majeure* in general has been restated in Cass civ 2, 15 November 1984, *Gaz Pal*, 1985, I, 296, note F Chabas.

12 See [609] above.

unknown. But the practical repercussions of holding the defendant liable were potentially far reaching. As it became clear that, following the decision in *Résine de Bordeaux*, property owners could be held liable for damage to neighbouring properties because of the mere consideration that the fire had started on their land, the French parliament was forced to respond to the public outcry and the pressure from insurance companies who feared for a backlash from property owners whose premiums would have to go up. In the result the Code was amended in order to limit the liability of property owners for fire to instances of fault.

[614] Noteworthy is the manner in which the *Code civil* has been amended in the wake of the *Résine de Bordeaux* case. Article 1384(1) *Code civil* was not repealed. Instead, two new paragraphs were inserted in 1384 which qualify the operation of Art 1384(1) *Code civil*. Thus the statutory amendment has been integrated in the overall tort-liability scheme of the *Code civil*. More importantly, it means that the legal basis for the decisions in both *Résine de Bordeaux* and *Jand'heur* stands.[13]

(iii) The distinction between fait personnel and fait des choses

[615] The decision in *Jand'heur* was considered by the *Cour de Cassation* twice. It will be recalled that the French Supreme Court cannot normally substitute its decision for that of the appellate (trial) court.[14] If an appeal to the *Cour de Cassation* (*pourvoi en cassation*) is successful, the appellate decision is merely quashed and the matter is referred to a different appellate (trial) court for re-consideration. The latter body is not bound by the decision of the *Cour de Cassation*. Thus it is perfectly possible for the second appellate court to confirm the decision of the first appellate court, thereby effectively ignoring any "hints" given by the *Cour de Cassation*. However, in the event, the losing party is free to approach the *Cour de Cassation* a second time. The outcome of this re-consideration by the *Cour de Cassation* is legally binding on the parties in the dispute at hand. And this is also what happened in the *Jand'heur* case. A comparison of the texts of *Jand'heur I* and *Jand'heur II* reveals an intriguing difference in the motivating parts of both decisions. In *Jand'heur I* the strict liability of the guardian of a thing is said to be triggered, inter alia, "by reason of the dangers to which it (ie the thing) may expose others".[15] No such limitation

---

13   The English text of Art 1384 *Code civil*, as amended, is reproduced in the Documentation section of the book.

14   See [409] above.

15   Compare the (English) text of both decisions in Tomlinson 1988:1366-1367.

of strict liability to dangerous things appears in *Jand'heur II*. This omission raises a serious question as to how to distinguish between the act of things and the act of humans. Specifically, the regime of strict liability for the act of things in Art 1384(1) risks swallowing the general rule of tort liability for fault in Arts 1382-1383 *Code civil*.

[616] In *Jand'heur I* the Advocate General argued that a proper basis for limiting the application of Art 1384(1) could be the degree of danger posed by the things under one's guard. In practice, injuries inflicted by non-dangerous things would then continue to require proof of fault. The *Cour de Cassation* did not actually rule that the delivery van which had hit the girl constituted a "dangerous" thing. This question of fact was considered to be dealt with more appropriately by the trial court upon referral. As it turned out, the appellate court in question not only abstained from labelling the vehicle as dangerous, it ignored the decision in *Jand'heur I* entirely. And in *Jand'heur II* a different Advocate General appeared to display far less caution than his colleague. In the result, *Jand'heur II* does not distinguish between dangerous and other goods.[16] The consequences thereof continue to occupy the minds of French scholars to date. Roland and Boyer (1988:120) argue that the current legal regime is impractical because, in the end, things are necessarily operated by human beings. The French courts have grappled with the distinction between *fait de la chose* and *fait de l'homme* by holding that Arts 1382-1383 continue to govern situations where there has been no involvement of a "thing" whatsoever, including situations where any such thing displays no causal link with the injury. A collision between pedestrians is an example.[17]

[617] Even where the thing simply acts as intended, eg someone uses a bat to hit someone else over the head, is this a case of *fait de l'homme* rather than of *fait du bâton* (Roland and Boyer 1988:117). In effect, some commentators argue that a case of *fait de la chose* exists only in situations where the thing which inflicted the harm escaped human control.[18] But such a narrow approach fails to deal with instances where things did not escape control and instead have been operated in a negligent fashion. For instance, does it make sense to insist on liability for (proven) fault if the

---

16   A further difference between the texts of *Jand'heur I* and *Jand'heur II* is that only the former decision uses the qualification of movable with respect to things in Art 1384(1).

17   Paris, 29 March 1962, *JCP* 62, II, 12874, note Esmein; TGI Riom, 1 December 1965, *D*, 1966, 116; Lyon, 21 November 1972, *JCP* 73, IV, 339, as cited in Roland and Boyer 1988:117.

18   *Mazeaud* and *De Juglart*, *Leçons de droit civil* II, Vol 1, no 530 as cited in Roland and Boyer 1988:117.

driver of a car opens the door of the vehicle and accidentally hits a passing cyclist on the basis that the door was within the perfect control of the tortfeasor? The French courts operate on the basis that flexibility is required in drawing the line between *fait personnel* and *fait de la chose*. Thus the *Cour de Cassation* has held in favour of liability on the basis of *fait de la chose* where two motorbike riders pass one another but the elbow of one touches the elbow of the other in the process and this causes one of the riders to fall and die. The *Cour de Cassation* ruled that motor bike and driver constituted one entity (Cass civ, II, 21 December 1962, *D*, 1963, Somm 70; *Gaz Pal*, 1963, 1, 285; note Tunc, *Rev tr dr civ*, 1963. 732). Furthermore, it is established case law (*jurisprudence constante*) that where the damage is caused by a ski attached to the boot of a person skiing, liability is triggered by the *fait de la chose*. Apparently, the courts are open to the suggestion that the use of skis increases the speed of the person skiing which in turn increases the likelihood of serious injury in case of a collision. Any damage inflicted is therefore just as much, if not more, attributable to the ski (*fait de la chose*) as to the person skiing (*fait personnel*). Alternatively, one could argue to the same effect that ski and person are one.[19] By contrast, it has been held that no *fait de la chose* exists where someone slips outdoors in a ski resort on steps covered in ice as this is a situation of "*comportement normal de la chose*" (Cass civ II, 15 March 1978, *D*, 1978, inf rap 406). Similarly, one cannot claim compensation by invoking Art 1384(1) when colliding with a car which has broken down but is parked clearly visibly at the side of the road according to regulation (Cass civ II, 30 June 1971, *D*, 1972, 461, note AD; Cass. civ, II, 11 January 1995, *D*, 1995, inf rap, 39; *JCP*, 1995, éd G, IV, 625; Viney 1995:264, no 3853).

(iv) Contributory negligence and accountability

[618] To escape liability under Art 1384(1), the defendant must be able to point at a *cause étrangère*. The latter notion of "foreign cause" is sufficiently broad to cover instances of *force majeure* or *cas fortuit*, as discussed already.[20] Fault of the victim or of a third party (*fait d'un tiers*) is yet another form of *cause étrangère* which may have an exonerating effect. French case law has come full circle in this regard. At first, the courts tried to "accommodate" fault of the victim by treating it as an

---

19   Roland and Boyer (1988:119) cite the example of Grenoble, 8 June 1966, *JCP* 67, II, 14928, note WR; Durry, *Rev trim dr civ*, 1967, 637.

20   See [611] above.

instance of *force majeure* wherever the victim's fault was sufficiently major to be the main cause of the damage.[21] Later on the courts tried to balance things somewhat better by reducing the degree of liability of the defendant in accordance with the degree of fault of the victim. In the 1982 *Desmares* case the French Supreme Court returned to the all-or-nothing approach of the early days, however, by ruling that fault of the victim does not exonerate the defendant, whether wholly or in part.[22]

[619] The decision in *Desmares* produced a public outcry. In the result an Act of Parliament was passed that severely restricts the instances where fault of the victim can act as a defence. The so-called *Loi-Badinter* of 5 July 1985 has introduced a new regime of liability for traffic accidents (Act no 85-677 of 5 July 1985, *JCP*, 1985, III, 57405). The Long Title of the Act lists as objectives both an improvement in the situation of victims of traffic accidents and an acceleration of the compensation procedures. Drivers of motor vehicles are henceforth liable for injuring pedestrians, cyclists and passengers in cars except if intent or *faute inexcusable* on the part of the victim can be shown. Not even this escape hatch exists where the victim is younger than 16 or over 70 years of age, or incapacitated by more than 80%. In a further episode of legislature-judiciary dialogue the *Desmares* approach has now been abandoned by the *Cour de Cassation* in favour of a recognition, once again, of a reduced liability of the defendant in the face of proof of fault by the victim. The case involved injury to a young girl who, accompanied by her father, had stopped to watch the burning of lawn clippings on a neighbouring property (Cass civ, II, 6 April 1987, *D*, 1988, 32, note Mouly; *JCP*, 1987 II, 20828, note Chabas). This case (*Waeterinckx*) is reproduced in the Documentation section of the book.

[620] A century after the decision in *Teffaine*, the *Cour de Cassation* decided in the *Blieck* case (Cass civ 29 March 1991, *DS*, 1991, 324; *JCP*, 1991, no 216-73, *Rev tr dr civ*, 1991, 541) that the scope of application of Art 1384(1) can be expanded even further. In *Teffaine* the focus was on the meaning of things (*choses*) one has under one's guard. In *Blieck* it was held that the category of persons for whom one can be responsible is not necessarily limited to the categories listed in Art 1384(4)-(8) *Code civil*.

---

21   See the exceptions of liability listed in *Montagnier* and *Jand'heur*.

22   *"[L]e comportement de la victime, s'il n'a pas été pour le gardien imprévisible et irrésistible, ne peut l'exonérer, même partiellement"*, headnote of Cass civ, II, 21 July 1982, *D*, 1982, 449, note Larroumet; *JCP*, 1982, II, 1986, note Chabas. The full text of the *Desmares* decision has been reproduced in the Documentation section of the book.

The case involved damage caused by an intellectually handicapped person who had started a forest fire. At the time of the incident that person had been in the care of a special centre but not under its actual control. In fact, it was an integral part of the centre's therapy that no constant supervision would be exercised. Because of the nature of the therapy, the trial court considered that it could not hold the centre liable for lack of supervision. Instead, liability was based on Art 1384(1) *Code civil*. A plenary session of the *Cour de Cassation* affirmed the decision of the lower court. If the decision in *Blieck* is confirmed in subsequent cases before the *Cour de Cassation*, any remaining doubts as to whether Art 1384(1) can be more than merely a general introduction to the rest of Art 1384 *Code civil* will be laid to rest for good (Berg 1994:103).[23]

[621] The conceptual approach of the French law of tort, with fault as its traditional basis for liability, has had a pervasive influence in the legal systems of Belgium and The Netherlands. Articles 1382 and 1383 of the Belgian *BW* are identical to their French counterparts. Similarly, Art 1401 of the Dutch *BW* is a repetition, almost word for word, of Art 1382 *Code civil*. In the new Dutch code the concept of fault appears to have been replaced with a new notion of accountability (*toerekening*). A considerably longer Art 6:162 *NBW* stipulates in its first subsection that anyone who commits a tortious act upon someone else for which the former can be held accountable (*welke hem kan worden toegerekend*), is under an obligation to compensate any damage suffered by the latter. Subsection 2 of Art 6:162 defines tort (*onrechtmatige daad*) as an infringement of a legal entitlement, an act or omission in violation of a legal obligation or of an unwritten rule of acceptable social behaviour, provided there is no justification for the infringement, act or omission. Most interesting is the third and final subsection of Art 6:162 where the concept of fault has been re-introduced by the back door. Specifically, a person can be held accountable for a tort which has been committed because of the fault of that person or because of another reason attributable to that person in accordance with the law or the generally accepted principles of social interaction (*de in het verkeer geldende opvattigen*).[24] Van Dam (1989:87)

---

23 Compare and contrast Art 1386 bis of the Belgian *BW*, inserted by an Act of 16 April 1935. This Code provision gives discretionary powers to the court to order intellectually handicapped people to pay full or partial compensation for any damage caused, "depending on the circumstances of the case and the condition of the parties".

24 Article 6:163 NBW adds that no obligation to compensate exists where the rule that has been violated does not have as its goal the protection against damage such as it has been suffered by the victim.

observes that the new concept of accountability risks being as ambiguous as the notion of fault in the past. In particular, the new term is sufficiently broad to be able to accommodate all sorts of judicial policy considerations. On the other hand, the Dutch *NBW* also makes (express) provision for so-called instances of liability based on risk taking. Dealt with in Part 6.3.2 of the *NBW* are liability for faulty goods, dangerous products, buildings and animals. The liability of the driver of a motor vehicle for injury to pedestrians or cyclists is governed by special legislation outside the *NBW*. Except for the defence of *force majeure*, this is an instance of strict liability.[25]

6.3 Tort Law in Germany

(a) The more casuistic approach of the BGB

[622] The principle of liability in tort on the basis of a general Code provision is not universally accepted.[26] A clause similar to Art 1382 *Code civil* does not feature in the *BGB*. Kötz (1987:9) points out that this omission was deliberate. The drafters of the *BGB* held fears that the (fragile) unity of German law might suffer from a general tort provision which would have required extensive judicial interpretation. The idea clearly was to have the legislature (rather than the courts) as the main initiator as regards the legal regulation of torts. To avoid unnecessary detail in the Code itself, a compromise was worked out whereby the tort provisions have been limited to 30 in total, including three provisions of a more general nature: Paragraphs 823, I, II and 826 *BGB*. All three of these more general tort provisions establish liability on the basis of fault, and the latter notion covers both intent (Paras 823 and 826) and instances of negligence (Para 823). The more specific tort provisions include some reminiscent of the tort provisions in the French *Code civil*. Thus, Para 833 *BGB* regulates the liability of animal keepers and Para 836 *BGB* deals with liability for collapsing buildings. Unlike the approach of the *Code civil*, the *BGB* comprises an express provision on contributory negligence: Paragraph 254 *BGB*. The latter provision can be found towards the beginning of Book 2 on Obligations. The tort provisions themselves are grouped together in a Title 25 on Delicts.

---

25 Article 31 *Wegenverkeerswet* (WVW) For a general discussion of tort and the Dutch *NBW* see Van Maanen 1986:201 ff.

26 See Ferrari 1993:813 for a comparative study of the French and German approaches to tort law.

[623] The aim of drafters of the *BGB* to contain judicial activism in tort law met with partial success only. On the one hand, no statutory basis for a regime of strict liability exists in the *BGB* and the German courts have always refused to read one into the *BGB*. Instead strict liability in Germany has more typically been introduced by way of special legislation. Zweigert and Kötz (1987II:347) give examples which pre-date the codification of 1896, eg the 1838 Prussian *Railway Act* although several post-*BGB* examples exist as well, inter alia, the *Road Traffic Act* of 1952 − which imposes strict liability upon the driver except upon proof of force majeure (*höhere Gewalt*). Whether strict liability should remain the creature of statutory law or be admitted into the Code has become a question of some importance for the contemporary German jurist (von Mehren 1981:29; Kötz 1970:15). To "admit" strict liability into the Code may be seen as destroying the conceptual unity that the drafters of the *BGB* considered so important. On the other hand, the dogmatics of the *BGB* has not prevented the German law of tort being shaped heavily by case law.[27] A comparison of the texts of the three general tort provisions in the *BGB* may suggest that, because of its relatively higher degree of generality, Para 826 on the infringement of public morals (*die guten Sitten*) would have been eminently suitable to function as a catch-all provision, capable of accommodating any new developments in society affecting the law of tort. This did not happen, however. Instead, the courts use Para 823, I *BGB* as the legal basis for important developments in tort law. Paragraph 823, I introduces fault-based liability in instances of damage to "the life, body, health, freedom, property or other right (*sonstiges Recht*) of a person". In turn Para 823, II *BGB* prohibits infringements of statutes outside the *BGB* that are intended for the protection of others ("*ein den Schutz eines anderen bezweckendes Gesetz*"). The main application is criminal law legislation.

(b) Paragraph 823, I BGB and the judicial creation of a general right of personality (Persönlichkeitsrecht)

[624] The recognition of a general right of personality as one of the "other" rights in Para 823, I *BGB*, has been described as the most important change in tort law since codification (Larenz and Canaris 1994:491). Its classification alongside the expressly listed rights in Para 823, I is not self evident. Even so, German courts have consistently

---

27   See the discussion of the German law of tort by means of a case study in Markesinis (1994).

interpreted the protected rights in Para 823, I to be absolute rights, thus entitling the holder of these rights to invoke them *erga omnes*. The general right of personality – a concept sufficiently broad to cover one's good name, reputation, honour and privacy – constitutes one such absolute right.[28]

[625] The leading case is a decision by the *Bundesgerichtshof* in 1954 concerning a certain Dr Schacht.[29] Dr Schacht had been the Minister of Economic Affairs during the Hitler period. The defendant had published a magazine containing an article that criticised the establishment of a new bank by Dr Schacht. Dr Schacht instructed his attorney to approach the journal and to ask for the publication of certain corrections in the contents of the article. The journal's editor decided to publish an extract of the lawyer's letter in the column "Readers letters". From the manner in which the letter had been published, it appeared that the attorney had acted in a private capacity, expressing his own, personal views rather than those of his client. This caused the attorney who had originally been retained by Dr Schacht to bring a court action in his own right. In the first instance the *Landsgericht* held the publisher liable by application of the criminal code as well as the civil code: defamation is a crime in the *Strafgesetzbuch* (*St. GB*) and Para 823, II *BGB* holds liable those who infringe a statute intended for the protection of others. The appellate court (*Oberlandesgericht*) disagreed. The *Bundesgerichtshof* held that it was irrelevant whether or not the defendant had been guilty of a crime. Rather, the plaintiff's general right of personality had been infringed. This general right of personality was held to deserve recognition as a basic constitutional right, especially since the German Constitution already embodied, in Arts 1 and 2 *GG*, "the right of people to have their dignity and free development of personality protected against infringement by all".[30] Undoubtedly, both constitutional provisions are a direct reaction

---

28 In France, privacy (*la vie privée*) is expressly protected by Art 9 *Code civil*, as inserted by Act no 70-643 of 17 July 1970. At the level of the EC a Directive on the protection of individuals with regard to the processing of personal data and on the free movement of such data was adopted on 24 October 1995 (*OJ* 1995 L 281/31).

29 BGH 25 May 1954, *BGHZ* 13, 334; *NJW* 1954, 1404; *JZ* 1954, 698. A translation of the case appears in Markesinis 1994:376.

30 "*Nachdem nunmehr das Grundgesetz das Recht des Menschen auf Achtung seiner Würde ../.. und das Recht auf freie Entfaltung seiner Persönlichkeit auch als privates, von jedermann zu achtendes Recht anerkennt ../.. muss das allgemeine Persönlichkeitsrecht als ein verfassungsmässig gewährleistetes Grundrecht angesehen werden*": *BGHZ* 13,334, 338; Van Dam 1989:37.

against the gross violations of human dignity which had occurred in the Nazi period (Markesinis 1994:411).

[626] The *Bundesgerichtshof* has invoked this general right of personality in situations of recording a conversation without the consent of the speaker, passing on medical data to third parties, and the use of photos for commercial purposes (BGH 20 May 1958, *BGHZ* 27, 284; BGH 2 April 1957, *BGHZ* 24, 72; BGH 26 June 1981, *BGHZ* 81, 75). Another example is the refusal by the *Oberlandesgericht* of Frankfurt to entertain a claim by Lufthansa in the early 1980s against a defendant who had produced a sticker depicting two copulating cranes, accompanied by the word "Lusthansa".[31] A Para 823, I action for violation of privacy has a residual character. Thus, it is not normally available if a more specific rule covers the point, eg the protection of name under Para 12 *BGB*. Where it is decided that the plaintiff's claim can proceed on the grounds of breach of the all-embracing right of personality and privacy, the courts consider the merits of the case in light of all the surrounding circumstances. As the approach is highly casuistic, hard and fast rules are difficult to state. Markesinis (1994:412) identifies two threads of thought in the judgments. First, on the whole, freedom of expression prevails over the right of privacy where the former is directed at informing and educating the public at large and not, merely, to pursue sensationalism. Secondly, the likelihood of successfully bringing a privacy claim decreases as the public profile of the plaintiff increases. In this regard the German approach to the disclosure of true private facts tends to be one of trying to distinguish between (a) the "intimate", (b) the "private" and (c) the "social" sphere of the plaintiff: the first receives quasi total protection, whereas the last gets little or none.

[627] The typical remedy for breach of Para 823, I is monetary compensation. The size of any sums ordered to be paid tends to be low.[32] Even though it has not been specifically provided for in the tort provisions of the *BGB*, injunctive relief is available (Markesinis 1994: 413-414).

---

31 OLG Frankfurt, *NJW* 1982, 648. Lufthansa also has a (one) crane as its emblem.

32 Any sums awarded during the period of 1980-1993 almost invariably were (well) below DM 10,000: Markesinis 1994:415.

6.4 Product Liability

(a) National developments

(i) France

[628] French product liability law has traditionally been based on the liability of the vendor for latent defects (De Courrèges 1992:103). According to Art 1603 *Code civil* the seller has two main obligations: to deliver and to warrant the thing that is the object of the sale. Article 1604 *Code civil* defines delivery as the transfer of the thing in the power and possession of the buyer.[33] Case law has supplemented the obligation to deliver with a duty to inform and even advise the buyer. Thus a professional dealer or producer must describe the goods, list its conditions of use and warn against the possible risks of damage. In a 1982 decision by the *Cour de Cassation* it was held that the seller of an anti-parasite product for use on farm land is under an obligation to warn about its potentially harmful effects for the eyes.[34] Specifically, the mere warning that prolonged contact with the skin ought to be avoided was held to be insufficient. Both the duty to inform (*obligation de renseignement*[35]) and the duty to protect the physical safety of the other party (*obligation de sécurité*)[36] are obligations that apply to contracts in general. Their legal

---

33 The transfer of the legal title is an automatic consequence of the (consensual) agreement and thus it is not the object of a separate obligation.

34 Cas civ, I, 14 December 1982, *Bull civ*, I, n 361; *Rev tr dr civ*, 1983, 544, note G Durry. On the other hand, the contractual duty to inform does not encompass a duty for the producer to warrant against "risks of development" that were unknown at the time of bringing a new product onto the market: Cas civ, I, 23 May 1973, *Bull civ*, I, n 181; Cass civ, I, 8 April 1986, *Rev tr dr civ*, 1986, 779, note J Huet. It has been suggested that this decision was influenced by the EC Directive on Product Liability: Calais-Auloy 1996:123-124. See also [639]ff below.

35 The specific contents of the obligation to inform can vary widely. It may include a duty for the professional party to warn the non-professional party about any risks of (physical or economic) damage. This duty to warn is referred to as an *obligation de mise en garde*. A clear example is the duty of medical doctors to advise their patients about the potential side-effects of a particular type of medical treatment (Cass civ, I, 29 May 1984, *D*, 1985, 281, note Bouvier F; Cass civ, I, 23 April 1985, *D*, 1985, 558, note S Dion). Another example is the lack of warning about the flammable character of certain insulation material for buildings (Cass civ, I, 13 May 1986, *Bull* civ, I, n 128). As it has been observed already, this duty to inform is mitigated by a duty of each party to inform itself. See [515] and [520] in Chapter 5. See also: Cass civ, I, 19 March 1985, *Bull civ*, I, n 98; Cass com, 19 November 1985, *Lexis* n 984; *contrary*: Cass civ, I 17 February 1987, *Bull civ*, I, n 57.

36 The duty to provide safety was first introduced in contracts for the transport of persons. Nowadays this duty is deemed to be included in all contracts where one of the parties runs the risk of incurring physical injury. Schmidt-Szalewski (1995:137) gives examples where the duty is incurred by hotel managers, manufacturers of goods, hospitals, playground managers and professional salespeople.

basis is Art 1135 *Code civil* which stipulates that contracts oblige the parties not only to what is expressed in them, but also to all the consequences that equity, custom or the law imply.

[629] Article 1625 *Code civil* specifies that the warranty obligation in contracts of sale has a double angle to it. First, the seller is under a duty to ensure the peaceful possession of the thing sold. Secondly, and more importantly for our purposes, the seller is liable for any hidden defects (*vices cachés*) which make the thing unfit for its intended use. The courts generally prefer a broad, functional approach to the notion of defect.[37] Also, it is irrelevant whether the thing sold is new or secondhand and whether the seller is a professional or not: the relevant Code provisions – Arts 1641-1648 *Code civil* – apply regardless. A most restrictive requirement is, however, that cases must be brought within a short period of time (*dans un bref délai*) after, typically, the discovery of the defect – usually a few months (Art 1648 *Code civil*). But judicial creativity has once again been able to grant a remedy where deemed appropriate.[38]

[630] Parties without contractual rights, eg bystanders, have to fall back on the law of tort. It will be recalled that Art 1382 *Code civil* lays down a general duty of care, whereas Art 1384(1) has formed the basis for the development of a legal regime of quasi strict liability for damage caused by things under one's guard.[39] As regards product liability an additional distinction is made between the usage and the internal structure of a product. The physical owner of the goods is responsible for the manner in which they are used (*garde du comportement*), but the manufacturer is strictly liable for their intrinsically dangerous qualities (*garde de la structure*) (Cass civ, II, 5 June 1991, *Bull civ*, II, no 204, 145; De

---

37 For a general discussion of hidden defects in contracts of sale, see Ghestin and Desché 1990:762 ff.

38 First, determinations as to what constitutes a short period can vary considerably from one case to another, from a few weeks to – exceptionally – over a year. The courts may, for instance, take into account that negotiations with a view to an amicable settlement have taken place before the commencement of court proceedings (Cas civ, I, 16 July 1987, *D* 1987, inf rap, 182). Even the fact that the purchaser is a foreigner domiciled abroad can be a relevant consideration (De Courrèges 1992:106). Secondly, where the purchaser of a defective product is unable to bring an action based on liability for a latent defect, the more general Code provisions on contractual liability, especially Art 1147 or 1184 *Code civil*, may still trigger a remedy of damages for failure to supply a "conforming" product (De Courrèges 1992:108 and 110). Finally, the time restrictions of Art 1648 *Code civil* may be avoided all together by bringing a court action for mistake as to substance, even if the mistake is actually the result of the hidden defect (Ghestin and Desché 1990:856).

39 See [603]ff above.

Courrèges 1992:113; Howells 1993:109). Thus the product user is not subject to a presumption of fault regarding the usage of the product nor a presumption of being its most appropriate insurer.

[631] To date no special legislation to implement the 1985 EC Directive has been adopted. An explanation for this inaction may be found in concerns, as expressed by Howells (1993:101), that any new legislation may leave French consumers worse off, especially if the new Act were to become the exclusive source of redress for injured consumers as well as making provision for the so-called development risks defence as permitted under the Directive.[40]

(ii) Germany

[632] The drafting of the *BGB* was influenced by the perception that irregularities in the performance of contracts could be attributed either to impossibility (*Unmöglichkeit*) or to delay (*Verzug*). When it became clear that this approach was too rigid to do justice in the wide variety of instances of alleged breach, the former *Reichsgericht* developed the concept of positive breach of contract (*positive Vertragverletzung*) (*RGZ* 54, 98; Horn, Kötz, Leser 1982:105 cite Staub, *Die positiven Vertragsverletzungen,* Berlin, 1904; Link and Sambuc 1992:131). It is a residual head of liability, to be used only where the *BGB* provides no other remedy for breach of contract. The scope of positive breach of contract has been much expanded because of the implication into contracts of a "network of duties" designed to protect the interests of the parties (Horn, Kötz and Leser 1982:106). They are duties of care and protection that stand alongside the main obligations of the contracting parties.

[633] A positive breach of contract gives rise to a liability to compensate for the resulting harm. Besides instances of goods that are defective per se, the doctrine is also relevant where goods are rendered defective by faulty instructions (Howells 1993:124). Of more limited use in product liability cases is the Code provision for a warranty by the seller that the thing is "free from defects which diminish or destroy the value or fitness for ordinary use, or the use provided for in the contract".[41] Unlike in claims for a positive breach of contract there is no need to prove fault, but the remedy is limited to rescission (*Wandlung*) or price reduction (*Min-*

---

40 See [639] below. Technically, France is in breach of its EC obligations as the deadline for implementation of the Directive has long since passed: see the comments in fn 50 below.

41 Paragraph 459 *BGB*. English translation by Howells 1993:124.

derung); consequential damages are not normally recoverable.[42] The non-availability of damages can be explained by the consideration that warranty claims are based on the fundamental idea that the buyer, who pays good money, should receive a good product in exchange. Since a warranty concerns only the product proper, it does not cover the consequential damage which typically gives rise to product liability claims (Link and Sambuc 1992:126). Two important exceptions to the rule that the vendor's liability for defects does not involve any liability in damages are provided in Para 463 *BGB*. Where the vendor has guaranteed that the object sold has a specific attribute or where the vendor deliberately keeps quiet about the defect, damages are available in addition to the traditional remedy of rescission or price reduction (Horn, Kötz, Leser 1982:127; Link and Sambuc 1992:128).

[634] Notwithstanding attempts to use and adjust the *BGB* provisions on contract law during the early history of German product liability, the so-called fowl pest case (*Hünnerpest*) proved instrumental in switching the focus decisively to tort law.[43] In this case the owner of a chicken farm sued the manufacturer of a fowl pest virus after several thousands of his chickens had died from being vaccinated with contaminated serum. The serum had been supplied by the defendant to the plaintiff's veterinary surgeon. The trial court found for the plaintiff on the basis of various contract theories, but those were all rejected by the *Bundesgerichtshof*. One such theory is known as *Drittschadensliquidation* or the theory of transferred loss. Under this theory third parties can obtain a remedy by having, *in casu*, the vet sue the pharmaceutical company on behalf of the owner of the chickens. In the circumstances this was not considered appropriate as there was no "union of interest" between vet and plaintiff: the vaccine had not been bought specifically for the farmer (Markesinis 1994:495; Howells 1993:125). A second contractual theory – again rejected by the German Supreme Court – has been called *Vertrag mit Schutzwirkung für Dritte* or a contract with protective effect for third parties. Under this theory third parties can benefit from the subsidiary obligations of the contract which are implied according to the rule in

---

42   Horn, Kötz, Leser 1982:125. An exception is Para 635 *BGB* involving contracts for work or services. That provision regulates the liability of contractors in instances of a lack of product safety that amounts to a defect. Here compensation is an alternative remedy to cancellation or price reduction.

43   BGH decision of 26 November 1968, BGHZ 51, 91. Horn, Kötz, Leser 1982:153; Howells 1993:125. An English translation of the case can be found in Markesinis 1994:493.

Para 242 *BGB* to the effect that contracts must be performed in good faith. Even though their French counterparts appear more relaxed as regards this particular issue, a major concern of German courts, however, has been to avoid the relativity of the contractual bond being undermined entirely. In addition to the above contractual theories, the *Bundesgerichtshof* also dealt with several other submissions by the plaintiff aimed at justifying a regime of strict or semi-strict liability. However, in tune with a long-established practice, the Supreme Court refused to "discover" strict liability in the absence of legislative intervention and it continues to do so to date (Markesinis 1994:86-87).

[635] The 1968 decision of the *Bundesgerichtshof* in the above-mentioned fowl pest case held in favour of the plaintiff on the basis of Paras 823, I and II *BGB*. It will be recalled that Para 823 II creates liability in tort for the violation of protective statutes.[44] This notion of protective legislation includes food and drugs laws. Interestingly, whereas 823 II involves a reversal of the burden of proof, liability claims based on 823 I do not normally benefit from this procedural aid. Even so, this time the *Bundesgerichtshof* was prepared to extend the reversal of the burden of proof. A simple presumption of fault was deemed inadequate by the Court since:

> [A]ll too often the owner of a business can show that the defect in the product might have been caused in a way that does not point to his fault. ... Consequently, where damage has arisen within the range of the manufacturer's business risks, he cannot be regarded as exonerated merely because he points out that the defect in the product might have arisen without any organisation fault of his; he must, on the contrary, supply positive and complete evidence that the defect in the product is not due to his fault.[45]

[636] Having already reversed the onus of proving fault for purposes of Para 823 II *BGB*, the Court in 1968 saw no good reason why the same should not also be done with Para 823 I. Relevant considerations in this regard were the special features of product liability and in particular the victim's de facto inability to know what goes on in the manufacturer's business. Case law of the post-1968 era tends to be discussed by German scholars under the different headings of defects in manufacture, defects in design, defects in instructions, monitoring and the duty to recall (Vieweg 1996:218-221). Markesinis (1994:89) anticipates that these distinctions are likely to remain in use notwithstanding the adoption of specific product

---

44   See [623] above.
45   Translation by Lawson and Markesinis: Markesinis 1994:502.

liability legislation in the wake of EC Directive 85/374/EEC on the approximation of the laws of the member states concerning liability for the defective products.[46] As regards development risks, for instance, the general (German) approach has been one of limiting the producer's obligations to do what is "economically reasonable and technologically feasible".[47] But this negligence approach to tort law has not prevented the courts from improving the situation of the victim by imposing post-marketing surveillance obligations on the producer. These obligations continue to be relevant since the liabilities created by the European Directive cease once a product is put into circulation.

[637] The *Product Liability Act* came into force on 1 January 1990. The Act applies to products that have been brought on the market since that date. The Act is based on the principle of protected rights. These include life, body and health, and things. The Act expressly requires that an object other than the defective product itself be damaged. However, this does not affect cases involving the supply of a defective part which causes damage to the product into which it has been incorporated.[48] Liability for damage to property arises only where the damaged property is usually used for private purposes. In addition, the property must actually have been used for (mainly) private purposes. Link and Sambuc (1992:152) give the example of damage done to an excavator while the owner of a construction business uses the equipment for a private purpose during the weekend. The Act does not cover this type of situation. On the other hand, the plaintiff who uses a car for recreational purposes most of the time, and only makes occasional business trips, does not lose the protection of the Act. Clearly, the emphasis of the Act is on consumer protection proper.

---

46 *Gesetz über die Haftung für fehlerhafte Produkte*, 1989 *Bundesgesetzblatt* I, 2198. The 1989 *Product Liability Act* is discussed in Dielmann 1990:425. The text of the Act – both in the original language and in English translation – is reproduced in Schulz and Halbgewachs 1993:342. Useful commentaries that incorporate pre-Act developments can be found in Hoffman and Hill-Arning 1994:27; Howells 1993:123; Link and Sambuc 1992:151. See also the pre-Act commentary in Zekoll 1989:809.

47 When a recyclable lemonade bottle exploded in the face of a three-year-old child causing it to lose an eye, the *Bundesgrichtshof* insisted that the development risk doctrine did not absolve the manufacturer from having to adopt a high standard of care. *In casu*, the producer should have considered not only the specified uses of its bottles, but also foreseeable misuses, the long time lag inherent in the distribution chain and the wide variety of consumers using the product: *BGH* 7 June 1988, *BGHZ* 104, 323; (1988) *NJW* 2611; Howells 1993:131; Markesinis 1994:514.

48 Paragraph 2 of the Act defines "product" as a movable thing, including parts of other movable or immovable things.

[638] According to Para 3(1) of the Act, a product is defective if it does not provide the safety that can reasonably be expected considering all the circumstances. The producer must account for all uses of the product by the consumer which are not entirely unusual or unreasonable. The required safety standard is that which can be expected at the time when the product is put on the market. It is immaterial whether the producer is at fault, but contributory negligence on the part of the person who has suffered loss or injury is taken into consideration when determining the amount of damages. Like all German strict liability statutes the Act sets limits to the amount of damages which can be claimed. Immaterial damages, ie compensation for pain and suffering, are not claimable under the Act. But, of course, the Act only establishes a parallel regime to that of the *BGB* and it is up to the parties to decide whether to base their claims on the BGB and/or on the 1989 Act (Markesinis 1994:546).

(b) Developments at the level of the European Community

(i) Product liability sensu stricto

[639] A Directive on the Approximation of the Laws, Regulations and Administrative Provisions of the Member States concerning Liability for Defective Products was adopted on 25 July 1985.[49] The member states were given three years for bringing their laws into line. Only three countries – the United Kingdom, Italy and Greece – met the deadline for implementation (Bourgoignie 1996:35).[50] On the other hand, the Directive does not abolish national laws that already allow claims for damages on grounds of contractual or non-contractual liability, provided that these national (pre-existing) laws serve to attain the same objective as the EC law, ie the effective protection of consumers (Jolowicz 1990:381). The Directive is the product of a decade-long gestation period. Much of the delay in adopting the Directive has generally been attributed to its contentious nature (Stapleton 1994:47; Howells 1993:29; Jolowicz 1990:370). Questions were raised about the jurisdiction of the EC to act in this area (Stapleton 1994:53). But there were also differences of opinion as to the substance of the Directive. Most contentious were questions as to

---

49   Directive 85/374/EEC, OJ 1985 L210/29 The full text of the Directive is reproduced in Kendall 1994:391; in Markesinis 1994:534; and in Stapleton 1994:360.

50   All other member states – except for France – have since acted to implement the Directive. Initiated by the Commission, infringement proceedings under Art 169 EC resulted in a Court decision declaring France to be in breach of its Community obligations: *Commission v France*, case C-293/91, [1993] ECR 1. No action to enforce the Court decision (pursuant to Art 171 EC) has been brought as yet.

whether there should be a development risks defence, a limit on damages for death and personal injury, and whether primary agricultural produce and game should be excluded. In the result a compromise was reached by leaving these matters to the discretion of the member states (Arts 15-16 Directive).

[640] Technically, the Directive is based on Art 100 EEC. This Treaty provision concerns the establishment and functioning of the common market. According to the Preamble of the Directive, the approximation of the national laws on product liability is necessary, because the existing divergences may distort competition and affect the (free) movement of goods within the common market. Furthermore, consumer protection is also a stated goal of the Directive. Article 1 of the Directive establishes a regime of strict liability on the part of producers or importers into the Community for damage caused by a defect in their products. However, they are strictly liable whether the person killed or injured is a consumer or not. Some commentators infer from this that to evoke the Directive in the context of consumer protection is somewhat misplaced (Lewis 1992:169; see also Jolowicz 1990:370 and Stapleton 1994:60-64). On the other hand, compensation for damage to property – other than the defective product itself – is expressly limited to goods for private use or consumption and which were used by the injured persons mainly for their own private use or consumption (Art 9 Directive). The term consumer itself is not defined in the Directive.

[641] The Preamble of the Directive stipulates that liability without fault on the part of the producer is the sole means of adequately solving the problem of a fair apportionment of the risks inherent in modern technological production. That problem is said to be peculiar to our age of increasing technicality. Under the Directive a product is defective "when it does not provide the safety which a person is entitled to expect" (Art 6 Directive). Circumstances to be taken into account include the presentation of the product, reasonable expectations as to the use of the product and the time when the product was put into circulation. The EC definition of a defective product is not unproblematic (Stapleton 1994:234). The consumer expectation test assumes an ability of the consumer accurately to assess what level of safety can be expected. An inherent problem is further that consumers' expectations are conditioned by their everyday environment which is highly influenced by the manufacturers of products themselves. At times it may even be difficult to define what the consumers' expectations are (Howells 1993:11-13). Geddes (1992:22) makes a number of tentative (but useful) suggestions as to how to define a defective product. First, it is clear that a product may be defective even though it fulfils its design function in precisely the manner in which the manufacturer intended. It is thus no defence for producers to say that, at the time of putting the product into circulation, they did not know of the risks associated with its use unless they can also show that the state of scientific and technical knowledge at the time was not such as to enable the existence of the risk or defect to be discovered. Secondly, it is perfectly possible that hazards associated with a product's use may only arise in relation to a particular class of person, eg, children. Adequate warnings of the dangers to that class must be given if liability is to be avoided. Thirdly, a product may be defective where it causes injury when it is being used (or even misused) so long as it was reasonably to be expected that it would be used in that way. However, a product does not become defective merely because it wears out through use. Similarly, a product is not defective if it meets the existing requirements at the time it is put into circulation but safety regulations are tightened afterwards.

[642] Liability for damage caused by a defective product rests with its producer or, in case of imports of products that originate outside the EC, its importer into the Community. Where the producer cannot be identified, each supplier of the product can be treated as its producer. The same rule applies to importers who cannot be identified (Art 3.3 Directive). Liability is not reduced when the damage is caused by both a defect in the product and by the act or omission of another person, except where the latter is the injured person or someone for whom the injured person is responsible (Art 8 Directive). The liability of the producer arising from the Directive cannot be limited or excluded by contract (Art 12 Directive).

(ii) General product safety

[643] In principle, a product can be free of any defect and still be unsafe. Liability for damage caused by such an unsafe but defect-free product does not come within the ambit of the 1985 Directive (Lewis 1992:168). An obvious way of avoiding unsafe products causing harm to consumers is to prohibit them. Initially, the Community adopted a piecemeal approach to the problem. A Directive of 1987 prohibits the manufacture, marketing, import and export of so-called dangerous imitation products (Directive 87/357/EEC, *OJ* 1987 L 192/49). The 1987 Directive aims at protecting consumers – children in particular – from the dangers associated with products which can be confused with foodstuffs. One year later, in 1988, Council Directive 88/378/EEC was adopted which seeks to approximate the laws of the members states concerning the safety of toys (*OJ* 1988

L187/1). The 1988 Directive expects the member states to take all steps necessary to ensure that toys cannot be placed on the market unless they meet certain essential safety requirements as set out in an Annex to the Directive (Art 3 of Directive 88/378/EEC). The 1988 Directive sets up a system of presumed compliance. It involves a certification by the manufacturers themselves that their products conform with Community law. To this effect a "CE" label is placed on the toys. The Directive also establishes a safeguard mechanism which member states invoke if toys bearing the "CE" symbol turn out to be dangerous. The Directive has been in force since the beginning of 1990. Reportedly it has worked well so far (Lewis 1992:168).

[644] In response to criticism that the EC lacked a general product safety policy, Council Directive 92/59/EEC on general product safety was adopted in 1992 (*OJ* 1992 L228/24). The object of this Directive is to ensure that all products placed on the market are safe (Art 1.1 Directive 92/59/EEC). The term product is defined broadly to mean any product intended for consumers or likely to be used by consumers, which is supplied in the course of a commercial activity but without a need for consideration. Products whose safety requirements are already covered by specific Community rules continue to be governed by these (more specific) rules (Art 1.2 Directive 92/59/EEC). Article 13 of the 1992 Directive also states expressly that it is "without prejudice" to the 1985 Directive on liability for defective products. Article 2 of the 1992 Directive contains a rather long-winded definition of a "safe" product. A core element of the definition is that, in order to be safe, products may not present any risk or only the minimum risks compatible with their use. In the absence of specific Community legislation on the safety of a particular product, it is considered safe when it conforms to the specific, if any, national rules of the country where it is in circulation, including the health and safety requirements for its marketing. In the absence of specific national rules, alternative benchmarks include, for example, any codes of good practice on health and safety which may exist in the sector concerned. The bottom line is the state of development of the product and reasonable expectations of consumer safety. However, the competent authorities of a member state may always impose restrictions on the marketing of a product if it presents a danger to consumers notwithstanding its conformity with the above provisions. These national restrictions may even involve the withdrawal of the product (Art 4 Directive 92/59/EEC; Kendall 1994:37-38).

[645] The overall, albeit indirect, effect of the 1992 Directive is to create a system of strict and unlimited liability for the placing of defect-free but unsafe products on the consumer market (Lewis 1992:169). Primary defendants in any claim for damages are the manufacturers of the unsafe product, including anyone presenting themselves as the manufacturer. When the manufacturer is not established inn the Community, liability lies with the manufacturer's representative in the Community or, alternatively, the importer.[51] But the Directive does not leave the position of distributors of the product untouched either. A distributor is defined as any professional in the supply chain whose activity does not affect the safety properties of the (unsafe) product. Distributors are required to act with due care in order to help to ensure compliance with the general safety requirement of the Directive. They are under a negative obligation not to supply goods which they know or should know to be unsafe. They are also under a positive obligation to participate in monitoring the safety of products placed on the market. Specifically, they are expected both to pass on information as regards product risks and to co-operate in the action taken to avoid these risks Art 2-3 Directive 92/59/EEC). These aspects of the 1992 Directive are reminiscent of German tort law (which refuses to accept that the legal duties of the manufacturer cease at the point of production) and French contract law (which extends the obligations of the professional vendor beyond the point of sale).

References

Berg, M, "Recente ontwikkelingen in het Franse vermogensrecht 1989 tot en met 1993", (1994) 11 *Nederlands Tijdschrift voor Burgerlijk Recht* 103.

Bourgoigmie, Th, 1996, "The 1985 Council Directive on product liability and its implementation in the Member States of the European Union", in Goyens, M, (ed), *La Directive 85/374/CEE relative à la responsabilité du fait des produits: dix ans après*, Centre de la consommation, Louvain-la-Neuve.

Calais-Auloy, J, "La responsabilité du fait des produits en droit français", in Goyens, M, (ed), 1996, *La Directive 85/374/CEE relative à la responsabilité du fait des produits: dix ans après*, Centre de la consommation, Louvain-la-Neuve.

de Courrèges, M, 1992, "France", in Kelly, P, and Attree, R, (eds), *European Product Liability*, Butterworths, London.

Dielmann, HJ, "The New German Product Liability Act", (1990) 13 *Hastings International and Comparative Law Review* 425.

Ferrari, F, "Comparative Remarks on Liability for One's Own Acts", (1993) 15 *Loyola of Los Angeles International and Comparative Law Journal* 813.

Geddes, A, 1992, *Product and Service Liability in the EEC*, Sweet & Maxwell, London.

---

51 The term "producer" in Art 2 of the Directive is sufficiently broad to cover, expressly, "other professionals in the supply chain, insofar as their activities may affect the safety properties of a product placed on the market".

Ghestin, J, and Desché, B, 1990, *Traité des contrats. La vente*, LGDJ, Paris.

Hoffman, WC, and Hill-Arning, S, 1994, *Guide to Product Liability in Europe*, Kluwer, Deventer.

Horn, N, Kötz, H, Leser, H, 1982, *German Private and Commercial Law: An Introduction*, Clarendon Press, Oxford.

Howells, G, 1993, *Comparative Product Liability*, Dartmouth, Aldershot.

Jolowicz, "Product Liability in the EEC", in Clark, DS (ed), 1990, *Comparative and Private International Law: Essays in Honor of JH Merryman on his Seventieth Birthday*, Duncker & Humblot, Berlin.

Kelly, P, and Attree, R, 1992, *European Product Liability*, Butterworths, London.

Kendall, V, 1994, *EC Consumer Law*, Chancery Law Publishing, London.

Kötz, H, "Taking Civil Codes Less Seriously", (1987) 50 *Modern Law Review* 1.

Kötz, H, "Haftung für besondere Gefahr-Generalklausel für die Gefährdungshaftung", (1970) 170 *Archiv für die Civilistische Praxis* 1.

Larenz, K, and Canaris, CW, 1994, *Lehrbuch des Schuldrechts*, II, (Special Part, second volume), 13th ed, Verlag CH Beck, München.

Lewis, X, "The Protection of Consumers in European Community Law, (1992) 12 *Yearbook of European Law* 139.

Link, KU, and Sambuc, T, 1992, "Federal Republic of Germany", in Kelly, P, and Attree, R, (eds), *European Product Liability,* Butterworths, London.

Markesinis, BS, 1994, *The German Law of Torts. A Comparative Introduction*, 3rd ed, Clarendon Press, Oxford.

Roland, H, and Boyer, L, 1988, *Droit civil. Obligations.I Responsabilité délictuelle,* 3rd ed, Litec, Paris.

Rudden, B, "Torticles", (1991-1992) 6-7 *Tulane Civil Law Forum*, 105.

Schmidt-Szalewski, J, 1995, "France", in Herbots, J, (ed), Contracts. Volume I, in Blanpain, R, (gen ed), *International Encyclopaedia of Laws*, Kluwer, The Hague.

Schulz, A, and Halbgewachs, R, 1993, "Germany", in Hodges, CJS, (gen ed), *Product Liability. European Laws and Practice*, Sweet & Maxwell, London.

Stapleton, J, 1994, *Product Liability*, Butterworths, London.

Tomlinson, EA, "Tort Liability in France for the Act of Things: A Study of Judicial Law-Making", (1988) 48 *Louisiana Law Review* 1299.

Van Dam, CC, 1989, *Zorgvuldigheidsnorm en Aansprakelijkheid*, Kluwer, Deventer.

Van Maanen, GE, 1986, *Onrechtmatige Daad*, Kluwer, Deventer.

Vieweg, K, 1996, "The Law of Torts", in Ebke, WF, and Finkin, MW, (eds), *Introduction to German Law*, CH Beck, Kluwer, Munich, The Hague.

Viney, G, "Chronique. Responsabilité civile", (1995) 24 *La Semaine Juridique* 264.

von Mehren, AT, "Doctrinal Premises and the Law of Delict: Some Comparative Observations on German and Swiss Law", (1981) 16 *Revista Juridica de la Universidad Interamericana de Puerto Rico* 21.

Zekoll, J, "The German Products Liability Act", (1989) 37 *American Journal of Comparative Law* 809.

Zweigert, K, and Kötz, H, 1987, *An Introduction to Comparative Law*, II, 2nd ed, Clarendon Press, Oxford.

Chapter 7

Labour Law

7.1 Introduction

[701] The discipline currently known as labour law is of a relatively recent origin. As a study object in its own right – separate from the study of contract, tort or even criminal law – labour law became only fully recognised at the European universities after World War II. Especially German scholars were instrumental in developing this new academic discipline. Kahn-Freund has singled out Hugo Sinzheimer (1875-1945) as the founding father of labour law as it was Sinzheimer who brought about "the conception of labour law as a unified, independent legal discipline" (Kahn-Freund 1981:75).

[702] German scholarship traditionally defines labour law as employee protection law (*Arbeitnehmerschutzrecht*). And this expression captures the essence of the subject of labour law rather well (Vranken 1989:100). Technically, the employment relationship is based on contract. Yet, simply to apply the rules of general contract law is not entirely unproblematic as the relationship between employer and employee is fundamentally and inherently unequal. The employment relationship is fundamentally unequal because the nature of the inequality goes to the very core of the relationship. The relationship is also inherently unequal because the inequality is built in and therefore unavoidable. The inequality of the employment relationship involves a situation whereby one party (the employee) is economically dependent on the other party (the employer) for his or her livelihood. And the subordinate nature of the employment relationship is exacerbated even further by the consideration that it is an on-going relationship as opposed to other contracts such as sale, for example.

[703] Because of the fundamental and inherent nature of the inequality in employment relationships the civil law and common law share a common starting point. By and large, however, the European and the English or common-law approaches to labour law have tended to differ over the years. The Continental approach historically has been one of tackling the problem of inequality head on. Specifically, a tradition evolved of direct legislative intervention in the employment relationship. In the result relatively comprehensive employment "codes" comprise a range of statutory rights for the protection of individual employees in their relationship with the employer. Significantly, these statutory rights go beyond the protection of employees against unfair termination actions at the initiative of the employer[1] and also cover, inter alia, the conditions under which temporary work arrangements can be entered into, part-time work, privacy, working time and even the impact of strike action on the individual contract of employment.

[704] In recent years there has been growing pressure on law makers to allow for more flexibility in the regulation of labour law. In Europe the call for the deregulation of labour law became manifest from the mid-1980s onwards (Vranken 1986:143). But some statutory restrictions have always continued to apply even when the economic recession was at its deepest. Thus the enactment of the 1985 Act on the Improvement of Employment Opportunities (*Beschäftigungsörderungsgesetz*) in Germany was triggered by a desire to stimulate employment, including temporary employment. Yet the Act limits the permissible length of fixed-term contracts for new employees to 18 months with no opportunity for renewal (Weiss 1994:50). In France the conditions under which limited-term contracts can be entered into are governed by Sections L 122-1, 2 and 3 of the Labour Code (Javillier 1988:128). Calls for more flexibility in the regulation of working time resulted in the replacement of the 1838 Act on Working Time (*Arbeitszeitordnung*) by the 1994 Act on Working Time (*Arbeitszei-trechtsgesetz*) in Germany. The 1994 Act allows for an extension of the regular daily working hours of 8 to 10 hours, provided an average of 8 daily hours is not exceeded within a period of 6 months or 24 weeks (Weiss 1994:71). The French equivalent is Law No 93-1313 of 20 December 1993 on Labour, Employment and Vocational Training which seeks, inter alia, to encourage flexibility by introducing new forms of working time organisation on an annual basis. Each time the underlying idea is to maintain or even increase employment levels without, however, abandoning all protective employment regulation (*European Industrial Relations Review* 242:18-19 and 255:24-25). Typically, the above statutory rights of individual workers are enforceable in a specialist labour court.[2]

---

1 Protection against unfair dismissal is the most commonly found form of statutory protection in the civil law as well as the common law. In a number of instances, action of the member states was triggered by the adoption of a Recommendation on this issue by the International Labour Organisation in 1963 (ILO Convention No 119, 1963 concerning Termination of Employment at the Initiative of the Employer).

2 Labour courts owe their origin to the probiviral court or *conseil de prud'hommes* (literally, "court of wise men"), set up at Lyon pursuant to a Napoleonic law of 1806. See Vranken 1988:497.

[705] In the common law the problem of individual inequality between employee and employer is by preference tackled indirectly, ie at a collective level and involving the representatives of labour and management. In practical terms this necessitates, on the side of labour, involvement by the union in negotiating collective agreements detailing terms and conditions of employment for individual workers. Historically, English labour law has gone furthest in openly promoting state abstention from "interference" in the autonomy of the collective bargaining parties. In Australia and New Zealand, by contrast, a conscious decision was made at the turn of the century to reject collective laissez-faire. Legislation for the settlement of industrial (collective) disputes by means of compulsory conciliation and arbitration has only in recent years become controversial and more attention is now being paid to the idea of a statutory minimum floor of rights for employees in both these countries. In common with the English approach, however, Australia and New Zealand continue to display an adversarial approach to labour law. Reinforcing this conflict mentality is an assumption in those countries that labour relations are essentially about conflicts between parties that have diametrically opposed interests.

[706] Undeniably, labour relations are power relations and this impacts on the outcome of collective bargaining in the civil law as well as in the common law (Blanpain 1993:18). But because of the extensive individual employment laws in the civil law, the collective bargaining stakes are less high. Also, supplementing this individual employment legislation in the civil law is legislation that aims at actively promoting a co-operative approach to the employer-employee relationship at the level of the individual enterprise. Various forms of institutionalised worker participation exist in Europe. These are premised on the assumption that a minimum of commonality of interest exists between employer and employee. The promotion of this core of common interests is considered to be in the public interest. The focus of this chapter is on the two main forms of institutionalised worker participation, ie works councils and employee representation on the supervisory boards of companies. Attention is paid to both national and supranational developments in this regard.[3]

---

3 Currently there appears to be a revival of interest in worker participation. A special issue of the *British Journal of Industrial Relations* was devoted to this topic in 1995. See, in particular, the President's Introduction (at 315), Keller (at 317) and Sadowski, Backes-Gellner and Frick (at 493).

7.2 Works Councils

(a) Establishment, composition and competence

[707] The works council (*comité d'entreprise* or *comité d'établissement*; *Betriebsrat*) is an institution whose presence in civil law countries is widespread. Enabling legislation has been adopted in Austria, Belgium, France, Germany, the Netherlands and Spain. The detail of the national laws tends to differ. But, in essence, works councils in each of these countries are bodies established at the place of work where employer and employee can meet and confer on a footing of equality. Interestingly, the representative status of the works council is not limited to the unionised segment of a company's workforce. Even though in practice union members occupy a dominant position in the employee seats on the works council, the employee representatives on the works council are elected by and for all company workers.

[708] In France and Belgium employees are entitled to a number of representatives on the works council equal to the number of representatives from management. Meetings of the works council in these countries are chaired by the employer or a representative of the employer. In Germany – and this model is followed in Austria, the Netherlands and Spain – works councils are exclusively composed of employees. The threshold for the establishment of a works council is lowest in Germany where a works council must be established in every plant with more than five adult employees.[4] The minimum size requirement is 35 in the Netherlands, 50 in France, and 100 in Belgium.[5]

[709] The function of the works council is described most constructively in Para 2, 1 of the German Works Constitution Act (*Betriebsverfassungsgesetz*) where it is said that:

> The employer and the works council shall work together in a spirit of mutual trust having regard to the applicable collective agreements and in co-operation with the trade unions and the employers' associations represented in the establishment for the good of the employees and of the establishment.[6]

---

4   Section 1 of the 1972 Works Constitution Act (*Betriebsverfassungsgesetz*). The same low threshold applies in Austria.

5   The relevant legislation for the Netherlands is: the Works Councils Act 1971 as amended in 1981; for France: the Labour Code; for Belgium: the 1968 Works Councils Act. A comparative discussion can be found in Blanpain 1994:12.

6   Translation by the International Labour Organisation 1976:76.

The French Acts of 1982 and 1984 use language that is more one sided when it states the purpose of works councils to be:

> To ensure the collective expression of the employees and to allow their interests to be taken into account in decisions regarding the management and the economic and financial evolution of the enterprise, organisation of work, occupational training and techniques of production.[7]

The actual powers of the works council in influencing decision making by management tend to be limited largely to information sharing and consultation rights. The entitlement to information concerns primarily economic and financial matters. The information rights of Belgian works councils are especially comprehensive. According to a Royal Decree of 27 November 1973 certain information must be provided on a one-off basis, whereas other information rights are triggered annually, periodically or occasionally (Art 2 of the Royal Decree concerning the Regulation of the Economic and Financial Information to be provided to Works Councils, *BS*, 28 November 1973, as amended). Basic information to be given within two months of the election or re-election of the employee members of the works council relates to: the company statutes; the competitive position of the company in the market; production and productivity; the financial structure of the company; budget and calculation of cost; personnel costs; planning and general prospects for the future; scientific research; public assistance; and the organisational chart of the company. Annual information rights comprise the updating of the basic information above as well as copies of the balance sheet and the profit-and-loss account. The purpose of this annual information is to allow the works council to get an idea as to the position and evolution of the company in the previous year, and about the company's plans and prospective for the future. This annual information is supplemented with periodic information that allows the works council to see how any particular year is unfolding and the extent to which the projected goals are being met. This periodic information covers data as regards sales, orders, market, production, costs, stock, productivity and employment. In addition, occasional information must be provided whenever the need arises. Specifically, the duty to inform is triggered by events – both external and internal – which may have a significant impact on the company such as structural changes in the industry or the introduction of new technology. Significantly, the above information rights relate both to the so-called technical unit of production (which is the lowest level at which Belgian works councils are established) and the larger legal,

---

7   Section L 431-4 of the Labour Code. See Despax and Rojot 1987:195-196.

economic or financial group to which this unit may belong. In principle, this means that the works council of a plant controlled by a multi-national company is entitled to receive information about that company as a whole.

[710] Blanpain (1994:22) has identified a number of questions which arise when evaluating the real merits of information systems, especially where the coverage of this information is seemingly extensive. The most important questions concern (1) the subject matter of the information; (2) the entity about which information has to be given; (3) the timing of the information; (4) the addressee of the information; and (5) the relationship between the headquarters of multinational enterprises and their subsidiaries. It is also important to stress that, whereas information sharing constitutes the lowest degree of the participatory rights of the works council in the management of companies, knowledge is a *conditio sine qua non* for the successful exercise of any of the higher levels of worker participation to be discussed next.

[711] The information rights of the works council form a basis upon which its consultation rights can build. If the disclosure of information means that the employer makes available data, consultation entails an exchange of ideas which may culminate in the works council formulating an advisory opinion. This advice does not require unanimity, not even a majority vote. Consultation is indeed primarily designed to enable the employer to appreciate the different points of view which may exist. And of course, because of its very nature, any such advisory opinion of the works council is not binding on the employer (Vranken 1986:344). Generally speaking, the consultation rights of the works council tend to relate to the social impact of any economic or financial decisions by management. Under French law the consultation rights of the works council extend to the organisation, management and general functioning of the company (Javillier 1988:291). For instance, the works council must be consulted over contemplated changes to the economic or legal organisation of the company including – but not limited to – mergers and acquisitions. Other areas of consultation rights are, inter alia, the research policy of the company and employment conditions such as health and safety or working time.

[712] As stated above the legal requirement for management to ask for the advice of the works council does not normally entail an obligation to follow that advice. However, over the years the advisory powers of the works council have been strengthened in a number of countries in an attempt to force the employer, at least in some instances, to take the opinions of the works council seriously. In France, if no advice is sought where to do so is a legal requirement, the relevant management decision is considered legally void and unenforceable (Vranken 1986:345). In the Netherlands, the Works Council Act of 1971 was amended in 1979 to the effect that, where the works council contests an employer's planned decision in a prior consultation area, that employer is precluded from taking any action on the decision for at least one month. During this period, the works council can appeal to the Company Division of the Amsterdam Appellate Court. If, after having weighed the interests involved, the employer's plans are found to be "clearly unreasonable" (*kennelijke onredelijkheid*), the court can force the employer to withdraw the decision, either partly or completely (Bakels and Opheikens 1982:233; Blanpain 1994:26). In Germany this right to delay or even veto decisions is supplemented by a real co-decision right in 12 specifically enumerated areas of so-called "social matters".[8] In these areas the right of co-decision or co-determination means just that: management cannot take any decisions without the consent of the works council. But co-determination entails more than simply conferring veto powers. Both sides are given an equal voice in the decision-making process (Weiss 1994:181). Therefore, in principle at least, the works council as well as the management can take the initiative. Paragraph 87 of the 1972 Works Constitution Act lists the areas of joint decision making. They include, inter alia, the beginning and termination of the daily working hours, (including breaks and the distribution of working hours over the days of the week); any temporary reduction or extension of the normal working hours in the establishment; the time and place for the payment of remuneration as well as its mode; the establishment of general principles on annual vacation; and the intro-duction and use of technical devices designed to monitor the behaviour or performance of the workers.

(b) Relationship with trade unions and collective bargaining

[713] Cordova (1982:135) argues that trade unions were born as protest organisations, conceived primarily to represent workers, to negotiate on their behalf and to engage, if necessary, in industrial action so as to obtain

---

8   The participation rights of the German works council are divided into three broad areas, covering not only social but also personnel and economic matters. Personnel matters include personnel planning and vocational training as well as, significantly, the hiring, transfer or dismissal of employees. The general understanding is that social matters are only those relating to the social consequences of economic decisions. See Weiss 1994:181.

concessions from the employer. This perception as to the proper role of unions has conditioned a trade union mentality which found it difficult to accommodate certain non-adversarial forms of employee participation at first. The gradual acceptance of employee participation by the union is best illustrated by retracing somewhat the origins of the system of institutionalised worker participation at the plant level in Germany (Weiss, Simitis and Rydzy s.d.:2ff). The German model as it exists today is not at all an invention of the organised labour movement. On the contrary, employers during the last century voluntarily established some form of employee participation. They had essentially two reasons in mind. First, in a reaction against the growth of the union movement, the idea was to keep unions out of the plant. Secondly, a further goal was to provide employer policies at the plant with a better legitimation. Union support for the idea of worker participation came only later, due to political change and change in the strategies of the labour movement. As regards the latter, the awareness slowly grew that the managerial powers could be limited by establishing democratic structures within the plant, especially if employee participation could be controlled by the union.

[714] Under the first German Works Council Act of 1920, works councils were set up as separate institutions from the unions and they were to represent all employees at the plant, both organised and non-organised. Since 1920 the unions have tried to do away with this institutional separation and in more recent years they have succeeded, both in Germany and elsewhere, in legitimately controlling works council activities. Even if there is still – at least in principle – institutional separation between unions and works councils, there are currently close links affecting both the composition and the functioning of works councils. The results for the most recently held elections confirm that trade union members occupy three out of every four seats on German works councils against the backdrop of an overall participation rate of close to 80%.[9] In France the participation rate is below 70% but there as well more than two out of three votes go to union members.[10]

[715] More problematic is the co-ordination of the functions of the works council and the traditional role of the union as regards collective bargaining. Two basic approaches can be detected. France and Belgium are illustrative for the first approach. Under this approach works councils are expressly denied the right to enter into legally enforceable collective

---

9   *European Industrial Relations Review* 1994:248:7 (1994 elections).
10. *European Industrial Relations Review* 1995:255:6 (1993 elections).

agreements. Thus the exclusive bargaining rights of the union are preserved. Of course, the possibility that the works council de facto engages in bargaining can never be excluded, but any resulting agreements are legally unenforceable (Vranken 1986:346). A second approach, adopted in Germany and the Netherlands in particular, addresses the issue in a more constructive fashion. Under German law, for instance, management and works councils are free to enter into voluntary plant agreements (*Betriebsvereinbarungen*) on various matters relating to labour-management relations. However, since works councils are required by law to co-operate faithfully with management, strike as a means of resolving conflicts is expressly prohibited. This limits the power of the works council in inducing management to sign any such agreement. Yet another restriction is that plant agreements between works council and management can be made only in areas not already or normally covered by collective agreements.

[716] On the other hand, in matters where the works council has been given co-determination rights (most notably social matters), plant agreements between management and works council are compulsory. Here the relationship between collective and plant agreements becomes less transparent and conflicts between collective agreements and works council power are solved in a different manner. Briefly, although it continues to be the prerogative of the collective bargaining parties to regulate matters themselves, this does not necessarily imply a complete loss of power for the works council. First, the position of the works council is only affected if the plant is effectively covered by a collective agreement. In the past, collective agreements in Germany have predominantly been concluded at the level of the industry or region rather than at the level of the individual enterprise. Secondly, co-determination, as a practical matter, is only excluded if the collective agreement is sufficiently specific so as to cover all aspects of the matter (Weiss 1994:188). The works council benefits from the inevitably wide scope for interpretation this second requirement entails. Besides, because of the centralised nature of collective bargaining in Germany, few industry-wide agreements cater adequately for the often specific needs of individual enterprises.

7.3 Employee Representation on Company Boards

(a) No uniformity in Europe

[717] In a number of countries employee representatives sit on the boards of companies. As far as the private sector is concerned, this is at present mainly a Western European phenomenon although a limited form of board representation also exists in Japan and the United States (Blanpain 1994:38). But even within Europe no uniformity can be found. Certainly, not all European legal systems provide for board-level representation of employee representatives. Where board-level representation does exist, one of two principal models tends to have been adopted. They are the German and the Dutch models of representation. Together they have been a primary source of inspiration in the drafting of the proposed EC legislation to be discussed later in this chapter.

[718] A proper understanding of the European approach to worker participation on company boards requires a basic familiarity with the rules of company law. Specifically, European companies tend to be organised along a two-tier structure. The first body, the management board or directorate, deals with the day-to-day management of the company. A second body within the same company has as its task the supervision of the management board. This second body carries the not particularly original name of supervisory board. It is this board that appoints and discharges the management board. The supervisory board meets on average between two and four times a year. Typically, it does not deal with issues of daily management itself. Rather, the supervisory board decides upon general policy matters such as whether and where to invest or disinvest, and whether and how to diversify the company's lines of production. Worker representation under both the German and the Dutch model is at the level of the supervisory board, not the management board. It follows that board level representation in Europe does not entail co-management by the company's workforce but rather it is limited to the co-supervision (along with the representatives of the shareholders) of the management in any particular company.

(b) The German model

[719] Not one but three models of board level representation co-exist in Germany. The oldest model was introduced in the aftermath of the Second World War. It is the most far-reaching model in terms of the degree of employee participation it triggers, but its application is limited to large companies (more than 1000 employees) in the mining, iron and steel industries. The so-called Montan law of 1951 provides for equal representation of shareholders and employees on the supervisory board (*Aufsichtsrat*). The second model was established by the Works Constitution Act of 1952, which is the predecessor of the 1972 Works Constitution Act that is in force today. It applies to medium-sized companies employing

500 employees or more. These employees are represented on the supervisory board in a minority capacity: only one third of the board members must be employee representatives. The third model is contained in the Co-Determination Act (*Mitbestimmungsgesetz*) of 1976. It provides for quasi-equal representation of employees on the supervisory board, but the 1976 Act applies only to companies with a workforce of at least 2000 employees. Under this third model employee representation is quasi-equal, because the chairperson is, in practice, a representative of the shareholders and it is the chairperson who has the casting vote in case of a tie.

[720] The practical functioning of board-level representation can be explained by means of the following example from the mining, iron and steel industries. As a rule the supervisory board under the *Montan* model consists of 11 members. This means that the shareholders and the employees each appoint five members. These 10 people jointly appoint the 11th person who holds the chair. Under German law the chairperson must be a "neutral" in order to overcome any deadlocks which may arise between the representatives of the shareholders and the workers.[11] Of the five employee representatives on the supervisory board two are nominees from the works council whereas the other three are union nominees. Historically, labour law systems in Europe tend to differentiate between blue-collar and white-collar workers. This somewhat outmoded distinction continues to be applied in the 1951 legislation to the effect that the works council must nominate an employee from each category. The three union nominees need not be company employees. In practice, two of the three external members are always union members whereas the third "additional" member must be independent: that person may neither belong to the union nor to the company's workforce nor have an economic interest in the company (Weiss, Simitis, Rydzy 1989:88-89). The purpose of this rather elaborate system for the allocation of seats on the supervisory board is to avoid that one particular faction on the side of labour – the union in particular – dominates the proceedings of the supervisory board.

[721] Once the composition of the supervisory board has been determined, the board under the *Montan* model proceeds to appoint the management board. One of the members of the management board carries the title of labour director (*Arbeitsdirektor*), and is charged with all social and personnel matters. The appointment (or discharge) of the labour director requires the consent of the employee representatives on the supervisory board who have a veto right. This reflects the significance of the

---

11   In practice the chairperson is often a leading academic or ex-politician.

Arbeitsdirektor for the interests of the workers. The 1952 and 1976 models contain slight variations on the 1951 model of employee participation on company boards. Thus, under the 1976 model, the function of labour director exists but the employee representatives on the supervisory board have no veto powers. Under the 1952 model the employee representatives on the supervisory board are elected by the workforce at large, either directly or upon nomination by the works council.

[722] The effectiveness of the German approach to board level representation is influenced by certain built-in limitations. One such limitation concerns differences between the three models as to the question of who should be represented on the side of the workers. The position of so-called leading personnel (*leitende Angestellte*) is especially problematic. Only the 1952 Act excludes managerial staff from representation. The 1951 Act covers managerial staff, but does not treat it as a separate group. And the 1976 model expressly divides the company's workforce into three distinct categories. All three groups – blue-collar workers, white-collar workers and managerial staff – are guaranteed at least one representative on the supervisory board. Unfortunately for the other workers, perhaps, the interests of the *leitende Angestellte* often are more in line with the views of the management board than with the rest of the workforce.[12]

[723] The main weakness in board level representation has been identified by Weiss, Simitis and Rydzy (1989:90) as the determination of German law to attempt to address the issue of employee participation within the traditional framework of corporations law. In the result the legal status of the employee representatives on the supervisory board is identical to that of the other members of the board: they have the same rights and obligations as the representatives of the shareholders. The repercussions are significant. First, German law allows members of the board freely to discuss company matters among themselves, but they are prohibited from disclosing information to other persons (whether inside or outside the enterprise). This duty of secrecy inhibits communications between the employee representatives and their constituency. This can lead to isolation of the representatives, alienation of the constituency and, ultimately, a loss of legitimacy for the representatives on the supervisory board. Secondly, protection against employer reprisals may be necessary for those members

---

12   Weiss, Simitis, Rydzy 1989:90. Executive staff in the 1976 Codetermination Act is defined in the same way as in the 1972 Works Constitution Act for purposes of the works council. As for the position of executive staff in the Works Constitution Act, see Weiss 1994:172.

of the board who are also employed by the company if they want to be able effectively to influence policy making in the supervisory board. Members of the works council enjoy protection against dismissal and have a right to participate in vocational training programs without loss of pay. Yet, because of the principle of equality among all members of the board, the specific situation of the employee representatives on the board is not taken into account.[13]

[724] Ultimately, the practical usefulness of employee representation on company boards lies in the close, informal links which have developed between the board and the works council. Often the worker representatives on the board are equally members of the works council. German management by and large is convinced of the need to remain on good terms with the works council. It therefore also tends to avoid conflicts with those council members who sit on the board. It does so by discussing delicate issues with these employee representatives at informal meetings prior to matters being raised at the board itself. The net effect is a preventive one. It may also explain why most decisions of the supervisory board are taken unanimously, the presence of employee representatives on the board notwithstanding (Weiss 1994:199).

(c) The Dutch model

[725] The Dutch model of employee representation was introduced by the so-called Structure Act of 1971 (the full title of the Act is Act on the Structure of Limited Liability and Private Companies Act 1971). The Act applies to large ("structured") companies in terms of capital and size of workforce. As regards the latter, what is envisaged are companies which have a works council by virtue of employing 100 or more workers. The Dutch model starts from the premise that there is no room on the supervisory board for either employees or representatives of the union. Rather every effort is made to ensure that the board comprises members who enjoy the confidence of both labour and capital and not persons representing a particular interest. This philosophy appears to reflect a great sense of pragmatism reminiscent of legislative changes introduced in the early 1970s as regards the functioning of the work council. Specifically, a first Works Councils Act of 1950 had sought to promote the pursuit of

---

13 Obviously, the shareholders' representatives do not need protection against dismissal nor do they need a right to participate in vocational programs in order to become qualified for their job. The representatives on the shareholders' side are normally qualified experts in economic and financial issues: Weiss 1994:197-198.

shared interests between employers and employees. A second Works Councils Act of 1971 did not abandon the co-operation concept entirely. But the Dutch legislature deliberately opted for the regulation of works councils that henceforth would have a dual mission. Instead of treating the works council exclusively as an opportunity for labour and management to meet and confer for purposes of promoting the general interests of the enterprise, it was acknowledged that the works council is also a body for the defence of the more specific interests of the workers (Art 2 *Wet op de Ondernemingsraden*; Bakels and Opheikens 1982:210-211).

[726] In order to avoid unnecessary confrontation and to guarantee a smooth decision-making process the supervisory board, under the Dutch model, co-opts its own members subject, however, to a veto right of both the works council and the meeting of shareholders. Specifically, the works council, the shareholders and the management board are all entitled to nominate candidates when a vacancy arises. The supervisory board next informs the general meeting of shareholders and the works council of the name of the person it wants to co-opt. The appointment takes effect unless the shareholders or the works council object to the proposal by the supervisory board on grounds that the suggested person is "unfit for the performance of the duty of supervisory director" (Blanpain 1994:42). Such a veto can be overturned only by a court decision.

7.4 Developments at the Level of the European Community

(a) Social policy of the Community in general

[727] The 1957 version of the Rome Treaty did not pay much attention to issues of social policy. In part, this can be explained by a prevailing perception among the drafters of the Treaty that the development of a social policy would be the inevitable by-product of a successful economic integration to be achieved first. A major exception is Art 119 EC on equal pay. But even this and the few other provisions in the Treaty Title on Social Policy remained largely "dormant" during a first, neo-liberal phase of the Community (Blanpain and Engels 1995:116).

[728] The official turning point came in the form of a Solemn Declaration, issued by the Heads of State and Government of the member states, at Paris in 1972. The significance of the Declaration lies in that the member states openly acknowledged that, henceforth, progress as regards social policy was to be of equal importance to the pursuit of economic integration. The adoption of a Social Action Program in 1974 resulted in a so-called golden period of social harmonisation during which major initiatives were taken, especially in the field of labour law. Between 1975 and 1980 EC laws (Directives) were passed addressing the issues of equal pay (Directive 75/17/EEC, *OJ* L45/19) and equal treatment (Directive 76/207/EEC, *OJ* L39/40) as well as the protection of worker rights in instances of collective redundancies (Directive 75/129/ EEC, *OJ* L 48/29), transfer of undertakings (Directive 77/187/EEC, *OJ* L 61/26) and employer insolvency (Directive 80/987/EEC, *OJ* L283/23).

[729] The social integration policy of the Community came to a virtual halt during the 1980s. The Single European Act constituted a major amendment of the 1957 Treaty of Rome, but its emphasis was almost exclusively on finding ways to speed up the completion of the internal economic market. One exception was the introduction of qualified majority voting in matters of occupational health and safety (Art 118a EC as inserted by Art 21 SEA). However, any other Community initiatives in the fields of labour law and social security law continued to require unanimity in the Council of Ministers. The Community did not remain immune to criticism that the Single European Act reflected too narrowly an economic focus, though. A first corrective measure was by way of a political gesture only. In 1989 a Community Charter of (12) Fundamental Social Rights of Workers was adopted, but this document is not legally enforceable.[14] A few years later, the negotiations for a Treaty on European Union at Maastricht tried to bring about change that would be both politically and legally relevant. However, it would be wrong to assume that no new social legislation was enacted in the more immediate aftermath of the 1989 Charter. The Charter was accompanied by an Action Programme which resulted in the adoption of Community legislation (again Directives) on the employer's obligation to inform workers of the conditions applicable to the contract of employment relationship (Directive 91/353/EEC, *OJ* L288/91), collective redundancy (Directive 92/56/EEC, *OJ* L245/92, corrigendum in L311/92), and working time (Directive 93/104/EEC, *OJ* L307/18). Other social legislation centered on aspects of health and safety which, because of its more technical nature, tends to be less controversial. But, all in all, the progress towards the goals of the Community Charter has been disappointingly slow and it has been observed that, in order to secure their

---

14   The United Kingdom is not a signatory to the Charter. See the discussion in Hepple 1990:643.

approval, many of the legislative proposals had to be diluted severely (Hepple 1993:155).

[730] It was against this background that the EC leaders met at Maastricht in December 1991. A proposal to revamp substantially the Title on Social Policy in the 1957 version of the Rome Treaty was deemed totally unacceptable by the United Kingdom. By way of compromise, the provisions on social policy reform were put in a separate agreement outside of the Treaty itself. But even that was going too far for some member states. In the result, a Protocol to the Treaty on European Union allowed the member states minus the United Kingdom to enter into an Agreement on Social Policy. The Agreement widens the scope for qualified majority voting as regards matters of labour law, especially in the fields of working conditions, information and consultation of workers, equal treatment and "the integration of persons excluded from the labour market" (Art 2(1) of the Agreement on Social Policy). By contrast, it is expressly stipulated that unanimity remains necessary with respect to dismissal protection, the collective representation of workers (including co-determination matters) and social security. And certain topics – most notably pay, the right of association and the right to strike or lock out – have even been excluded from Community action altogether.

[731] The practical significance of Maastricht for the social policy of the Community remains to be seen. Problematic is that no clear demarcation lines exist between each of the above three categories of decision making by qualified majority. Especially the term "working conditions" is potentially very broad. In principle, a liberal interpretation of the term would henceforth allow for qualified majority voting to apply to most initiatives in the area of labour law (Weiss 1992:3). In practice, the immediate future may very well hold only consolidation and little development by way of new initiatives. These sentiments are reflected in a three-year social "action" programme adopted in April 1995 (*European Industrial Relations Review* 257:12-19). Reinforcing this tendency to consolidate rather than innovate is the concept of subsidiarity.[15] There is a concern that a shift away from centralised decision making at the level of the Community may eventuate, especially since it may prove difficult to satisfy the "value-added" test that subsidiarity entails (Hepple 1993:159).

---

15   See [231] above.

Commissioner for Social Affairs. The draft Directive on Procedures for Informing and Consulting Employees of Undertakings with Complex Structures, in particular Transnational Undertakings (*OJ* C297/3) is best known as the Vredeling proposal. The controversy surrounding the Vredeling proposal would finally be laid to rest with the adoption, some one and a half decades later, of the 1994 European Works Council Directive.[17]

[735] On a more positive note, attempts at a functional approach to employee participation did meet with more success. In 1975 a Directive on collective redundancies was passed (Directive 75/129/EEC, *OJ* 1975 L48). The Directive, as amended in 1992 (Directive 92/56/EEC *OJ* L245/3), introduces a duty for the employer to inform and consult with the employees' representatives on the social implications of certain dismissal actions. Community action in this field was triggered by the *AKZO* case. *AKZO* is a Dutch-German multinational company. In 1973 the company undertook a process of restructuring which involved the redundancy of some 5000 of its workers. *AKZO* had a number of subsidiaries in different European countries. Its strategy was to compare the cost of dismissal in the various countries and to carry out the dismissals in that country where the cost was the lowest. This led to outrage in some European quarters and to a demand for a European rule so as to make a repetition of any such company strategy impossible (Blanpain and Engels 1995:259).

[736] The 1975 Directive on collective redundancies only applies to terminations of the employment relationship at the initiative of the employer, ie, mainly dismissals. These dismissals must affect at least 10 employees and must be for reasons not related to the individual workers concerned. Information concerning the collective redundancies must be given on beforehand, ie before the decision to dismiss is taken. To enable the workers' representatives to make constructive proposals which mitigate the social impact of the planned employer action, all relevant information must be provided. The Directive specifies that this includes information, in writing, about the reason for the redundancies, the number of employees to be made redundant, the number of employees normally employed and the period over which the redundancies are to be carried out. A copy of the information given must be forwarded to the competent public authority. The sharing of the information with the representatives of the workers

---

17　A detailed study of the Vredeling proposal can be found in Blanpain and Blanquet 1983. See Docksey 1986:281 for a discussion with particular reference to the United Kingdom. The European Works Council directive 1994 is analysed in [740] ff below.

must be followed by consultations "with a view to reaching an agreement" (Art 2, 1 of the Directive). Clearly, this expression indicates that what is required goes beyond consultation in a strict sense. On the other hand, the intention was not to introduce a formal right to co-determination: there is indeed no requirement of actually reaching an agreement between both parties.

[737] The same notion of consultation with a view to reaching an agreement features in yet another example of functional worker participation at the level of the EC. The 1977 Directive on safeguarding the employees' rights in the event of a "transfer of undertakings, busines-ses or parts of businesses" (Directive 77/187/EEC *OJ* 1977 L 61) is aimed at enabling employees to remain in employment with the new employer on the same terms and conditions that applied with the transferor. More generally, the purpose of the Directive is to ensure that the inevitable restructuring of companies within a progressively unified economic market does not adversely affect the workers.[18]

[738] More recently, the concept of employee participation has also been embedded in a 1989 Directive on the improvement of safety and health at work (Directive 89/391/EEC *OJ* 1989 L 183). According to this framework Directive – the Directive needs to be supplemented by more "individual" Directives of which several have been adopted to date – workers should receive all the necessary information concerning the safety and health risks at their place of work. Consultation and participation, involving the right of workers and/or their representatives to formulate proposals, is also provided for. Some doubt exists, however, as to whether the Directive may be rather too vague for it to really further worker participation (Jacobs and Zeijen 1993:119).

[739] To date the biggest success of the EC in promoting worker participation has been the adoption in 1994 of a Directive for the establishment of European works councils, or equivalent procedures for informing and consulting employees, in companies with a "Community dimension" (Directive 94/45/EC *OJ* 1994 L 254/64). Known as the European Works Councils Directive it has been heralded as a major milestone in the (relatively young) history of EC social policy.[19] The Directive unquestionably represents the first successful attempt by the

---

18   The practical application of the Directive has not been entirely without problems: Blanpain and Engels 1995:265-276.

19   *EIRR* 1994:250:14. See von Maydell (1993:1401) for a critical review of the impact of the EC on national labour law and policy.